AF606020

The Virtue of *Sōphrosunē* in Plato's *Gorgias* and *Phaedrus*

SUNY series in Ancient Greek Philosophy

Anthony Preus, editor

The Virtue of *Sōphrosunē* in Plato's *Gorgias* and *Phaedrus*

KRISTIAN SHEELEY

SUNY
PRESS

The cover painting (oil on canvas) is *The Danaïdes* by John Singer Sargent, between circa 1922 and circa 1925; from Museum of Fine Arts, Boston; in the public domain.

Published by State University of New York Press, Albany

Printed in the United States of America

EU GPSR Authorised Representative:
Logos Europe, 9 rue Nicolas Poussin, 17000, La Rochelle, France
contact@logoseurope.eu

For information, contact State University of New York Press, Albany, NY
www.sunypress.edu

Library of Congress Cataloging-in-Publication Data

Name: Sheeley, Kristian, 1966– author.
Title: The virtue of sōphrosunē in Plato's Gorgias and Phaedrus / Kristian Sheeley.
Description: Albany : State University of New York Press, [2026]. | Series: SUNY series in ancient Greek philosophy | Includes bibliographical references and index.
Identifiers: LCCN 2025029558 | ISBN 9798855805529 (hardcover : alk. paper) | ISBN 9798855807028 (epub) | ISBN 9798855805543 (PDF)
Subjects: LCSH: Plato. Gorgias. | Plato. Phaedrus. | Temperance (Virtue). | Moderation.
Classification: LCC B371 .S54 2025 | DDC 184—dc23/eng/20250910
LC record available at https://lccn.loc.gov/2025029558

For indeed these things that we are disagreeing about do not happen to be at all small, but are more or less those things that it is most fine to know about [. . .]; for the chief point of them is either to know or ignore who is happy and who is not.

—Plato, *Gorgias* 472c

I am still not able to "know myself," as the Delphic inscription enjoins, and it seems laughable for me to think about other things when I am still ignorant of myself. [. . .] For me, the question is whether I happen to be some sort of beast even more complex in form and more tumultuous than the hundred-headed Typhon, or whether I am something simpler and gentler, having a share by nature of the divine."

—Plato, *Phaedrus* 229e–230a

Contents

Abbreviations		ix
Introduction		1
Chapter 1	The Ideology and Type of Soul Callicles Represents in *Gorgias*	21
Chapter 2	Socrates' Fitting Response to Callicles	67
Chapter 3	Pedagogy, *Erōs* Without Virtue, and Mortal Moderation in *Phaedrus*	109
Chapter 4	Genuine *Sōphrosunē* in *Phaedrus*	155
Conclusion		205
Bibliography		211
Index		217

Abbreviations

Ap.	*Apology* (Plato)
EN	*Nicomachean Ethics* (Aristotle)
Grg.	*Gorgias* (Plato)
Ly.	*Lysis* (Plato)
Phd.	*Phaedo* (Plato)
Phdr.	*Phaedrus* (Plato)
Phlb.	*Philebus* (Plato)
Plt.	*Statesman* (Plato)
R.	*Republic* (Plato)
Smp.	*Symposium* (Plato)
Sph.	*Sophist* (Plato)
Tht.	*Theaetetus* (Plato)
Ti.	*Timaeus* (Plato)

Introduction

Of all the philosophical issues that matter to us, questions about *how to live* are the most unavoidable. It might be possible to live without definitively committing oneself to particular views concerning the nature of reality, knowledge, beauty, the self, death, and so on, but we cannot help but make choices that affect ourselves and the well-being of others. To be sure, decisions about how to live are closely connected to social and political issues, metaphysical questions, epistemological problems, and maybe even aesthetics. Still, during the time we spend seeking answers to philosophical questions, we cannot postpone the ethical choices that confront us in daily life. Regardless of how oppressive the social conditions in which we live happen to be, we retain the ability to decide how we respond to these conditions. The goods that we value above all others influence the decisions we make, our decisions form our habits, our habits form our characteristics, and our characteristics shape our identities as well as our ways of life. In my view, the approach to ethics that focuses on virtue found in Plato's dialogues—an approach that is now called "virtue ethics"—can be an invaluable guide when we think carefully about how to apply its insights to our own contemporary individual and social contexts. Plato shows that the virtues are relevant to one's own well-being when he connects them with happiness and inner harmony. But he also compellingly illustrates how pervasively virtue (or the lack thereof) determines how well we tend to the well-being of others in the social and political spheres of our lives. We must decide how to care for ourselves and those around us today just as the people of the ancient world did. We may never gain the full and final answers to our philosophical questions that would make further inquiry unnecessary, but we can make progress in the search for these answers, and we can substantially improve our lives, our minds, and the lives of others over the course of this search.

This book examines Plato's reflections on virtue in two of his dialogues, the *Gorgias* and the *Phaedrus*. While these two texts cover a wide range of philosophical questions, both provide substantial, critical examinations that compare the various goods and ends that humans commonly pursue, such as wealth, pleasure, fame, political power, and certain traits of character. They investigate the nature of the good human life by paying close attention to questions of how to best cultivate one's moral character, what goods we should value most, and how we should build our relationships with others. Through this study, I aim to shed light on why, and to what extent, virtue can lead to both a harmonious inner life and healthy, fulfilling relationships. Of course, Plato wrote his dialogues at a time and in a culture very distant from our own, making some aspects of his works alien to modern readers. However, their explorations of fundamental human concerns such as moral goodness, happiness, interpersonal relationships, and philosophical reflection give contemporary readers the opportunity to gain insight about such issues in modern life. Accordingly, I seek to identify true insights found in Plato's texts that can guide ethical life today.

Historically, the *Gorgias* and the *Phaedrus* have not often been included in the first tier of texts that readers examine when studying ancient Greek virtue ethics. Aristotle's *Nicomachean Ethics* is obviously a core text for studying Greek philosophical conceptions of virtue (and rightly so), but even many of those who look to Plato's discussions of virtue do not devote the same amount of attention to the *Gorgias* and the *Phaedrus* as they do to other dialogues.[1] Scholars tend to regard the *Republic* and the *Philebus* as Plato's most seminal or mature ethical texts. Other dialogues that focus on a single virtue are often studied by those interested in that virtue. As I will discuss in chapter 1, some scholars see the *Gorgias* as an early attempt by Plato to lay out an ethical theory that he later improves on in the *Republic*. Similarly, in chapter 3, I note that many scholars take interest in the *Phaedrus*' discussions of erotic love and rhetoric, but it is not a text that scholars often look to for substantial insights about virtue. I do not criticize the *Republic*, *Philebus*, or any other dialogue—on the contrary, I often look to them for additional insight or guidance. Instead, I highlight the value we can find in the ethical discussions of the *Gorgias* and the *Phaedrus* when we interpret them well, and I pay special attention to their reflections on the virtue of moderation (*sōphrosunē*), as I explain in more

1. For example, in *Plato's Ethics* (1995), Terence Irwin devotes significantly less attention to the *Gorgias* than the *Republic*, and he devotes almost no attention to the *Phaedrus*.

detail below. Rather than being immature or insignificant attempts by Plato to understand virtue, the *Gorgias* and the *Phaedrus* contain profound ethical reflections that are universally relevant.

This book aims to contribute to both Plato scholarship and contemporary conversations about virtue ethics and philosophical pedagogy. My contribution to the scholarship on the *Gorgias* and the *Phaedrus* is, first, to highlight the important pedagogical context we must observe when reading these dialogues, and second, to elucidate the philosophical points that follow from reading the dialogues in this way, especially with regard to the process of cultivating moderation and the extent to which this virtue is crucial for a good life. I shed light on how and why Plato has Socrates speak in a way that is aimed at pedagogically and ethically benefitting his interlocutors as well as the readers of the dialogue. The pedagogical dimension of these dialogues fundamentally shapes the content of their discussions as well as their dramatic action. Socrates responds to different types of pedagogical needs that Plato represents through the characters of Callicles and Phaedrus, both of whom represent certain prominent types of people found in ancient Athens (and in the contemporary world).[2] Socrates ultimately aims to motivate his interlocutors to value and cultivate wisdom, courage, moderation, and justice, but he recognizes that due to each interlocutor's unique beliefs and moral character, he must adapt his accounts to fit their needs. He simultaneously makes strong ethical arguments and rhetorically packages them in a way that makes them accessible and compelling. So, instead of taking all claims about virtue in the *Gorgias* and the *Phaedrus* at face value or out of context, we should appreciate the way in which they are aimed at turning Socrates' interlocutors toward the path to virtue, as is especially clear in the dialogues' contrasting accounts of *sōphrosunē*. Specifically, in the *Gorgias*, Socrates characterizes *sōphrosunē* as the ability to restrain and impose limit on one's desires, since this conception of *sōphrosunē* has the most potential to benefit Callicles (and the type of soul he represents) given his moral character and his views. In the *Phaedrus*, on the other hand, Socrates gives a more nuanced and rich reflection of *sōphrosunē,* since Phaedrus and those

2. As I discuss further below, Callicles may stand for anyone who is committed to the unrestricted pursuit of political power, pleasure, or other conventional goods, and there is a plethora of such people in any given generation. Phaedrus represents those who are not yet committed to a given set of values and way of life, but who are tempted to become like Callicles. Many people, and especially young adults, find themselves at such a crossroad at some point in their lives.

like him are more equipped to receive and benefit from such a reflection. A study that makes sense of the differences between the accounts of *sōphrosunē* in the *Gorgias* and the *Phaedrus* from a pedagogical point of view has not been written before.

I contribute to contemporary discussions surrounding virtue and philosophical pedagogy by applying some of the key insights of the *Gorgias* and the *Phaedrus* to contemporary life. I argue throughout the book that these dialogues can deepen our understanding of virtue and why it is so valuable. Some of the strongest points in the *Gorgias* include Socrates' critique of the Calliclean conception of the good life, his arguments about the value of self-restraint, and his reflection on the types of goods that are most necessary for human happiness. Likewise, in the *Phaedrus,* Socrates effectively shows why Lysias' conception of moderation is flawed and incomplete. In doing so, he gives an insightful account of what erotic love (*erōs*) is, illustrates how we can handle it virtuously or viciously, and shows us that *sōphrosunē* is a multifaceted virtue that brings us substantial benefits, including healthier intimate relationships, self-knowledge, inner harmony, and a clearer view of reality. The notion of moderation we find in the *Phaedrus* is not reducible to habitual self-restraint or dogmatic rule following. Instead, moderation is the virtue through which we understand our own human limitations while at the same time cultivating our potential to achieve happiness and wisdom. My concern with the applicability of Plato's ethical thought to contemporary life sets this book apart from many others that aim solely to interpret the primary philosophical texts. While interpreting Plato well is obviously important for my goals, I simultaneously aim to show why the activity of thinking through Plato's dialogues can bring us some clarity in our own efforts to understand how to live well. In each chapter, I discuss how the primary ethical, pedagogical, or moral psychological points found in the dialogues might enhance our contemporary efforts to live happy and meaningful lives.

Interpreting Plato's Dialogues

Plato's method of writing and the type of engagement it demands from the reader have a significant impact on a project such as my own that examines virtue, moderation, friendship, and rhetoric in the context of his dialogues. Importantly, Plato's chosen literary genre, the dialogue, has characteristics that require readers to take unavoidable interpretive risks. Platonic writing contains especially powerful tools for training readers to think independently, as several aspects of his dialogues prompt the reader to directly participate in the discussions they depict. The following are just a few examples of important features of the dialogue genre that readers need to directly engage with. First, Plato never speaks in his own voice in the dialogues. Second, the characters he portrays often fail to articulate a solution to the philosophical problem raised in the dialogue. Third, the solutions that are given to philosophical problems are often explicitly provisional or incomplete in some way.[3] Fourth, the actions, settings, and characters of a given dialogue share significant connections to the philosophical content discussed in the dialogues.[4] These features of Plato's writing strongly suggest that he means for us to engage with the dialogues by contributing our own critical, philosophical reflection. If the dialogues present these challenges to us, then we must work through the interpretive puzzles they pose, critically assess each step of the discussion they depict, and complete the investigations that they artfully begin.

Moreover, Plato's dialogues contain various kinds of discourse that demand creative interpretation and critical, independent thinking on the part of the reader. He frequently interweaves ethical, political, epistemological, metaphysical, and aesthetic inquiries to show us that topics we often separate from one another have a much closer relationship than it first appears. Characters often use myths and images to make philosophical points or to make important additions to their philosophical discussions. The myths and images in the dialogues challenge the reader to interpret them, to identify the various meanings they may have, to connect them to the concepts discussed in the dialogue, and to explore any shortcomings they may have. The dialogues that end in *aporia* motivate both the interlocutors and the reader to let go of their previously unexamined opinions, since these opinions are likely similar or identical to the ones refuted in the dialogue. *Aporia* can also incite a desire to continue investigating a given question in

3. However, in the "Eleatic dialogues," characters often provide very definite answers to the questions they raise, but such answers can also serve as a kind of irony that prompts further inquiry between the reader and the dialogue itself. For example, in the *Statesman,* the reader should assess whether the Stranger's final definition of the statesman is really as complete as he and young Socrates conclude it is.

4. John Fritz (2016) thoroughly analyzes Plato's use of the dialogue genre by paying special attention to how the dialogues' characters, settings, and the time at which they take place influence how we should interpret their philosophical content.

the future. The arguments in the dialogues that are provisional, incomplete, or even flawed place the reader on a fruitful philosophical path while also challenging her to criticize and improve upon them. All of these aspects of Plato's dialogues prevent the reader from passively accepting a doctrine on the basis of the author's authority. Instead, they prompt the reader to practice philosophy for herself in the very act of reading them.[5]

Another aspect of Plato's dialogues that is especially crucial for my purposes is their depiction of concrete, paradigmatic examples of philosophical pedagogy.[6] They almost always feature interlocutors who are inexperienced in philosophy (such as young men or older men who care little for philosophy) speaking with Socrates or another character who is an experienced philosopher.[7] When the experienced philosopher (I will focus on Socrates for the sake of simplicity) speaks to less experienced interlocutors, it is usually for the sake of guiding them in their thinking and motivating them to pursue a more philosophical life. Socrates considers wisdom and the rest of the virtues among the most important goods a human can possess, and he seeks to benefit others by turning them toward the pursuit by which one attains them, namely the practice of philosophy: "It is the greatest good for a man to discuss virtue every day and those other things about which you hear me conversing and testing myself and others, for the unexamined life is not worth living for men" (*Ap.* 38a). Even if Socrates sometimes appears to speak abrasively in these discussions, he almost always aims to pedagogically benefit his interlocutors by ridding them of (or at least getting them to seriously question) their unexamined assumptions, bringing them to recognize that they lack the wisdom they think they possess, and showing them that real wisdom is something worth seeking.[8]

---

5. See Christopher Rowe (2007) for a thorough treatment of Plato's strategies as a writer. Rowe argues throughout that Plato's goal is to persuade the reader to take up a new outlook that she will have to try to better understand and develop over time.

6. Mitchell Miller's method of interpreting Plato's dialogues pays close attention to the pedagogical dynamic between the characters. For example, see his *The Philosopher in Plato's* Statesman (1980) and *Plato's* Parmenides: *The Conversion of the Soul* (1986). Ruby Blondell (2002) also makes an important contribution to this topic in Plato scholarship by examining the variety of ways that Plato uses literary characters to enhance his philosophical analyses of moral character.

7. I thank Ron Polansky for making me aware of this point in his unpublished notes.

8. Mark Brouwer and Ronald Polansky (2004) give an illuminating and succinct analysis of Socratic *elenchus*, which is followed by their interpretation of Plato's *Charmides* as an exemplary case of Socrates' method.

When reading the dialogues from this pedagogical perspective, we must pay careful attention to two different levels on which philosophical education happens—first, Socrates' (or the main speaker's) pedagogical relationship with his interlocutor, and, second, the ways in which the dialogue as a whole can foster the reader's philosophical development.[9] Plato does not explicitly tell us whether the characters Socrates speaks to gain any benefit from the discussion, and historically, we know that many of the real people that the characters are based on became infamous for their moral vice.[10] In my view, when Socrates' interlocutors appear to leave the conversation unchanged, this demonstrates an important point about philosophical pedagogy. As I will argue in chapter 1, Socrates makes the best attempt possible to benefit his interlocutors by way of discussion, but if they refuse to cooperate with his guidance, then they will not benefit from the discussion. In any case, Plato has Socrates make strong ethical points for the sake of the reader as well. Socrates' engagement with his interlocutors mirrors the dialogue's relationship to the reader, and readers can benefit from reading the dialogue carefully even when Socrates' interlocutors do not. Readers of all kinds can learn from the pedagogical dynamic between Socrates and his interlocutors, including those who are inexperienced in philosophy as well as mature philosophers interested in philosophically educating others. As I will argue, Plato fashions his characters so that they will resemble and represent types of people who are common among his readers, and readers who have something in common with Socrates' interlocutors can be especially impacted by reading and actively thinking alongside the characters.

In my view, these interpretive principles and commitments best respond to Plato's literary genre by taking into account the elements of the text that Plato would not have included if he had solely been interested in expounding his own views. In light of these interpretive principles, I am not interested in attempting to reconstruct Plato's personal views by defending theses with the general form "Plato believes X." The nature of the texts makes it impossible to reconstruct his views with certainty. This is not to say that all interpretations of Plato are therefore equally valid, since it is certainly possible to misunderstand the important ideas his dialogues

9. Jill Gordon (1999) and A. K. Cotton (2014) provide thorough reflections on how Plato's dialogues function as highly effective pedagogical guides for their readers.

10. Alcibiades, Meno, and Critias are just a few examples of infamous historical figures that Plato chooses to depict as Socrates' interlocutors. For biographies and other information about Plato's characters, see Debra Nails (2002).

express or to misidentify the path of investigation they encourage us to follow. Given these considerations, I aim to discover and make explicit some of the insights that the texts can lead us toward by carefully examining the ways that their form and content address key philosophical problems and contemporary concerns.

Many Platonic dialogues offer profound reflections on the good life, virtue, vice, and the various issues connected to them. Determining how to relate these reflections to one another is one of the difficult interpretive challenges Plato presents, and comparing dialogues requires extreme care. The ideas and arguments expressed in the dialogues are not like puzzle pieces that can be neatly fitted together without contradictions or incompatibilities, since they do not aim to present a complete, self-consistent philosophical system. In each dialogue, characters pursue a unique line of inquiry within a unique context—the characters differ, their assumptions differ, and the methods they use to investigate a given topic differ. For example, Socrates may use many figurative forms of speech, such as myths, images, and similes, when speaking with some interlocutors, while in others, he (or the main interlocutor) uses a more precise and dialectical method. On the other hand, there is clear overlap in many of the dialogues—discussions in separate dialogues sometimes bear resemblance to one another, the main interlocutor sometimes gives different versions of the same argument or concept, and so on. To use an example from later in the book, I argue that Callicles' soul and his views have much in common with the "tyrannical soul" discussed in *Republic* IX.

Many fruitful comparisons have been made between dialogues that take either similar or contrasting approaches to dealing with the same questions. Scholars frequently compare certain pairs (or sets) of dialogues based on some type of similarity in their themes or content. The *Gorgias* and the *Phaedrus* are one such pair of dialogues that scholars have compared in the past, primarily because both deal substantially with rhetoric.[11] In addition to their focus on rhetoric, both dialogues contain substantial reflections on the nature of the virtues and why they matter for human life. Regarding the virtue of moderation, the *Gorgias*' critique of immoderation is a pri-

11. Two prominent book-length studies of the *Gorgias* and the *Phaedrus* as a pair have been written by Seth Benardete (1991) and Tushar Irani (2017), though neither takes virtue as its primary focus, as I do here. Marina McCoy (2008) provides a valuable analysis of both dialogues in addition to the *Protagoras* and others.

mary focus of its ethical discussions, and Socrates enumerates convincing reasons why the ability to restrain desire in certain situations is so crucial for a good life. Similarly, the *Phaedrus* critiques "mortal moderation," that is, the practice of restraining some desires for the sake of fulfilling others, and its subsequent discussion of genuine moderation gives us a profound approach to gaining a deeper understanding of this virtue. Further, reading the *Gorgias* and the *Phaedrus* together provides a clearer understanding of the pedagogical dimension of the dialogues. As I mentioned above, the main interlocutors in each dialogue represent different types of souls or moral personas that are common in ancient Athens and contemporary life. So, analyzing the *Gorgias* and the *Phaedrus* together sheds light on how Socrates' approach to defending virtue differs in each context in accord with the type of soul to whom he speaks.

When comparing the *Gorgias* and the *Phaedrus*, I reject the developmental approach that many scholars have used to interpret Plato's dialogues. Those who use this approach divide the dialogues into early, middle-, and late-period dialogues, and they claim to trace Plato's philosophical "development" by reading them in this sequence. They sometimes explain apparently weak arguments in one dialogue or differences between separate dialogues by claiming that Plato must have written one when he was at an earlier stage of maturity and another at a later stage.[12] Although the dialogues that are classified with each other in these early, middle, and late groupings certainly share similarities with one another, there is no testimony from Plato's contemporaries that he wrote one group when he was younger and another when he was older. None of my comparisons between the *Gorgias* and the *Phaedrus* take into consideration *when* Plato might have written either text. Instead, as I explained above, this book primarily looks to the pedagogical dimension of the *Gorgias* and the *Phaedrus* to make sense of the similarities and differences in their ethical content.

12. Leonard Brandwood (1990) attempts to establish the order in which Plato wrote his dialogues based on analyses of Plato's prose style, since there is little evidence to help us determine when Plato wrote them apart from the dialogues themselves. Debra Nails (1995) surveys different issues surrounding the problem of how to relate the content of Plato's dialogues to one another, and she offers a convincing criticism of the developmentalist approach (115–139).

Philosophy and Sophistry

Plato does not put Socrates in dialogue with the most famous ancient Greek sophists in the *Gorgias* and the *Phaedrus*, but his main interlocutors are nonetheless influenced by the sophistic movement in fifth- and fourth-century BCE Athens, represented by Gorgias (and his followers) and Lysias' speech.[13] The intellectuals known as the sophists held a wide range of views and perspectives, so it is difficult to make broad claims that would apply to all sophists, and I avoid doing so throughout the book. Still, in my view, Plato identifies two core ideas that help shape the sophists' way of thinking and arguing, namely Protagoras' famous dictum that "man is the measure of all things,"[14] and the commonly used distinction between nature (*physis*) and convention (*nomos*).[15] As Socrates puts it in the *Theaetetus*, a reasonable way to interpret Protagoras' "man is the measure" statement is that "as each thing appears to me, so it is for me, and as it appears to you, so it is for you—you and I each being a man" (*Tht.* 152a). Even if this interpretation does not represent how some ancient thinkers and orators interpreted Protagoras (or even what Protagoras himself meant), many at least adopt the basic orientation of rejecting socially accepted views of good and bad, justice and injustice, and so on in favor of one's own assessment of reality. From this Protagorean perspective, if those who decide the socially accepted rules are men just like oneself, then there is no reason to accept the social standards if they conflict with one's own desires or views about the good, justice, and so on. If man is the measure of all things, and all views stem from humans, then the conventions of society are not inherently truer or better than any given individual's idiosyncratic worldview or desires. While Socrates' interlocutors in the *Gorgias* and the *Phaedrus* do not push

13. Rhetoricians such as Gorgias and Lysias may not be sophists per se, but they are at least influenced by common ideas in the sophistic movement, and they are often classified as sophists for this reason (Barney 2006, 77n1). McCoy (2008, chapters 4 and 7) offers insightful analysis of Plato's accounts of rhetoric in the *Gorgias* and the *Phaedrus*.

14. Although Plato presents an important portrait of Protagoras and his views in the dialogue named after him, he confronts a particular interpretation of the view that "man is the measure of all things" most directly in the *Theaetetus*' discussion about whether knowledge is perception (151d–187a).

15. Rachel Barney (2006) has an illuminating discussion on the relativism associated with the idea that "man is the measure" as well as the distinction between nature and convention. She sees both of these concepts as essential aspects of the sophistic movement, even though individual sophists give several different versions of each view.

Protagorean relativism to its logical conclusions as Socrates does in the *Theaetetus*, they nonetheless reject customary views in favor of their own values and assessments of morality and reality.[16]

In the *Gorgias*, Callicles uses the common sophistic distinction between *physis* and *nomos* to give his own account of morality according to which there is no measure for goodness, justice, beauty, and so on apart from whatever the individual desires, and so it makes perfect sense for the strong to immoderately oppress the weak for the sake of fulfilling their own desires as far as possible (for example, see *Grg.* 482e–484c). For Callicles, common ideas about justice, moderation, and other similar virtues are simply the result of the power struggle between the weak mob and the exceptionally strong individuals; the former fabricate the laws for the sake of controlling and protecting themselves from the latter (491e–492c). Lysias' speech in the *Phaedrus* also aims to subvert socially accepted conventions about erotic relationships in favor of his own self-serving ends, arguing that a beautiful young man should give sexual favors to him, a (supposed) nonlover, rather than an intimate partner by way of the traditional Athenian homoerotic relationship. Phaedrus and Socrates also briefly reference "the wise men [*hoi sophoi*] of our day" (*Phdr.* 229c) who try to debunk traditional myths with naturalistic explanations early in the *Phaedrus*, an example of them elevating the "natural" view of things over the conventional myths of humans. Hence, the sophistic distinction between *physis* and *nomos* is an important component of the intellectual context that Socrates engages with in the *Gorgias* and the *Phaedrus*, and his arguments about virtue especially speak to those who hold (or at least take seriously) this basic perspective.[17]

Through Socrates' words, characteristics, and deeds, we can gather the main ways in which Plato contrasts sophistry with philosophy. In my view, Plato depicts a concrete model of the ideal philosopher in Socrates. Socrates' words and deeds demonstrate that living a virtuous and philosophical life involves thinking and choosing independently in order to realize virtue in any given situation rather than following a predetermined set of rules that are supposed to be universally applicable. In other words, virtue requires us to think for ourselves rather than follow the orders of another person,

16. In the *Theaetetus*, Socrates argues that the person defending the "man is the measure" doctrine is bound for self-refutation or inconsistency (169d–172c).

17. In my view, by assessing Plato's engagement with the sophists in the *Gorgias* and the *Phaedrus*, we can put his thought in dialogue with various contemporary philosophical worldviews, as I will discuss in chapters 1 and 2.

the rules of a given code of conduct, or the tenets of a preexisting ideology. Instead, we must cultivate virtue on our own (albeit with the help of philosophical friendships and community) and determine how to realize wisdom, courage, moderation, and justice in the context of our unique, individual lives. In this way, the philosopher has something in common with the sophists in Plato's dialogues. Socrates' conception of the virtues is not completely relativistic—he is clear that virtues are real (*Phaedrus* 247d–e, for example) and universally good, but his explanations of the virtues are not completely devoid of the sophists' emphasis on the importance of thinking and seeing the truth for oneself. According to Socrates, the virtues are not simply whatever a given individual wants them to be—it is not the case that "as each thing appears to me, so it is to me" (*Tht.* 152a) in the realm of virtue. Socrates avoids the hubristic mistake of too quickly concluding that there is no real universal human good, that all such ideas are mere convention, and that one therefore might as well seek to fulfill his own desires at any cost. However, it is up to each individual to determine how to realize the virtues in her own particular life and her community. Both the philosopher and the sophist subvert social norms in favor of a goal that they deem more valuable, but the philosopher does so in a way that more reliably leads to happiness (*eudaimonia*) for oneself and others.

The Virtue of *Sōphrosunē*

As we would expect, Plato's work suggests that the true philosopher commits herself to understanding reality as much as is humanly possible. But she also commits herself to living in a way that is most harmonious with the patterns that reality sets for good living. Cultivating virtue is essential for reaching *both* goals. The wise person knows what is truly good and how to live in such a way that she becomes as good as possible, a task that requires all the human virtues. Living philosophically also inevitably leads us to question the being who does all the questioning, namely ourselves, and so philosophy is also inseparable from the pursuit of self-knowledge. It is unclear whether any human can complete the project of becoming wise, but the philosopher—the person who loves wisdom—strives for wisdom with more enthusiasm and dedication than any other type of person. Plato's dialogues suggest that philosophy necessarily involves cultivating or perfecting our own souls (an activity that he calls "purification" in the *Phaedo* at 66e–67b) so that we will become better able to make our own progress in seeing reality for what it is. Developing the virtues is the primary way to cultivate the soul. The ideal philosopher for Plato rejects erroneous social conventions in favor of observing reality, which requires an understanding of "the Forms," and lives in conformity with them, as is especially clear in the *Phaedrus*. Understanding the Forms aids the process of cultivating true virtue, and the more virtuous we become, the better we can understand the Forms.

While all virtues Plato discusses are crucial for a good life, I narrow my focus in this book to the virtue of *sōphrosunē*. *Sōphrosunē* is on the short list of virtues Plato most often discusses, the others being wisdom, courage, justice, and (less frequently) piety. In her classic study of *sōphrosunē* in Greek literature, Helen North (1966) claims, "Plato contributed more generously to the development of *sōphrosunē* than did any other writer of any period" (151). *Sōphrosunē* is the primary topic of Plato's *Charmides*, a dialogue that ends in *aporia* after Socrates refutes the six definitions of this virtue offered by his interlocutors, and it is of course a deeply sophisticated reflection on *sōphrosunē* that should be read on its own terms. Naturally, much of scholarship on the *Charmides* discusses the nature of *sōphrosunē*,[18] but much less attention has been given to the accounts of this virtue in scholarship about the *Gorgias* and the *Phaedrus*, even though it plays a leading role in

18. For two recent books on the *Charmides*, see Voula Tsouna (2022) and Raphael Woolf (2023). Identifying the ways in which the *Charmides*' reflection on *sōphrosunē* is similar to and different from the accounts in the *Gorgias* and the *Phaedrus* is a substantial task that falls outside the scope of this book. If an answer to the question "What is *sōphrosunē*?" can be gathered from the *Charmides* itself, a strong possibility is the interpretation of Mark Brouwer and Ronald Polansky (2004). They argue that each of the six definitions of *sōphrosunē*, while refuted individually by Socrates as inadequate definitions, contribute to a "comprehensive understanding" of *sōphrosunē* (5). The six definitions that Charmides and Critias offer for *sōphrosunē* are quietness, modesty, doing the things of oneself, doing good things, self-knowledge, and knowing what one knows and does not know. These definitions cover both the characteristic behaviors of the moderate person and the inner "character and insight" that make an individual moderate. Further, Socrates embodies *sōphrosunē*: "*Charmides* completes an account of temperance, and [. . .] Socrates is the living embodiment of temperance throughout. His interaction with the interlocutors displays temperance in action. What is stated about temperance in the dialogue says nearly all that can be usefully said about it, about the sort of action that is temperate and about both the inner character and insight that lead to it. The accounts offered by the interlocutors are refuted because the interlocutors have an ambition that works against temperance, and they misconstrue what they say. Socrates, however, proceeds quietly, modestly, doing his own thing, doing good things, knowing himself, knowing what he knows and does not know, and having knowledge of the good and the bad" (12).

the ethical discussions of both dialogues and is especially pertinent to the questions they are most concerned with.

Sōphrosunē is notoriously difficult to translate into English, and most scholars agree that there is no English term that serves as a perfect equivalent. The most literal translation of *sōphrosunē* is "sound-mindedness," but it was most often translated as "temperance" in the nineteenth and early twentieth century. Later in the twentieth century and into the present day it has been increasingly translated as "moderation." In the introduction to their recent translation of the *Charmides* (2019), Christopher Moore and Christopher Raymond discuss the benefits and drawbacks of various English words that one can use to translate *sōphrosunē* (xxxiv–xxxvii). The words they consider are "sound-mindedness," "moderation," self-control," and "temperance," but they ultimately decide to take a novel approach by selecting "discipline" as their preferred translation.

Since I limit my focus to the accounts of *sōphrosunē* in the *Gorgias* and the *Phaedrus* (while touching on several other Platonic dialogues), I do not provide a comprehensive analysis of the wide variety of ways in which authors throughout antiquity conceptualize *sōphrosunē* as North does. In her chapter on Plato, she surveys the *Charmides,* the *Protagoras,* the *Gorgias,* the *Phaedo,* the *Symposium,* the *Republic,* the *Phaedrus,* the *Timaeus,* the *Sophist,* the *Statesman,* the *Philebus*, and the *Laws*. She notes similarities, differences, and developments across these many passages about *sōphrosunē*, identifying common trends of *sōphrosunē* conceived as "the restraint of appetite," the "orderly arrangement of the soul," and the rehabilitation of the nonrational desires under the guidance of reason. However, she wisely avoids the "danger of abstracting any definition from its context" and so always analyzes *sōphrosunē* "within the framework of specific dialogues" (152). In her interpretation of the *Gorgias*, North rightly claims that Socrates closely associates *sōphrosunē* with the ability to restrain desire for the sake of imposing order and harmony onto one's own soul (159–165), but she does not consider the pedagogical dimension of the *Gorgias*' account of virtue, as I argue below. When discussing the *Phaedrus*, she accurately detects the important distinction between human and divine *sōphrosunē* (176–181), but she does not give a comprehensive analysis of the latter, nor does she detail the benefits it brings to humans according to Socrates.

In addition to North's book, there are two other book-length studies that explore the rich variety of ways philosophers and other writers use the term *sōphrosunē*. Adriaan Rademaker (2005) examines the meanings of *sōphrosunē* in Homer, archaic poetry, the classical tragedians, Aristophanes, and the Attic Orators with the goal of clarifying the ways in which Plato uses the term. He then examines the *Charmides,* the *Protagoras,* the *Laches,* the *Gorgias,* the *Republic*, and the *Laws*, but not the *Phaedrus.* He argues that the most central meaning of *sōphrosunē* in Plato is representative of the most central meaning of this term in Plato's time (2), which is the *Republic*'s definition of this virtue as "the friendship and accord" (*philia kai sumphōnia*) of the soul's (or city's) three parts that reason should rule (442c–d). Later, I will argue that the harmony of the soul is only one facet of Plato's account of genuine *sōphrosunē* in the *Phaedrus.* Christopher Moore (2023) analyzes the use of *sōphrosunē* in ancient authors, including Heraclitus, Euripides, Xenophon, Plato, and Aristotle. He argues that all of these authors "share a basic assumption" that "*sōphrosunē* is the capacity to act well in the face of [. . .] the conflicting heterogeneity of our ends" (2), and as such it is a virtue of agency and "self-constitution" (14). Again, while I think this capacity is one important part of the conceptions of *sōphrosunē* we find in the *Gorgias* and the *Phaedrus*, it does not capture the multifaceted and sophisticated portraits of this virtue offered by Plato. Further, in my view, Moore's goal of finding a unifying or universal definition of the *sōphrosunē* necessarily leads him to interpret the texts about this virtue in a procrustean manner. Instead, I emphasize the extent to which the differing contexts shape the meaning of *sōphrosunē* in the *Gorgias* and the *Phaedrus.*

Throughout this book I often leave *sōphrosunē* untranslated, but when translating it I prefer to use "moderation," because it allows us to best appreciate how Plato starts with a popular, commonly used notion of *sōphrosunē* and transforms its meaning, the clearest example of which is found in the *Phaedrus.*[19] In the *Phaedo* (68e–69a), the *Republic* (553e–554e), and the first two speeches of the *Phaedrus,* Plato draws our attention to a mistaken definition of moderation that was very common in his time (and that is still common today), namely the ability to prevent our desires from leading us toward harmful extremes, or, put another way, restraining certain desires so that we can fulfill others, thereby maximizing our own experience of pleasure over a longer period of time. For example, we choose to eat and drink "moderately" to achieve the pleasant consequences of bodily health or to avoid gaining weight. Against Callicles' claims that it is best to live an *immoderate* life wherein one has the power to constantly satisfy all his desires, Socrates argues in the *Gorgias* that imposing limits on the soul

19. Nearly all translations of Plato's dialogues that I cite throughout the book use the term "moderation" as well.

through the development of moderation is necessary not just for avoiding certain unwanted consequences but also for achieving the state of inner harmony, completeness, and sufficiency that is foundational for a happy and well-lived life. So, in the *Gorgias*, the conception of *sōphrosunē* Socrates espouses is more sophisticated than the popular notion mentioned above, but not terribly far removed from it, and it functions as a sort of "civic" virtue (*R.* 429d–430e) that lies between the conventional notion of *sōphrosunē* and the genuine *sōphrosunē* we find in the *Phaedrus.* Socrates' second speech in the *Phaedrus* explicitly criticizes the conventional conception of moderation, calling it mere "mortal moderation" (256e), and he offers a profound reflection on the true nature of *sōphrosunē* that carries the term still further from its popular usage. So, although "moderation" is by no means a perfect match for *sōphrosunē,* it reflects the way in which Plato offers a transfigured and perfected portrait of this frequently discussed characteristic.

As I indicated above, I analyze Socrates' pedagogical goals and tactics in the *Gorgias* and the *Phaedrus* to make sense of the substantial differences in the way that each dialogue characterizes *sōphrosunē.* In both cases, Socrates helps the interlocutors transition toward a deeper understanding of *sōphrosunē* and a greater appreciation of its value, but the primary interlocutors he speaks with in each dialogue, Callicles and Phaedrus, represent two very different types of people or souls. Callicles represents those who value immoderation and the constant pursuit of more than one has (an idea summed up in by the Greek term *pleonexia*) as essential parts of the best possible human life. So, Socrates' tactic in this discussion is to criticize the flaws in Callicles' commitments and defend the value of self-restraint, since one must first recognize the futility of immoderation and feel shame (*aischos*) about his vices if he is eventually going to become open to cultivating genuine moderation. Self-restraint is much better for the human soul than Callicles' unfettered hedonism, but it is inferior to the fully developed, genuine *sōphrosunē* illustrated in the *Phaedrus.*

The *Phaedrus*' account of genuine *sōphrosunē* shows us how the same virtue is necessary to thrive in several apparently separate spheres of life. Phaedrus, while not a philosopher, shows signs of philosophical potential and an openness to learn from Socrates. Socrates' account of moderation in this context is therefore richer, fuller, and more connected to Socrates' notion of the philosophical life. Socrates paints moderation as the opposite of *hubris*, the moral flaw that leads us to overestimate our knowledge or abilities and treat others as if they are solely means for fulfilling our own desires. Put another way, the hubristic individual sees himself as a god among mortals and forgets his mortal limitations. Moderation is the virtue through which we see ourselves as we are, that is, as limited beings in need of education and self-transformation if we want to lead better lives. When it comes to our desires for wealth, pleasure, power, and so on, the *Phaedrus* suggests that habitual self-restraint is only a necessary step toward genuine moderation. Self-restraint, along with a dedication to philosophical activity and the cultivation of all the virtues, allows the soul to eventually become moderate and harmonized such that it actually comes to resemble the divine, unlike the hubristic individual who falsely thinks he is divine. In addition to greater self-knowledge, *sōphrosunē* improves the quality of intimate relationships, because the moderate lover treats his beloved reverentially and works for his benefit as they jointly pursue wisdom and virtue. Finally, the cultivation of moderation in the context of the philosophical life changes the soul such that it can gain a fuller (though perhaps never complete) understanding of reality.

Another way this book aims to illuminate Plato's reflections on the virtue of *sōphrosunē* is by considering its corresponding vices. Intriguingly, Plato does not contrast *sōphrosunē* with a single vice but with at least four different types of moral imperfection: *akolasia* and *pleonexia* in the *Gorgias*, *hubris* in the *Phaedrus*, and the tyrannical structure of the soul in the *Republic* (and I argue in chapter 1, section I.3, that Callicles is an example of a tyrannical soul). Callicles praises immoderation (*akolasia*), the literal translation of which is "lack of discipline," identifying it as the means to true freedom and happiness. The term *akolasia* here denotes the practice of deliberately *not* disciplining or limiting one's desires with the goal of satisfying all of one's desires as frequently as possible. Relatedly, *pleonexia* is usually translated as "greed," "grasping," or "taking more," as it signifies the active pursuit of an unlimited amount of pleasure, power, wealth, fame, or whatever else one happens to desire. The *Phaedrus* contrasts *sōphrosunē* with the famous term *hubris*, which also has a range of meanings in Greek literature but might be described by Plato as the perennial human mistake of supposing that we are wiser, more powerful, or more important than we really are. Socrates in the *Phaedrus* devotes much attention the role that virtue and vice play in the context of an intimate relationship, where *hubris* manifests as the manipulative, controlling, and even abusive behavior of a vicious lover who regards the satisfaction of his own desires as more important than the well-being of his beloved. In *Republic* IV, Socrates defines *sōphrosunē* as the "unanimity" (*homonoian*) or harmonious friendship between the three parts of the city and soul regarding the issue of which part should rule (432a). The tyrannical soul *completely* lacks the inner harmony of the moderate soul. The tyrannical soul's vice and disorder stem from the fact that both his reason and *thumos* are enslaved to his desires. This self-enslavement prevents reason from apprehending what is truly good for the whole soul and the souls of others. Instead, the tyrannical soul's numerous inordinate and misguided desires govern all of his decisions and interactions with others, which inevitably leads to a life of injustice, friendlessness, violence, and misery. While there is much overlap in the discussions of these four opposites of *sōphrosunē*, they do not collectively point to a single definition of *sōphrosunē* that is uniform across all three dialogues. Rather, each of these forms of moral imperfection correspond fittingly to the different conceptions of *sōphrosunē* found in each context.

The *Gorgias* and the *Phaedrus* make serious contributions to contemporary discussions of the value of virtue ethics, especially when it comes to refining our notions of moderation. Commonly, when considering how the virtue of moderation might benefit our own lives, we conceive of it in a fairly one-dimensional way that might be somewhat similar to the "mortal moderation" that Socrates criticizes in the *Phaedrus*. Again, a likely reason why English speakers make this mistake is that our language does not have a word that covers every meaning the term *sōphrosunē* carries in Plato and in ancient Greek literature more broadly. Plato shows us that moderation helps us thrive in several important spheres of life, and that reducing it to the ability to restrain desires prevents us from fully appreciating how much it pertains to other areas of our lives. Of course, the ancients were not the only people prone to *hubris*. It is a timeless human problem that can manifest in many different ways, such as the habit of thinking we know more than we do or living as if the satisfaction of our own desires took precedence over all else, including the well-being of others. At the end of chapter 4, I expand on why a serious study of Plato's reflections on *sōphrosunē* shows how crucial this virtue is for healthy intimate relationships, self-knowledge, a happy and harmonized mind, and finding meaning in the world. Many think of moderation as minimizing, weakening, or deliberately denying our own desires, but Plato shows us how to think of moderation as a healthy way of handling and pursuing the people and goods that we love. Outside of our intimate relationships, moderation enhances our understanding of our own human limitations as well as our potential for self-transformation. Philosophy as a wisdom practice is rooted in moderation, an idea that some have lost sight of today; through this wisdom practice, we discern real meaning and the ends most worth pursuing. To live philosophically, we must live moderately.

Book Outline

The first chapter of this book examines the type of person and the set of views that Plato represents through his depiction of Callicles. Callicles uses the common sophistic distinction between nature (*physis*) and convention (*nomos*) to argue that, according to nature, the best human life consists in the unlimited satisfaction of one's own desires, while human conventions or laws praise justice, moderation, and other such virtues only for the sake of keeping the strongest individuals under control. In his view, the best human life consists in gaining the power one needs to dominate others and constantly fulfill one's own inordinate desires. In other words, he thinks the good life consists in a commitment to *pleonexia*, or the constant striving to accumulate more than one currently possesses. I argue that while he appeals to nature to justify these views, his position actually implies that there is no real measure for goodness or value apart from the individual's own desires. Further, I explain why Callicles' soul is vicious and disordered, and why it shares many similarities with the tyrannical soul of the *Republic*. His inordinate, misguided desires for wealth, pleasure, and domination rule his soul, and as a result his capacity for reason is reduced to a mere instrument for satisfying these desires. I also argue in this chapter that the root of Callicles' vice is his ignorance of what is, in reality, best for his own well-being and that of others.

In chapter 2, I argue that Socrates gives a fitting response to Callicles by critiquing his views and offering an account of virtue that has the most potential to provide Callicles and those like him with pedagogical and ethical benefit. Socrates argues that there is a real measure for goodness and virtue (without giving much detail about what the measure is), and based on this measure, we can determine that some goods are more necessary for human happiness than others, namely the virtues, philosophical education, friendship, and inner harmony. I argue that Socrates characterizes the virtue of *sōphrosunē* as the ability to satisfy only the desires that will increase the individual's well-being by bringing him closer to a state of self-sufficiency, completeness, and inner harmony. Socrates emphasizes the value of self-restraint in this context because someone like Callicles, who prizes immoderation and unrestrained desire, must first understand the value of self-restraint before he will be ready to understand and pursue genuine *sōphrosunē*.

The second half of the book takes a similar interpretive approach to the *Phaedrus*. I argue that Socrates' account of virtue, and *sōphrosunē* in particular, differs from that of the *Gorgias* due to the *Phaedrus*' unique pedagogical context. In chapter 3, I begin by examining the type of soul Phaedrus represents. Phaedrus is "going in two directions" (*Phdr.* 257b). On the one hand, he is attracted to the way of life represented by Lysias that involves the pursuit of goods such as wealth, power, and pleasure through the conventional, often manipulative way of practicing rhetoric. On the other hand, Phaedrus also shows signs of potential for the philosophical life spent in pursuit of the virtues. Over the course of the dialogue Socrates seeks to guide Phaedrus' soul toward the latter way of life through his philosophical rhetoric. Next I show that Lysias' speech and Socrates' first speech play a crucial role in the *Phaedrus*' examinations of *erōs* and *sōphrosunē.* These speeches depict *erōs* as it is handled by those who lack virtue, and they illustrate a common (yet flawed) conception of *sōphrosunē* as the practice of restraining some desires for the sake of fulfilling others, which Socrates later calls mortal moderation.

By contrast, Socrates' palinode speech, which I examine closely in chapter 4, explains how one can handle the *erōs* he experiences virtuously, and it points out the key differences between mortal moderation and genuine *sōphrosunē.* I argue that genuine *sōphrosunē,* unlike mortal moderation, is related to the concept of the divine in two important senses. First, in the context of an intimate relationship, *sōphrosunē* is expressed as the activity of treating the person one loves with "reverence" (*sebomai*) as an image of divine beauty. Second, the person who possesses *sōphrosunē* accurately sees herself as a limited, imperfect human being, and so avoids the *hubris* of those who live as if they are gods, but at the same time, she actively cultivates her own potential to become similar to the divine by gaining internal harmony and a better understanding of Being. The development of moderation is best pursued in the context of a philosophical relationship and a philosophical life more broadly. Finally, I further illuminate the nature of genuine *sōphrosunē* by discussing three main benefits it brings to human life, namely happy (or "eudaimonic") intimate relationships, self-knowledge, and insight into Being. In all four chapters, I periodically discuss ways in which the insights expressed in these dialogues pertaining to virtue, moral psychology, the good life, and so on are relevant to contemporary moral life, and I elaborate further on these points in the book's conclusion.

Chapter 1

The Ideology and Type of Soul Callicles Represents in *Gorgias*

Plato's account of virtue in the *Gorgias* is best understood when we bear in mind that Socrates uses a *pedagogical* approach to defend his conception of the good life. That is, Socrates does not discuss the virtues in a vacuum, but with the aim of critiquing Callicles' ideology and persuading him that the virtues are more necessary for human happiness (*eudaimonia*) than anything else, both of which could potentially benefit Callicles' disordered soul. If we interpret the dialogue in light of this pedagogical context, though, one might wonder what we can learn from the *Gorgias* that is relevant today. Obviously, the characters of the *Gorgias* as well as its original audience lived in a culture that was significantly different from our own in many respects. However, choices concerning what goods we should care about most in life, how to treat other members of society, and how to critique socially received values are just as relevant to contemporary individuals as they were to Plato's ancient readers. These choices are among the primary focuses of the *Gorgias*. Moreover, Socrates' main interlocutors are young adults who stand at a crucial juncture in their ethical development, just like young adults today, insofar as they must decide how to build their identities, what ethical guidelines they will follow, and the way of life they will adopt. The first two chapters of this book address the mistaken scholarly view that the *Gorgias*' treatment of virtue can be taken out of its pedagogical context, as well as the question of how the dialogue's ethical inquiries are relevant to us today.

In my view, Callicles is not only Plato's depiction of a concrete person (either real or fictional) but also a symbol for a type of person (common in both ancient and contemporary society) who has certain ideological views and a certain moral character, and who occupies an early stage of ethical development. Specifically, Callicles represents those who are not morally virtuous, who do not have a strong desire to become virtuous, and who dismiss as fiction any version of traditional morality that values justice over injustice, moderation over immoderation, and so on. Callicles is an extreme example of the people in this category, because he does not simply lack virtue—he has clearly embraced vicious views, though we should leave open the possibility that his moral character still has potential for positive change at the time of the conversation in the *Gorgias*. Others who fall into this category may be only tempted to live like Callicles without having taken any real steps toward doing so. A significant portion of Plato's readers in liberal democracies with institutions like those (for example) in North America or Europe share some degree of similarity with Callicles, or at least feel some lure toward the sort of life he espouses.[1] Of course, virtuous people or those who do not otherwise share important similarities with Callicles still have plenty to learn from the *Gorgias*, but people who resemble or admire Callicles stand to benefit most from Socrates' account of virtue.

In this chapter, I illuminate the imperfections in Callicles' character and ideology, as well as the root of these imperfections, to show how the *Gorgias* can help us gain insight about happiness and moral virtue (*aretē*). Socrates' critique of Callicles' character shows us why self-centered, inordinate desires for conventional goods alone—and the vices such desires lead to—are inherently unsatisfying and self-destructive. Given the nature of the human soul, it is impossible for conventional goods alone to bring us to our ultimate goal, happiness, and the "higher" goods (as I call them) such as virtue and education are naturally more necessary for genuine happiness. To live happily, we must reach a certain end or limit through which we feel complete and in need of nothing, which means that simply fulfilling our nonrational desires repeatedly with no limit in sight is inevitably disappointing. This end or limit does not have to be a static goal or stopping point. Rather, it is something ongoing that we can maintain over time.[2]

---

1. Historically, the choice between Socrates' conception of virtue and the way of life advocated by Callicles is relevant only to men, since oppression on the basis of gender in many cultures prevented women from engaging in public life such that one could take either of the two paths. However, today, I think the choice between these two ethical paths is relevant to all people regardless of gender. As I will discuss in chapter 2, Socrates makes progressive suggestions regarding gender equality in both the *Republic* and the *Gorgias*.

2. In accord with this idea, Aristotle defines happiness as an "activity" (*energeia*). In *Nicomachean Ethics*, he calls "the human good" an "activity of the soul in accord with

Callicles' pursuit of an unlimited amount of conventional goods will never allow him to reach a lasting state of satisfaction and rest. Then, as now, regardless of our talents, career success, or social status, if we solely pursue goods that are not in themselves sufficient for happiness, then we will at best be unhappy, and at worst vicious and miserable.

Some scholars are disappointed in Plato's account of virtue in the *Gorgias*. Those who mistakenly remove the insights of the *Gorgias* from their pedagogical context, such as Terence Irwin,[3] Charles Kahn,[4] and Rachel Barney,[5] believe that the *Gorgias* is an early, imperfect attempt to defend the value of virtue using an argumentative approach that Plato later improves in the *Republic*.[6] I accept that the *Republic*'s account of virtue includes certain elements that the *Gorgias* does not—it describes each virtue in more detail, it analyzes the nature of the soul (which includes an analysis of *thumos*), and it gives a more thorough explanation of the relationship between the virtues.[7] However, in my view, the imprecision of the *Gorgias*' defense of virtue and its analysis of the soul are *fitting* with respect to the dialogue's pedagogical context, and they serve their functions well. The *Gorgias*' moral psychology relies on a twofold distinction in the soul between reason (*logos*)

virtue" (*EN* 1098a13). He also follows Plato when he argues that the human good (happiness) is complete and self-sufficient when he says that "the complete good" "by itself makes life choiceworthy and in need of nothing" (*EN* 1097b8–16).

3. Irwin 1995, 126.

4. Kahn 1996, 144.

5. Barney 2017.

6. One could also point to the *Philebus* as Plato's most mature reflection on ethics, since it is typically classified as a late-period dialogue. The *Republic* and the *Philebus* undoubtedly contain profound discussions of the good life, but there is no need to conclude that the differences between the *Republic*, the *Philebus*, the *Gorgias*, and other dialogues are due to Plato's level of intellectual maturity at the time of a dialogue's composition. Instead, various types of context that are present in the dialogues themselves better account for the differences between them.

7. However, even the *Republic*'s analysis of the soul is explicitly incomplete—Socrates decides to talk about the soul as if it has three parts (perhaps for the sake of expediency and for the benefit of Glaucon and Adeimantus), even though this method will not allow for a "precise grasp" on the soul (*R.* 435c–d). One key difference between the *Republic* and the *Gorgias* is the main interlocutors with whom Socrates speaks. In the *Republic*, Glaucon and Adeimantus are not seduced by the sophistic account of virtue that they elaborate in book II (and Socrates praises them for this at *R.* 367e–368a), while Callicles clearly *is* persuaded by some such account. Hence, Socrates has to take different approaches to discussing the similar issues due to the different pedagogical needs that these characters have.

and nonrational desire (*epithumia*), yet Callicles' intense and misguided desires have thumotic competition built into them. People like him want to constantly take goods *from* others and occupy positions of dominance, and this twofold desire is a psychological object of analysis that is worthy of its own attention. So, I will explain the nature of what is called *thumos* in other dialogues as it appears in the *Gorgias* and examine its relation to *logos* and *epithumia*, which will prove extremely revealing. From the pedagogical perspective, Socrates limits the conversation's focus to the contrast between reason and desire, since Callicles considers unlimited fulfillment of desire as the key to the good life. Instead of assuming that the *Gorgias*' account of virtue is the product of an early stage in the development of Plato's thought, or that its moral psychology is deficient because it is not the same as the *Republic*'s tripartite account of the soul, we should respect these parts of the dialogue on their own terms.

In sum, I argue in these first two chapters that Socrates' defense of virtue is an exemplary attempt to persuade souls like Callicles, who have no motivation to pursue Socrates' conception of virtue, that prioritizing wisdom, moderation, justice, and courage over all else constitutes the best and happiest way of life.[8] To support this argument, chapter 1, section I, analyzes the *Gorgias*' moral psychology in order to clarify how the interplay between the different aspects of the soul contributes to the formation of virtue or vice, which is where I explain my reading of how *thumos* (as it is called in other dialogues) relates to the twofold distinction between reason and nonrational desire in the context of the *Gorgias*.[9] Then, in sections II and III, I analyze Callicles' character and views, and Socrates' explanation for the source of his vice. In my view, if we first understand Callicles' soul, his worldview, and the ways in which he is ignorant, then we can better appreciate how Socrates tailors his defense of virtue to the sort of person

8. Of course, Socrates' arguments also aim to benefit Polus, Gorgias, and any others who may be present in the audience of the conversation. However, in addition to the fact that his conversation with Callicles takes up roughly half of the dialogue, Callicles embodies the type of person and ideological position that Socrates' arguments are most directly aimed at. As Eric Sanday (2012) points out, the conversation between Socrates and Callicles "directly addresses the decisive assumptions on which the results of [the conversations with Gorgias and Polus] are predicated" (198).

9. Throughout the first two chapters, I refer to reason and nonrational desires as "aspects" of the soul instead of "parts" or "forms" (*eidē*) as they are called in the *Republic* (e.g., 439e), since the *Gorgias* does not use the language of parts or forms to analyze the soul.

and ideological position that Callicles represents. Chapter 2 will then discuss the important components of Socrates' response to Callicles, including his core ethical views and his defense of self-restraint, as well as Socrates' pedagogical aims in the dialogue.

I. Diagnosing the Order and Disorder in Callicles' Soul

The most substantial discussion of virtue in the *Gorgias* occurs between Socrates and Callicles, taking up roughly the second half of the dialogue. When we take into account all of Callicles' words and deeds in the dialogue, we find a rich portrait of a person who challenges some of the fundamental tenets of the philosophical life as Plato portrays it. In effect, Callicles is a vivid symbol for the type of person who rejects socially established ethical and political standards with reckless abandon for the sake of gaining conventional goods such as pleasure, political power, popular approval, and so on. He is similar to Gorgias and Polus in that he uses rhetoric to manipulate the masses, but he shows more signs of a tyrannical nature than they do. Even though Callicles' tyrannical soul is vicious, disordered, and possesses only a mere semblance of virtue, it still has a detectable order or structure. The tyrannical soul's structure is apparent in its behavior patterns and in the internal power relations between its different aspects. Most significantly, Callicles' nonrational desires dominate his thought and behavior, which causes his love (*erōs*) to become unusually inflamed and directed toward unsatisfying objects.

Plato invites readers to analyze both Callicles' arguments and his soul as we critically engage with the text's core questions. For these reasons, a careful study of Callicles' soul and his views will help us to draw insights from the text effectively. So, section I.1 discusses the moral psychology of the *Gorgias* to clarify the conceptual schema we should use to understand the aspects of the soul that play the largest roles in shaping a person's moral character, namely reason (*logos*), nonrational desire (*epithumia*), and love (*erōs*). Then, section I.2 analyzes the important characteristics of Callicles' soul, paying special attention to his intense, improperly directed desires as well as his vices. Finally, section I.3 highlights the similarities between Callicles and the *Republic*'s account of the tyrannical soul for the sake of gaining more precision in understanding his character, the type of person he represents, and the consequences (both for oneself and others) of having a tyrannical soul.

I.1. The Moral Psychology of the *Gorgias*

There are two key moments in the *Gorgias* that help us to see the broader context of the dialogue and the issues at stake in its conversations. On an unspecified date,[10] Socrates and Chaerephon approach Gorgias, Polus, and Callicles, who must be in a public place such as gymnasium in front of other young aristocratic men,[11] since Gorgias has just finished giving a display speech (*Grg.* 447a) with the aim of recruiting students for rhetoric lessons. Gorgias claims that he has the ability to answer "whatever anyone asks" (447d), so Socrates asks him "who he is" (447d), or in other words, "what the power of [Gorgias'] art is, and what it is that he professes and teaches" (447c). This conversation leads Socrates to draw a crucial distinction between craft (*technē*) and "experience" (*empeiria*), and he argues that rhetoric is an *empeiria*, even though Gorgias and company consider it a *technē*. In this context, Socrates argues that the person practicing an *empeiria* "flatters" (463b) or panders to others by causing them as much pleasure and gratification as possible, which brings him various rewards in return (462d, 501b–c). The person practicing a craft, by contrast, does *what is best* for the people or objects he affects (464d), which is not always the same as what is most pleasant.[12] This twofold distinction brings up one of the main themes of the dialogue, namely the difference between what is really good and what is only apparently good. Crafts benefit, or promote the good, of the person or object they act on, while *empeiriai* do not, but only appear to do so by causing pleasure.[13] As I will discuss further below, this distinction between craft and experience mirrors the important moral psychological distinction between *logos* and *epithumia*.

The second key passage that develops the *Gorgias*' exploration of the difference between the real and merely apparent good is 466c–468d, which I discuss in more detail in section III.2 below. In his conversation with Polus, Socrates distinguishes between action and the goal of action, the latter of

10. Nails (2002, 326–327) lists several possibilities for the dramatic date of the dialogue, and she agrees with Dodds (1959) that Plato does not definitively set the dialogue in a particular year.

11. Nails 2002, 326.

12. I return to the *Gorgias*' treatment of rhetoric in chapter 2, section II.1.

13. Similarly, in *Republic* I, Socrates argues against Thrasymachus that crafts, "in the precise sense," benefit the persons or objects they act on rather than the craftsman himself, and that ruling a city is one such craft (341c–342e).

which is always "the good" (*to agathon*) (468b). By "the good" Socrates does not mean a Form (such as the Form of the Good in *Republic* VI and VII), but rather anything that is good or beneficial in some way, such as "wisdom and health and wealth and other such things" (467e). He states: "It is therefore in pursuit of the good that we walk whenever we walk, thinking it to be better; and, the opposite, that we stand still whenever we stand still, for the sake of the same thing, the good; isn't it?" (468b). In this conversation, Socrates gets Polus to agree that possessing "intelligence" (*nous*) is necessary for achieving what is really good (466e), since it is possible for someone without intelligence to do something that is bad or harmful to himself even though it "seems good to him" (468d). These premises lead to the conclusion that doing whatever appears best is not really power, as Polus initially asserted. Instead, real power is the ability to achieve what is actually good. Both this passage and the previous discussion of *empeiria* and *technē* at 448d–466a contextualize Socrates' conversation with Callicles, where the dialogue's moral psychological insights become explicit.

It is important to examine the moral psychology of the *Gorgias*, because not only does it underpin the dialogue's insights about the nature and value of virtue, but it also illuminates the ways in which Socrates tactically formulates his account of virtue with a view to benefitting souls like Callicles, as I will show in chapter 2. Gorgias, Polus, Callicles, and others who practice rhetoric in fifth-century Athens have a largely instrumental attitude toward *logoi*, construed broadly as words, speeches, reason, concepts, arguments, and accounts. Callicles, at least, sees rhetoric as the skill that allows him to use *logoi* as maximally effective tools for fulfilling his own desires for political power, wealth, pleasure, and so on. When we examine this attitude toward *logos* carefully, we find that it is (at least implicitly) rooted in a moral psychological structure that prioritizes the satisfaction of one's own desires above all else. As Socrates argues, the person with this type of soul is far from understanding the best way to care for oneself or to relate to others in the community. While having this instrumental view of *logos* is common, Callicles pushes this attitude and its goals (the acquisition of conventional goods) to the extreme. In Callicles, Plato gives us the most detailed portrait of the vice and moral psychological disorder that underlie the common, self-interested, instrumental attitude toward rhetoric and *logos*.

The *Gorgias* does not aim to provide an exhaustive, highly technical analysis of the soul. Instead, it makes insightful points about the aspects of the soul that are most relevant to moral decision-making, the nature of virtue and vice, and *eudaimonia*. In dialogues such as the *Republic* and the *Phaedrus,* the characters make "divisions" between different aspects of the soul in order to illuminate the nature of virtue and vice. The *Gorgias* makes similar distinctions in the soul, but not as sharply or explicitly as the other two dialogues. The three aspects of the soul that the characters discuss most substantially in the *Gorgias* are reason (*logos*), nonrational desire (*epithumia*), and love (*erōs*).[14] The conversation between Socrates and Callicles is especially concerned with the relationship between *logos* and *epithumia*, and even though characters do not provide explicit definitions of either term, their conversation points out important differences between the two. They primarily use the term *logos*[15] throughout the dialogue to refer to the causal order possessed by objects and the cosmos as a whole; a correct human *logos* (which can refer to our concepts as well as verbal or written explanations and arguments) is the account we give of the causal order of things. A true human *logos* corresponds to the ratios that govern the natural world. In other words, a correct human *logos* expresses insight into the order of things. It is not a separate apparatus or instrument that captures the object, as later thinkers often use this term.

According to the *Gorgias*, humans have the capacity to recognize the structure of the cosmos, the structure of things *in* the cosmos, and that which is truly *good* for (at least some of) these things. Craftsmen, for example, instill "a certain arrangement" in the object of their craft, "compelling one thing to fit and harmonize with another until he has composed the whole as an arranged and ordered thing" (503d–504a). The person who possesses

14. The term *boulēsis* also appears in the conversation with Polus as an act of the soul that is relevant to moral decision making. Plato does not use the term *boulēsis* in a technical way in the *Gorgias*, and it seldomly appears in the dialogue. In Socrates' conversation with Polus, it is more closely related to thinking than nonrational desire. Socrates says that everyone wishes for the good, and we always do what "seems best" (*doxē beltiston einai*) (466e) to us, though it is possible to be wrong about what is actually best for us (468d). The root of *boulēsis* (*boulē*) means "counsel," which also suggests that it is related to thinking and reasoning. Aristotle later uses *boulēsis* to mean "rational wish" (see especially *Nicomachean Ethics* III, chapter 4).

15. Socrates also uses the term *nous* a handful of times throughout the dialogue. At 466e he says that it is possible for someone to do what seems best without *nous* (translated as "intelligence" by Nichols); at 487a he says that a good interlocutor must have "knowledge, goodwill, and outspokenness [*epistēmēn te kai eunoian kai parrēsian*]"; and at 505b he calls the bad soul *anoētos*, which Nichols translates as "thoughtless." In my view, Plato does not use the term in a consistent way throughout the dialogue as he does with *logos*, *epithumia*, and *erōs.* Instead, it occurs in nontechnical contexts, and *logos* is the more substantial term when it comes to how reasoning or thinking are relevant to moral life.

a *technē* is a keen student of the real structures of the world. She understands the order that is best with a view to the causal arrangement of their objects. Arrangement and order in turn contribute to making something excellent, since "the virtue of each thing—of implement, body, soul too, and every living being—does not come to be present in the finest manner simply at random, but by arrangement, correctness, and art, which has been assigned to each of them" (506d). On a broader scale, the "the wise" (507e) observe the beauty and order of the entire cosmos: "Heaven, earth, gods, and human beings are held together by community, friendship, orderliness, moderation, and justness" (507d–508b). The human soul can apprehend the measures[16] for goodness, beauty, and order, and it can look to these measures to promote the good of humans, other living things, or objects.

By contrast, *epithumia* naturally strives for pleasure and gratification with no regard for whether the pleasures are beneficial or harmful. In other words, our desires for pleasure, food, sex, power, fame, wealth, and so forth blindly urge us to satisfy them, even in contexts where doing so would be detrimental to ourselves or others. Desires are not naturally inordinate or inclined to pursue the excessive, unlimited amount of goods that Callicles says we should. However, if an individual is negatively influenced by a poor upbringing or by vicious, ignorant role models, then he will "let his desires grow to be as great as possible and not chasten them" (491e–492a), endeavoring to fulfill them as much as possible in accord with the misguided view that doing so is the key to happiness. Desires therefore must be guided and regulated by correct reason in the person who seeks to avoid the different sorts of harm that *epithumia* can potentially bring. Importantly, desires are only ever satiated temporarily, as the image of the leaking jar illustrates (492e–494a). As one's desires grow stronger, they require either greater quantities of goods to satisfy them, or they require satisfaction more frequently, or both. Socrates says that the person who cares only about satisfying his own desires is like a person trying to fill a "perforated jar" with water, and he carries the water with a "perforated sieve" (493b). Filling the jar symbolizes the satisfaction of one's desires, and the holes in the jar symbolize the desires themselves, which shows that we never remain satisfied for long. Indeed, as our desires grow more intense or inflamed by bad influence (or,

16. In my analysis of the *Gorgias* and the *Phaedrus*, I use the concept of "measure" (*metrion*) from Plato's *Statesman* to describe the real, universal standards for goodness, beauty, or virtue for all things, including human beings. I expand on this concept of measure in sections II and III below.

as the holes in our jars grow larger), the amount of time we remain satisfied decreases, and we therefore experience more and more pain, since "all need and desire are painful" (496d). Without virtue and the right exercise of reason, desire neither observes the measure of a thing's well-being, nor does it discern how to apply that measure to a given context. If desire takes as its measure a good subject to limit, then it is in conformity with virtue and a true human *logos*, but if its primary object is an unlimited amount of conventional goods, then it is in this sense irrational.

Nonrational desires are not rooted in reason, but they are nonetheless responsive to reason to at least some degree. Without reason to order and regulate one's desires, their intensity and insatiability will likely grow over time.[17] The virtuous person, by contrast, desires only the types and amount of goods that reason identifies as best, such that reason and desire harmonize. The *Gorgias* suggests several different ways in which reason can influence desire, one of which is through the experience of shame (*aischos*). When an individual considers the strength or objects of his own desires shameful, his desires may recoil (at least temporarily), and he is likely to voluntarily restrain them. If he uses reason to restrain his desires habitually, then they may conform to reason more closely over time.[18] As I will discuss further in chapter 2, section II.3, cultivating one's sense of shame is an important part of the process of becoming virtuous. Cultivating a noble sense of shame involves learning what is truly shameful, namely committing vicious actions and having a vicious, disordered soul. The person who understands this will experience the appropriate level of shame about his own moral imperfection. Callicles currently does not feel shame about his own imperfection, but instead considers suffering injustice as more shameful than committing it (486b). One person can help another cultivate his sense of shame, as Socrates attempts to do in his conversation with Callicles (I also show this in chapter 2, section II.3). Such assistance involves helping the other person recognize that his desires are inordinate or improperly directed and begin the process of restraining them by bringing them into

17. Some bodily desires may naturally fade due to age, and not because of any regulation from reason or virtuous habituation. For example, Cephalus says that he has been released from desires for sex and alcohol in *Republic* I (328d–329c). However, his desire for money appears to be as strong as ever (331a–b), which is evidence that age does not diminish all desires.

18. I agree with Jessica Moss (2005), who argues that in the *Gorgias* "shame can sometimes neutralize the appetites' destructive force where reason on its own has failed: it can make the agent recoil from the pleasures of vice and aspire even to the pains of virtue" (17).

conformity with correct reason through rehabituation. The way that Socrates helps Callicles cultivate his sense of shame is analogous to the way parents discipline children who lack knowledge of how to act well for their benefit. It is worth noting the clear etymological link between discipline (*kolasin*) and the term Plato uses for immoderation, which is, literally, the lack of discipline (*akolasia*). For both Plato and Aristotle, discipline or punishment helps to remove immoderation.[19]

Desires are also responsive to reason when they are "punished" (*kolazesthai*) (476a) or rationally disciplined by another person or institution.[20] Disciplining the soul involves keeping it "away from the things it desires" (505b) and applying "pains and griefs" (525b–c).[21] If discipline can rehabituate our desires, then it can influence the intensity or even the objects toward which we direct them. Just so, discipline helps to rid the soul of its "injustice" and "immoderation" (*akolasias*) (478b), and so the person disciplined "becomes better in respect to his soul" (477a). Discipline therefore "moderates [*sōphronizei*] men and makes them more just and comes to be the medicine for baseness" (478d). In this context, "moderating" the soul means helping someone develop self-restraint, such that his desires do not lead him to act contrary to what the true *logos* indicates is best, as I will discuss further in chapter 2. If the person being punished is properly rehabilitated, then his behavior will no longer be shaped by inordinate desire for certain types of goods, nor will his desire lead him to treat others unjustly. However, in Socrates' view, punishment alone could not make someone virtuous—at best, it creates the ideal conditions in which one could choose to morally cultivate himself. Discipline does not simply give moderation or other virtues to the person punished. Rather, it begins the process of training that one needs to go through in order to achieve moderation. Just as physical training does not by itself create a good athlete (one also needs repeated

19. In *Sophist* 229e–230d, the Visitor outlines "admonition" and "cross-examination" as two ways that one person can help another experience the constructive kind of shame. In chapter 2, section II.3, I examine Plato's discussions of shame in more detail.

20. See Aristotle, *Nicomachean Ethics* 1119a34–b15 for a similar discussion of how desires can be disciplined and the potential benefits of doing so.

21. In the *Gorgias'* myth of the afterlife, Socrates claims that properly administered pains help to "cure" the soul of its vice both before and after death: "And some there are who are benefited and pay the just penalty, by gods and human beings—those who err in making curable errors; nevertheless the benefit comes about for them through pains and griefs both here and in Hades, for it is not possible otherwise that they be released from injustice" (525b–c).

practice at the sport, proper coaching, and so on), punishment alone does not make someone virtuous. Obviously, there is much to be said about the complicated relationship between reason, desire, and the potential impact of just discipline, and I will return to the *Gorgias*' treatment of punishment when I discuss Socrates' response in chapter 2. Nonetheless, it is at least clear that rational discipline can influence nonrational desire.

Interestingly, the distinction between *logos* and *epithumia* corresponds to several other important distinctions throughout the *Gorgias*. First, as I will discuss further below, it corresponds to the difference between Socrates' and Callicles' conceptions of the good life. Socrates argues that pleasure and the good are distinct (495a–499c) and that the philosophical life in accord with *logos* is best. Callicles, on the other hand, argues that pleasure is the good, and therefore that happiness and a good life result from letting one's desires grow as large as possible and gaining the power to constantly fulfill them (491e–492c). Second, the distinction between *logos* and *epithumia* corresponds to Socrates' division between *technē* and *empeiria*. The person with a *technē* promotes the order and well-being of the object of her craft (464c), and she can accurately explain why her work benefits or improves its object (465a). For example, the doctor can give an account that explains what causes a certain medicine to cure a certain disease. By contrast, someone with an *empeiria,* such as the pastry baker or the average rhetorician, simply aims to satisfy nonrational desires by producing as much pleasure as possible for himself and others (462c, 464d, 500e–501c). Third, the relationship between the characters Socrates and Callicles in the *Gorgias* mirrors the dialogue's points about the ability for *logos* to "punish" or reign in *epithumia.* Socrates attempts to persuade Callicles to stop pursuing unlimited pleasure by helping him cultivate shame, just as an individual can reign in his desire through reason, cultivating shame, or some type of punishment. Socrates thus symbolizes reason, and he "punishes" Callicles, who symbolizes *epithumia,* by way of refutation. Plato makes this point explicit at 505c—when Callicles starts refusing to cooperate in the discussion, Socrates observes that Callicles "does not abide being benefitted and suffering for himself this thing that the argument is about, being punished." While Socrates may or may not succeed in having any impact on Callicles, he nonetheless attempts to motivate Callicles to become self-restrained (so that he can eventually be virtuous),[22] just as

22. There are other Platonic dialogues in which Socrates speaks to young men at crucial point in their lives just before they assume an influential position in society, such as Glaucon and Adeimantus (*Republic*), Phaedrus, Meno, Charmides, and Alcibiades

reason should aim to regulate desire in accord with its views about what is best.

As I mentioned above, the third aspect of the soul that is most relevant for moral life according to the *Gorgias* is love (*erōs*). At first glance, it may appear that *erōs* is simply a type of *epithumia,* but several passages in the *Gorgias* indicate that Socrates does not use the term *erōs* to denote one particular desire (for example, the desire for sex or intimacy) that belongs to the same class as our desires for food, drink, money, pleasure, and so on. Rather, *erōs* is the attraction that the whole soul feels toward whatever appears best to it. The *Gorgias* does not contain a discussion devoted to the nature of *erōs*, so we can only attain a limited degree of precision about it in this context, but there are a few points in the text where it plays a crucial role. As I will discuss further in section I.2, despite the drastic differences between the souls of Callicles and Socrates, both of them are "in love"—Socrates is in love with philosophy and Alcibiades, and Callicles is in love with Demos, son of Pyrilampes, and the Athenian people (*demos*) (481d–482a). Callicles is ruled by his desires, and Socrates is not, yet both of them are in love. The experience of *erōs* is common to everybody, regardless of one's values or moral character. This suggests that *erōs* is not a type of *epithumia* but rather a more fundamental source of motivation—in other words, something that leads the soul—to pursue the persons or objects that appear best and most beautiful.

Although the *Gorgias* does not contain substantial discussions devoted to the nature of *erōs,* several passages share important similarities to the *Symposium*'s discussion of *erōs,* so examining passages from both dialogues helps to flesh out the *Gorgias*' suggestions about love. As Diotima says in the *Symposium,* love is a "leader" (*ho hēgoumenos*) (210a) of the soul that compels it toward whatever it regards as best and most beautiful (*Smp.* 205d–206a).[23] According to Diotima, everyone is in love with something,

---

in *Alcibiades* I (I acknowledge that this dialogue's authorship is debated). In these conversations, Socrates' goal need not be turning them into philosophers overnight, but rather motivating them to value and pursue virtue. In the *Gorgias,* Socrates certainly defends the value of philosophy, but his most pressing concern with Callicles is to persuade him to begin cultivating virtue.

23. Interestingly, the term "lead" (*proagō*) appears repeatedly throughout the *Phaedrus* (see 227c, 230a, and 261a as just a few examples). This term is related to *psychagōgia,* an important word in Socrates' definition of rhetoric. Socrates defines rhetoric: "Isn't the art [*technē*] of rhetoric, taken as a whole, a certain guiding of souls through words [*psychagōgia tis dia logōn*] not only in the law courts and other places of public assembly, but also in private?" (261a–b)

but different kinds of people love different kinds of things. We cannot help but strive for happiness (205a–b),[24] and all people suppose that attaining the best things will bring them happiness. So, every person is in love with whatever appears best to him or her (205d).[25] The soul's conception of what is best will change depending on whether reason or desire rules within it. Someone like Callicles who is ruled by *epithumia* directs his love toward the objects of *epithumia*, namely conventional goods such as pleasure, wealth, power, and so on. The person ruled by reason, on the other hand, directs his love toward wisdom, virtue, learning, and whatever else is, in reality, more necessary for *eudaimonia*.[26] Callicles' nonrational desires dominate his thought and behavior, which causes his *erōs* to become unusually inflamed and directed toward unsatisfying objects. The individual who primarily loves wisdom still feels some degree of love for these conventional goods insofar as they are good, but she loves wisdom most intensely as her top priority, and as a result she subordinates her desires for other goods to this principal love. In this way, the structure of one's soul, and, relatedly, her virtue or vice, determine how she directs her *erōs*.

The *Republic* and the *Phaedrus* both distinguish *thumos* as one of the three parts of the soul. In the *Republic* especially, *thumos* is associated with anger, competition, self-assertiveness, domination, and the social recognition one gains from victory.[27] The *Gorgias* acknowledges that the experiences

24. Diotima describes love as wanting to possess the good forever: " 'Now this desire for happiness, this kind of love—do you think it is common to all human beings and that everyone wants to have good things forever and ever? What would you say?' 'Just that,' I said. 'It is common to all' " (*Smp.* 205a–b).

25. Diotima names money, sports, and philosophy (or wisdom) as examples of different things that people regard as best and therefore love (205d).

26. In the *Republic*, Socrates also suggests that the virtuous person loves the highest goods when he says that "the right sort of love [*orthos erōs*] is by its nature the self-controlled [*sōphronōs*] and harmonious love of what is self-disciplined and beautiful" (*R.* 403a). See also 403b–c.

27. The *Republic* (440b–441c) and the *Phaedrus* (253d) also suggest that *thumos* is a natural ally to reason. For example, in the *Republic*, Socrates states: "When desires force someone contrary to the calculating part, he reproaches himself and his spirit is roused against that in him which is doing the forcing; and, just as though there were two parties at faction, such a man's spirit becomes the ally of speech? But as for its making common cause with the desires to do what speech has declared must not be done, I suppose you'd say you had never noticed anything of the kind happening in yourself, nor, I suppose, in anyone else" (440a–b). In other words, when an individual's reason and desire pull him toward different goods, both the *Republic* and the *Phaedrus* suggest

Plato elsewhere associates with *thumos* are present in the soul when Callicles behaves aggressively (for example, see 485d, 489b, 505b, all of which I will discuss further below) and praises the benefits of good reputation or honors (486c–d). However, the dialogue does not sharply demarcate these experiences from the *epithumiai*. It is possible that the *Gorgias* implies that *thumos* is separate from the desires. However, I think it is more likely that the *Gorgias* only makes a twofold division in the soul between reason and nonrational desires (with *erōs* being common to both), and that psychic phenomena that dialogues such as the *Republic* associate with *thumos* are amalgamated with some of the nonrational desires according to the *Gorgias*. In other words, some of the nonrational desires that the characters discuss in the *Gorgias* have a strong admixture of what is called *thumos* in other dialogues. Callicles' desires have a thumotic, competitive dimension, as expressed in his desire to dominate others; the pleasures he desires and the pleonexic way of life he aspires to involve taking goods *from* other people. For example, the inclinations toward domination and violence are two desires that Callicles says the naturally powerful man will fulfill by becoming a tyrant (492b). There is a thumotic element of Callicles' character, even if the dialogue does not distinguish *thumos* as a separate part.

Hence, Plato probably does not find it necessary to explicitly introduce *thumos* as a separate part of the soul in the *Gorgias*, since so much of the debate concerns the interplay between reason and nonrational desire in the good human life. The twofold distinction in the soul between reason and desire also makes sense from the perspective of Socrates' pedagogical goal in the conversation. Callicles regards the fulfillment of nonrational desire as the key to happiness, and he is ruled by his own desires. So, it is appropriate for Socrates to include the phenomena associated with *thumos* among the class of *epithumiai*, since his aim is to show Callicles that being internally ruled by anything besides reason is dissatisfying.[28] It is not my

that *thumos* can help reason win this inner conflict through a sort of self-reproach that helps to lessen the influence of the nonrational desires.

28. In the *Philebus*, where characters compare the value of pleasure and knowledge, *thumos* is also not demarcated as a separate part or aspect of the soul. Just as the characters focus on the twofold distinction between reason and desire in the *Gorgias*, so do they discuss the twofold distinction between knowledge and pleasure in the *Philebus*. Although *thumos* is not explicitly discussed in either dialogue, experiences and psychic phenomena elsewhere associated with it are clearly a concern when characters discuss the soul's *pathēs* at 47d–48b. Further, the concept of "measure" is common to both dialogues as well. Perhaps the reason for these similarities between the two dialogues is

primary aim to answer questions about whether the soul has parts and what they are, because this is not the *Gorgias'* primary aim either, but to properly diagnose Callicles' soul I will focus on the distinction between reason and his thumotic, inordinate, misguided desires.

I.2. Callicles' Character

Having discussed the moral psychology of the *Gorgias*, we can use the dialogue's own key concepts and terms to analyze the structure and disorder of Callicles' moral character. In doing so, this section will carry forward the discussion of vicious, inordinate desire and orderly arrangement of the soul discussed in the previous section. E. R. Dodds (1959) and Debra Nails (2002) agree that Callicles was a real person, though we have no other sources about him besides the *Gorgias*. Nails (2002, 75–76) shows that, at the time of the conversation in the *Gorgias*, Callicles is probably in his early thirties, a householder, a lover of a young man named Demos,[29] and in the early stages of his political career. Aside from his association with Gorgias, he also associates with Andron (487c), a member of the oligarchy of the Four Hundred in 411.[30] Plato depicts Andron in a group with Phaedrus and Eryximachus that gathers around the sophist Hippias in the *Protagoras*, which establishes a link (at least superficially) between Callicles and Phaedrus. While the historical question of whether Callicles was a real person is not extremely important for interpreting the *Gorgias*, the details about his life and pursuits (whether real or fictional) will shed light on the ways in which Plato employs this important character throughout the dialogue.

Just after Callicles steps into the conversation at 481b, Socrates identifies two objects of Callicles' "love" (*erōs*), each of which highlights important aspects of his character, values, and way of life. Socrates says that he and Callicles are similar insofar as they are both "lovers" (*erōnte*). However, Socrates directs his *erōs* toward philosophy and Alcibiades, while Callicles directs his toward Demos (son of Pyrilampes) and the Athenian *demos* (481d). Socrates refers to Demos and the Athenian people as Callicles'

that in both Socrates' interlocutors advocate unfettered hedonism, and this influences the approach Socrates uses to analyzing the soul, knowledge, reason, virtue, and so on. Of course, I merely point out these similarities here, and a more in-depth discussion of them deserves its own project.

29. According to Nails (2002), Callicles' beloved, Demos, was Plato's stepbrother (327).

30. Nails 2002, 29.

two "boyfriends" (*ta paidika*, 481d). Callicles' love leads him to constantly say what his boyfriends want to hear—he never "contradicts" Demos or the Athenian people (481d) but instead says whatever pleases them most, no matter how often it leads him to contradict what he said in the past. He is successful at gratifying them because he is "terribly clever" (481d). Callicles' desire to please his boyfriends completely dictates his life, as he follows this desire wherever it might lead him. He has no interest in remaining consistent in his words or actions, nor does he adhere to a set of principles or code of conduct save for the goal of pleasing Demos, the crowd, and himself.

For Callicles, gratifying the desire of his boyfriends is a means for satisfying his own immoderate and exceptionally intense desires (*epithumiai*). His obsession with pleasure is apparent at 491e–492c, where he lambasts the virtue of moderation. He praises "immoderation" (*akolasia*) and unfettered hedonism, arguing that the best possible life consists in letting one's desires grow as large as possible and having the power to constantly fulfill them.[31] Indeed, "virtue and happiness" consist in "luxury, intemperance, and freedom when they have support" (492c). As I will discuss further in section II below, Callicles' values are summed up well by the Greek term *pleonexia* (sometimes translated as "greed," "grasping," or "taking more"), because in this context it signifies the goal of obtaining an unlimited amount of pleasure, power, wealth, fame, or whatever one happens to desire. Securing affection from Demos ensures Callicles' own erotic satisfaction, and gaining approval from the majority of Athenians gives him political power he can use to obtain whatever he might want. Importantly, it is not only the intensity of Callicles' *epithumiai* and *erōs* that contributes to his vice but also the fact that he directs these desires *solely* toward conventional goods, as I will discuss further below.

Callicles has desires for many different things, such as pleasure, wealth, and dominance over others, but there is not one type of good that stands out to him among the others as the most desirable. Rather, he wants all of them at once.[32] Fulfilling all of these desires at the same time, though,

31. Plato even subtly highlights Callicles' intense desire for pleasure in apparently insignificant remarks that Callicles makes throughout the dialogue: "I certainly desire [*epithumō*] to do so" (481b) and "I don't know if I have ever had such pleasure as now. So for me, even if you should want to converse the whole day long, you'll be gratifying me [*charieisthe*]" (458d).

32. Raphael Woolf (2000) rightly observes that Callicles' words and desires contradict one another; although Callicles rejects the value of *nomoi* in his speeches, he also craves the conventional fruits of success such as popularity, good reputation, wealth, and so on (5).

is likely impossible for practical reasons. For example, he has a desire to have as much money as possible, but he also has the desire to experience physical pleasures as often as possible, and these cost money. He is not like the oligarchic soul in the *Republic*, for instance, who refrains from fulfilling some desires for the sake of accruing as much wealth as possible (*R.* 554a–b). Callicles' desires thus conflict with one another in that he cannot fulfill all of them simultaneously, and this is one way in which he is "dissonant" or in disagreement with himself (482b). His multifarious, competing desires inevitably clash against one another and cannot be satisfied simultaneously, and so in this sense he is at war with himself. Another way in which he is dissonant with himself is shown by his habit of making different claims at different times (481d–e). Just as his desires conflict with one another, so also his reasoning frequently contradicts itself. Habitual philosophical examination helps to bring one's reasoning into conformity with itself such that his views remain consistent over time, as Socrates exemplifies throughout the dialogue (and he points out explicitly at 508e–509a). Similarly, when it comes to competing desires, the virtues help to regulate and bring them into harmony with reason, so that they are not excessively intense, they are properly directed, and they are no longer in painful strife with one another. Of course, Callicles lives neither philosophically nor virtuously, and so continues to vainly pursue gratification of his conflicting desires.

Callicles' intense desire for an unlimited amount of pleasure or other goods also explains his devotion to rhetoric. Young men such as Callicles and Polus are so attracted to rhetoric because (as Gorgias himself says at 452e) it is an effective means for gaining power and gratifying one's desires in a wide array of situations, whether it be the courtroom, political arenas such as the Assembly or the council, private business, or even when dealing with experts such as the doctor or the trainer (452e). Becoming a master of persuasion is therefore a seductive prospect, especially for young, ambitious men in a democratic society such as Athens.[33] All of Callicles' pursuits are

33. Mark Munn (2000) states that, in Athens during Socrates' lifetime, "sovereignty in all matters lay with the Athenian *demos*, the forty or sixty thousand adult male citizens [. . .] The votes of the majority in the Assembly dictated the tasks to be carried out by the officers of the state, while majority votes in the jury-courts imposed penalties on those who failed to carry out the people's will" (64–65). Given this type of government, the ability to speak persuasively became extremely important; the individuals who often gained political power were "those who regularly came forward to speak in the Assembly, before the Council, or before any other board of public officers that had to deliberate on matters in the people's interest" (71–72).

thus self-serving, and they are rooted in his intense, misguided *erōs* and *epithumia*. Rhetoric is a means for persuading or gratifying his "boyfriends," and their gratification is a means for his own.

Further, Callicles is aggressive, and there are hints that he is not opposed to using violence or breaking the law to get what he wants. He behaves aggressively in the dialogue by being combative[34] instead of cooperative with Socrates throughout their conversation. He hurls insults at Socrates, calling him a "demagogue" (*dēmēgoros*) at 482c and often saying that his words are mere "drivel" (489b). When Socrates points out the incoherent consequences of Callicles' views, he refuses to continue the conversation for a time (505d). He praises tyranny (492b), whose defining features are, of course, the use of violence and disregard for established laws. He also extols Heracles for stealing cows in Pindar's story (484b–c), and he claims that those who spend too much time pursuing philosophy "need a beating" (485d). Relatedly, he prizes good "reputation" or honor (486c–d) and victory in the law courts (486b), both of which indicate a competitive and self-centered character. Importantly, Callicles' proclivity for violence or other forms of aggression is another symptom of his inordinate desire; if violence is the means for fulfilling his intense desire, then Callicles has no qualms about attempting to get away with as much aggression as he can. As I indicated above, Callicles' desire is amalgamated with the sorts of psychic phenomena elsewhere associated with *thumos*. He is an example of how nonrational desires become unusually inflamed, appetitive, and inclined toward domination in the vicious soul. He takes pleasure in violating norms and standards, and taking goods from others. When given the opportunity, people like him enjoy violently violating interpersonal standards. The goal of the pleonexic way of life he advocates is both satisfaction of desires and dominion over others.

Another important feature of Callicles' character that Plato frequently calls our attention to is his sense of shame.[35] On the one hand, Callicles does not feel shame about things that most other people do, as evidenced by the fact that he is not ashamed to say publicly that injustice is superior to justice in every way, unlike Gorgias and Polus (492d). He likewise feels

34. Callicles opens the *Gorgias* with a question to Socrates, and the first word of the dialogue is "war" (447a), which may foreshadow his penchant for violence.

35. For more on the importance of shame in Plato, see Jenks (2012), Brouwer and Polansky (2004), and Tarnopolsky (2010). In chapter 2, I will discuss the role of shame in the *Gorgias* in greater depth.

no shame at the prospect of living unjustly, seeing no reason to avoid committing injustice or causing harm to others so long as he can get away with it (492a–c). In his view, having a sense of shame about such things would be a symptom of weakness, since it would prevent one from committing injustice or living immoderately (492a). On the other hand, Callicles regards suffering injustice as shameful, and he seeks to avoid it by attaining as much political power as possible. He emphasizes the importance of being able to defend oneself against unjust accusations or violence from others (486b), and he sees the ability to defend oneself as the most valuable form of power. He avoids suffering injustice and just punishment, reacting angrily to any standards being imposed on him by anyone besides himself. So, even though he considers the prospect of suffering injustice shameful due to the pain and embarrassment it would involve, he lacks the sort of shame that is bound up with self-criticism, self-restraint, and moral decision-making. Much as his *erōs* and *epithumia* are too fixated on conventional goods, he feels too much shame about that which is less harmful, and too little shame about that which is most harmful.

Plato thus uses Callicles to represent anyone who is committed to the unrestricted pursuit of political power, pleasure, wealth, and other similar conventional goods. There are, of course, many such people in both historical and contemporary societies, since the inclination to follow one's desires wherever they may lead is natural enough, and the intensity of such desires tends to grow if we do not put some check on them. The way of life characterized by *pleonexia* is especially appealing to those who think they will excel against others in the social competition for conventional goods. As Callicles himself points out, those who are "stronger" (i.e., those who are born with certain natural talents or social advantages) than the average person are tempted to seek positions of social power and luxury (491e–492c). In the competition for power, pleasure, or wealth, injustice often leads to an advantage over others, so such people often commit as much injustice as they think they can get away with, especially when they are motivated by the pain of unfulfilled desire. This kind of vicious character reaches its extreme in the tyrannical soul who becomes an actual tyrant, as Plato shows in the *Republic*, and Callicles shares the tyrannical soul's key characteristics.

As I mentioned in the introduction, examining the type of soul Callicles represents is important not only for understanding the *Gorgias* but also because his moral persona remains relevant to contemporary life. Many of us share at least some common traits with Callicles, even if we might not think so at first glance. He makes explicit what many people may think but are prevented from saying by various social pressures. Plato explicitly points this out when Callicles says to Socrates that he will not shy away from saying what Gorgias and Polus thought but were too "ashamed" to say (482c–e). He boldly expresses what other people may not want to admit about themselves. Or, perhaps examining Callicles may bring our attention to aspects of ourselves that we are unaware of and need to examine. During at least some points in our lives, we cannot help but feel strong desires for various objects or goals, and these desires may lead us to act in harmful ways. As Socrates says in *Republic* IX: "Surely some terrible, savage, and lawless form of desire is in every man, even in some of us who seem to be ever so measured. And surely this becomes plain in dreams" (572b). While most of us do not reach the point of having a "tyrannical" nature like Callicles (as I discuss immediately below), many people base their lives around the goals of acquiring wealth, achieving higher social status, maximizing pleasure, and frequent consumption. To this extent, many modern individuals have something in common with Callicles, even if we live in a culture that is very distant from his. Even those who do not base their lives around achieving these goals, and who, for example, commit themselves to serving others, may occasionally feel some lure toward the Calliclean life. After all, we have a cultural fascination with the "outlaw," the type of person who boldly takes as much as he or she wants with no regard for laws or social limitations. Plato's portrait of Callicles' viciousness can help us confront the Calliclean inclinations we might have, which in turn can lead us toward a deeper moral self-understanding and self-harmony.

I.3. Callicles' Similarity to the *Republic*'s "Tyrannical Soul"

Much like Callicles, the tyrannical soul in *Republic* IX misdirects his *erōs* and *epithumia*. Hence, a brief study of the tyrannical soul will help to shed light on Callicles' character, the type of person he represents, and the cause of his severe moral imperfection. The *Republic* draws a distinction between a tyrannical soul and an actual tyrant—the two are similar in terms of their psychological structure and the nature of their vice, but the power that comes with being an actual ruler of a city allows this vice to reach its most extreme pitch, making the tyrannical soul who becomes a tyrant "the most wretched of all men" (*R.* 578b–c). Actualizing one's vicious intent through real, habitual action further develops and entrenches one's vice, and becoming a political leader drastically increases one's opportunity for such action. Callicles, of course, does not have the political power necessary to turn into a tyrant, so it is more accurate to understand him as a tyrannical soul with the potential to become a real tyrant should the opportunity present itself. In *Republic* I, Thrasymachus draws a distinction between "partially unjust men" ("temple robbers, kidnappers, housebreakers, defrauders, and thieves") and the tyrant who is perfectly unjust and therefore able to effectively take over an entire society without paying a penalty (344a–c). Callicles resembles the second kind—clever and shrewd, he is a demagogue and an aspiring tyrant who is waiting for his opportunity to ascend to the top of the social ladder.

Callicles and Polus cite tyrants as the happiest men and the paradigmatic examples of the way of life they desire most (470e, 471a–d, 492b). While the tyrant's public image is one of success, indulgence, and happiness such that many people envy him, the *Republic* clearly argues that a glimpse into his inner life reveals that he is "the most wretched [*athliōtaton*][36] of all men" (*R.* 578b).[37] Socrates suggests that such a person experiences severe inner torment due to his insatiable desire for pleasure, power, fame, and whatever else he might happen to desire at a given time. As a result, the tyrant's life does not turn out to be the series of constant pleasures for which he hopes. Instead, his life consists in attempting to stave off the intense pains that will ensue if he fails to constantly satiate his inordinate desires. When he inevitably fails to perpetually satisfy his desires, he suffers immensely: "Then it is necessary to get contributions from every source or be caught in the grip of great travail and anguish" (574a). The tyrannical soul's insatiability is reminiscent of the *Gorgias*' image of the leaking jar (*Grg.* 493a–b), where Socrates says that the person with intense desires can never become fully satisfied.[38] Moreover, if he ever fails to keep pleasures

36. *Athlios* is the same word that Socrates frequently uses in the *Gorgias* to describe the misery of the vicious soul.

37. Just after this claim, Socrates compellingly summarizes the reasons why the tyrant is the most miserable of all mortals: "Therefore, the real tyrant is, even if he doesn't seem so to someone, in truth a real slave to the greatest fawning and slavery, and a flatterer of the most worthless men; and with his desires getting no kind of satisfaction, he shows that he is most in need of the most things and poor in truth, if one knows how to look at a soul as a whole. Throughout his entire life he is full of fear, overflowing with convulsions and pains, if indeed he resembles the disposition of the city he rules" (579d–e).

38. Socrates' myth at the end of the *Gorgias* suggests that the vicious person's actions and suffering cause lasting damage to his own soul. When Rhadamanthus examines the soul of a tyrant after death, he sees "scars" caused by the tyrant's own injustice: "[Rhadamanthus] perceives that there is nothing healthy in the soul [of the great kind or some other king or potentate], but it has been severely whipped and is filled with scars

constantly flowing in, then the result is great pain, since "all need and desire are painful" (496d). In both cases, uncontrolled desire leads to a significant amount of suffering. The *Republic* and the *Gorgias* thus agree that a life of misery is the cumulative effect of failing to subordinate desires to the measure identified by correct reason.

Worse still, the tyrannical soul's pain has no benefit; it is simply pointless suffering brought on by his own vice. In some contexts, pain promotes well-being, such as the pain caused by the doctor as she heals the body or the pain of punishment that (ideally) improves the soul morally (*Grg.*, 525b–c). Thus, it is not simply pain but *useless* and *excessive* pain that makes the tyrant's life miserable, and this pain is caused by his own vicious, disordered soul. We should embrace pain when it promotes genuine well-being, as Diotima points out in the *Symposium*:

> But according to my story, a lover does not seek the half or the whole, unless, my friend, it turns out to be good as well. I say this because people are even willing to cut off their own arms and legs if they think they are diseased. I don't think an individual takes joy in what belongs to him personally unless by "belonging to me" he means "good" and by "belonging to another" he means "bad." That's because what everyone loves is really nothing other than the good. (*Smp.* 205e–206a)

The correct use of reason helps us to identify and pursue the pleasures and pains that actually promote our physical or mental health. The tyrannical soul, however, is too ignorant to seek only the pleasures or pains that are conducive to happiness, as I will discuss further in section III.2. So, instead, such souls indiscriminately pursue as much pleasure as possible by gratifying their intense desires as often as they can, but they end up with the sort of pain that brings nothing but a miserable life. This misery is not only the pain of insatiable desire but also the soul's despair at its own emptiness and lack of fulfillment. Such a person may even try to deceive himself

---

from false oaths and injustice, which each action of his stamped upon his soul, and all things are crooked from lying and boasting, and there is nothing straight on account of his having been reared without truth; and he sees the soul full of asymmetry and ugliness from arrogant power, luxury, wanton insolence, and incontinence of actions; and having seen it he sends it away dishonorably, straight to the prison, having come to which it is going to endure fitting sufferings" (524e–525a).

into thinking he is happy when he successfully achieves some goal, but the misery and despair return persistently.

Just like the *Gorgias*, the *Republic* names moderation and shame as two important qualities that can help to rectify the inordinate, misguided desires that foster vice. The tyrannical soul lacks both qualities, so his numerous and intense desires govern all of his decisions and interactions with others. Socrates likens the tyrant's soul to a nest holding a "great winged drone" that symbolizes his misguided *erōs* (572e).[39] The drone rules in the soul, and the "other desires" (*epithumiōn*) (573a) intensify or "foster" (573a) it until it grows strong enough to eliminate any shred of shame or moderation:

> Then, when the other desires [. . .] buzz around the drone, making it grow great and fostering it, they plant the sting of longing in it. Now this leader of the soul takes madness [*mania*] for its manned guard and is stung to frenzy. And if it finds in the man any opinions or desires accounted good and still admitting of shame [*epaischunomenas*], it slays them and pushes them out of him until it purges him of moderation [*sōphrosunēs*] and fills him with madness brought in from abroad. (573a–b)

Without moderation or a sense of shame, the tyrannical soul does not hesitate to use "deceit" and "force" (573e) wherever necessary to increase his consumption of whatever he wants, nor is there any "terrible murder" or "deed" that he will not commit if he thinks it necessary (574e). *Erōs* becomes the "tyrant" within his soul (575a), and it completely controls his thoughts and actions. It is in this sense that the tyrannical soul is "mad." Just like Callicles, the tyrannical soul displays misdirected, inordinate *erōs* and *epithumia*. Callicles' desires are not only excessively intense but also wholly self-centered. As a result, he can care about objects—and even other people—only insofar as they are means to his own satisfaction.[40] Properly

39. Just as *erōs* is a primary source of motivation, or a leader of the soul, in the *Gorgias* and the *Phaedrus*, so also the deeply misguided *erōs* of the tyrant leads the soul toward what it erroneously regards as good in the *Republic*.

40. Callicles' entire way of life resembles Socrates' characterization of an *empeiria*, which he contrasts with *technē*: "I was saying, I suppose, that cookery does not seem to me to be an art, but experience; whereas medicine, I said, examines the nature of him of whom it takes care and the cause of the things that it does, and it has a reasoned account to give of each of these things, medicine does. But the other—its care is wholly with pleasure, and it proceeds altogether artlessly toward pleasure, without having examined

directed *erōs* leads us to care for the well-being of others, but the tyrannical soul's perversely directed *erōs* aims only to fulfill his own nonrational desires.[41]

Another consequence of the tyrannical soul's vice is that it renders him incapable of any real friendship. The misguided *erōs* and *epithumia* that rule within the tyrannical soul force him to constantly attend to their satisfaction and nothing else. He can relate to others only through relationships of domination or submission: "[Tyrannical souls] live their whole life without ever being friends of anyone, always one man's master or another's slave. The tyrannic nature never has a taste of freedom or true friendship" (576a). To the tyrannical soul, every other person is either an object to be exploited or a threat to one's own gratification that he therefore fears and obeys. Similarly, in the *Gorgias,* Socrates points out that the person who leads the way of life that Callicles advocates will have no friends; if one allows his desires to be immoderate, then he "would be a dear friend neither to a human being nor to a god," because he is unable to "share in common" with others (*Grg.* 507e). In other words, excessive desires compel us to prioritize our own satisfaction over sharing goods in common with others, and the ability to care for and meet the needs of others is a necessary condition for friendship. Callicles' relationship to his beloved, Demos, is consistent with this view of friendship, since Callicles seems to say only the things that Demos wants to hear in order to obtain erotic satisfaction from him.[42] Thus, people like Callicles have only relationships of domination, or, at best, relationships based on utility[43] rather than true friendships that involve care for the other's well-being.

---

to any degree the nature of pleasure or the cause, all in all irrationally, making virtually no distinct enumeration, but by routine and experience saving only the memory of what usually comes about, by which then it also provides pleasures" (500e–501b). Instead of caring about his own good or the good of others, Callicles irrationally pursues unlimited pleasure for himself, "neither examining nor caring about anything but gratification alone" (501b–c).

41. Aristotle makes a similar distinction in *Ethics* IX when discussing the nature of self-love: "The good person ought to be a self-lover—he will both profit himself and benefit others by doing noble things—but the corrupt person ought not to be—he will harm both himself and his neighbors, since he follows his base passions" (1169a11–14).

42. Contrast this self-centered approach to relationships to the philosophic couple's relationship in the *Phaedrus*' palinode, where each person cares for and prioritizes the well-being of the other (*Phdr.* 252e–253b).

43. Aristotle has a similar line of thinking in *Ethics* XIII when he argues that complete friendship requires virtue (*EN* 1156b7–15), whereas anyone can have friendships based on utility or pleasure.

II. The Socratic Explanation of Callicles' Vice

In addition to providing a nuanced portrait of Callicles' vicious character in the *Gorgias*, Plato also gives us the material we need to discern the root of Callicles' vice. While some might regard Callicles (and people like him) as one who fully understands what is morally good and bad but nonetheless pursues a morally corrupt life due to some twisted, deranged goal to cultivate vice for its own sake, several important passages in the *Gorgias* allow us to give a different diagnosis of his moral condition. Callicles is vicious due to his ignorance of what goods are most essential for human happiness, and this ignorance in turn gives rise to his misdirected, overly intense *erōs* and *epithumia* for pleasure, power, reputation, wealth, and so forth. To make the *Gorgias*' insights about the root of Callicles' vice more explicit, I will first discuss the dialogue's distinction between (what I call) "higher goods," namely the virtues, philosophical education, friendship, and inner harmony, and "lower goods," which include conventional goods such as wealth, pleasure, political power, and honor or fame. Although the *Gorgias* does not use the terms "higher goods" or "lower goods," it draws a distinction between the goods that are necessary or essential for happiness (*eudaimonia*) and those that are not. So, I use the term "higher goods" to designate the former and "lower goods" for the latter. In the next chapter, I will explain why the higher goods are more essential for happiness in more detail—at this point, I only call attention to this distinction in order to show that Callicles' ignorance leads him to exclusively care about the lower goods. In section III.2, I elucidate the *Gorgias*' suggestions that all people seek the good and love what appears best to them, that nobody commits injustice voluntarily, and that all people would agree about what is truly good if they only understood it. Finally, section III.3 shows that Callicles resembles the tyrannical soul of the *Republic* in another important respect, namely that a core cause of vice in both of them is their ignorance about what goods are most necessary for happiness.

II.1. The Highest Human Goods

For Socrates, regardless of our identity or social context, *none* of us can be happy if we do not have enough moral virtue, education, and friendship. These goods are therefore universally necessary for human happiness, and so everyone should prioritize them above all other goods. Polus and Callicles, by contrast, believe that the more conventional goods they acquire, the happier they will be. When Polus confidently asks if Socrates thinks the "great king" of Persia is "happy" (*eudaimona*), Socrates says he does not know, since he must first learn "how he stands in regard to education [*paideias*] and justice [*dikaiosunēs*]" before he can make that judgment (*Grg.* 470e). The king's opulent wealth and enormous power are irrelevant to the question of whether he is happy. For reasons Socrates explains later in the dialogue, those who are vicious and severely ignorant about the nature of reality fall into inevitable misery. He closely associates philosophy, or the philosophical life, with a virtuous and educated life when he refers to the ideal of virtue he has been advocating as "this life in philosophy" (*ton bion ton en philosophia*) (500c). Philosophy is not simply theoretical discourse for Socrates but also a way of life built around pursuing the virtues. Virtue also goes hand in hand with friendship (*philia*), since one cannot have friendship without it:

> This in my opinion is the goal looking toward which one must live, straining to direct all one's own and the city's things toward this, that justice and moderation will be present for him who is to be blessed; thus must one act, not allowing desires to be intemperate and striving to satiate them—an endless evil, living a robber's life. For such a one would be dear friend neither to another human being nor to god; for he would be unable to share in common, and he in whom there is no community would not have friendship [*philia*]. (507d–e)

Socrates implies that having friends is necessary to be "blessed" or happy, and the alternative is a lack of genuine "community" and a life of painful isolation. The vicious person does not care for the well-being of others, nor do others care for him. He only uses others for the sake of fulfilling his own desires, and others likewise relate to him in a purely self-interested way, that is, to get something from him or to avoid being hurt by him. Since one must care about the good of others and treat them virtuously to maintain friendships, the vicious person has no friends, and he therefore lacks a good that is crucial for a happy life.

The *Gorgias*' approach to explaining *why* the higher goods bring happiness focuses on the limit or measure that they give to human life, as opposed to the limitlessness of *pleonexia*. Measure gives beautiful, harmonious order to the soul and therefore makes it more perfect and sufficient, both of which are necessary for happiness. In Plato's *Philebus*, Socrates says that, whatever the good is, it must be "perfect" (*teleon*)[44] and "sufficient" (*hikanon*), meaning that nothing could be added to it that would make it better, and that the person who has it needs nothing else to be happy (*Phlb.* 20d). If there is such a thing as the good, then it must have these qualities, since these are what make it more valuable than anything else and therefore deserving of the name "the good."[45] In the *Gorgias*, after Socrates compares the immoderate life to a leaking jar, he claims that the moderate life would allow for the jars to remain full and satisfied. His jars are "healthy and full," and therefore his soul is "at rest" (493e). Placing a limit on desires through moderation allows one to satisfy his desires and *erōs*, which removes the pain of desire as much as possible. Moreover, the measure imposed by virtue and education not only eliminate pain but also give the soul the qualities it needs to flourish in life:

> The wise say, Callicles, that heaven, earth, gods, and human beings are held together by community, friendship, orderliness, moderation, and justness; and on account of these things, comrade, they call this whole an order, not disorder and intemperance. [*phasi d' hoi sophoi, ō Kallikleis, kai ouranon kai gēn kai theous kai anthrōpous tēn koinōnian sunechein kai philian kai kosmiotēta kai sōphrosunēn kai dikaiotēta, kai to holon touto dia tauta kosmon kalousin, hō hetaire, ouk akosmian oude akolasian*]. You, however, seem to me not to turn your mind to these things, wise though you are about them, but it has escaped your notice that geometrical equality has great power [*mega dunatai*] among both gods and human beings, whereas you think one must practice taking more; for you have no care for geometry. (507e–508a)

Virtue allows us to experience a sense of inner peace and fulfillment. It gives

44. The term *teleon* can also be translated as "complete."

45. In *Republic* VI, Socrates makes a similar point when he says that we need the good to be happy, and that nothing is worth having unless it is good in some way: "You have many times heard that the idea of the good is the greatest study and that it's by availing oneself of it along with just things and the rest that they become useful and beneficial. [. . .] And, if we don't know it and should have ever so much knowledge of the rest without this, you know that it's no profit to us, just as there would be none in possessing something in the absence of the good. Or do you suppose it's of any advantage to possess everything except what's good? Or to be prudent about everything else in the absence of the good, while being prudent about nothing fine and good?" (*R.* 505a–b).

the soul a certain invisible, beautiful order that is analogous to the beauty of the cosmos, and this beauty is evident when the soul is at rest with itself or in peaceful unity with others through community and friendship. The person who has achieved this state is "powerful" and free, because he has attained his ultimate goal, happiness, and so does not need anything else. Thus, the higher goods identified in the *Gorgias* allow the soul to achieve the state of perfection and sufficiency discussed by the *Philebus*.

Another reason why the higher goods are essential for human happiness is that they help us to remain in "harmony" with ourselves. Socrates uses the concept of harmony in at least two different senses throughout the *Gorgias*. The first way one can remain in harmony with himself is by not holding contradictory opinions. Socrates carefully ensures that his views harmonize with one another by repeatedly examining them, whereas Callicles frequently expresses opinions that contradict each other (e.g., 481d–e, 482b). Socrates stresses that it is more important for an individual's views to harmonize than for an individual to harmonize (i.e., share the same set of contradictory opinions) with the majority of people: "And yet I think, you best of men, it is superior that my lyre be out of tune and dissonant, and the chorus I might provide for the public, and that most human beings disagree with me and say contradictory things, rather than that I, being one man, should be discordant with myself and say contradictory things" (482b–c). Education and philosophical inquiry in a community of friends can help bring our contradictory opinions to light if we are unaware of them, as Socratic *elenchus* frequently shows us. Similarly, the person who commits herself to virtue will not make the mistake of consciously contradicting herself solely for the sake of gaining approval from others.

The second sense of the term "harmony" refers to the state of peaceful agreement between the different aspects of the soul, as opposed to the disorder and conflict within the soul that Callicles exemplifies. Just as there is conflict between contradictory opinions, so too is there conflict between inordinate desires for conventional goods. The person who is in harmony with himself does not experience the pain of inordinate desire, nor does he experience the inner turmoil that comes from conflict between different aspects of the soul, whether it be different desires competing against one another or desires competing against reason. The harmonious soul in possession of the higher goods has a tranquil beauty that mirrors the beautiful structure of the cosmos.

Once we achieve this inner harmony through the higher goods (to at least some degree), we can fully actualize the potential benefits of conventional goods such as wealth or political power. Socrates states this idea succinctly in the *Apology*: "Wealth does not bring about excellence [*aretē*], but excellence makes wealth and everything else good for men, both individually and collectively" (*Ap.* 30b). His point applies not only to wealth but also to all the conventional goods that the characters discuss in the *Gorgias*, such as pleasure, health, wealth, political power, fame, protection from danger, and so on. Importantly, Plato is not suggesting that the lower goods are inherently bad. Rather, they are simply less essential for happiness—and therefore less good—than the higher goods. Having the lower goods without the higher ones will inevitably cause the opposite of happiness, namely misery (*athlios*). If this is so, then obtaining a high quantity of lower goods does little to remedy such misery; obtaining high amounts of wealth or pleasure might bring temporary pleasure or relief from pain, but not *eudaimonia*. The vicious person will abuse the lower goods by using them for vicious ends, in which case they bring more harm than benefit.

If happiness is bound up with giving our souls and lives a certain ideal measure through the higher goods, then we must wonder: *what is* the measure that the virtuous soul instantiates? Socrates implies that there is some standard or source of measure that the virtuous soul looks toward, and it is not simply imaginary or created by the human mind. He compares the virtuous person to a craftsman who refers to an ideal model to help him produce something good and beautiful: "Won't the good man, who speaks with a view to the best, say what he says not at random but looking off toward something? Just as all the other craftsmen look toward their work when each chooses and applies what he applies, not at random, but in order that he can get this thing he is working on to have a certain form [*eidos*]" (503d–e). Other Platonic dialogues suggest that this measure could be either the Forms or some divinity, and the use of the term *eidos* in this passage suggests that Forms could be the answer. However, the *Gorgias* contains no explicit discussion of the Forms or the nature of divinity, nor does it give a clear answer about what the good person "looks off toward." Rather, the *Gorgias* focuses on what qualities this measure must have in order to make us happy, and it argues that the higher human goods help us to instantiate or live in accord with this measure (whatever it is) in our own lives. A different kind of inquiry that the *Gorgias* does not contain would give more specific suggestions about the ultimate source(s) of goodness and beauty, and we find such an inquiry in the *Phaedrus*, as I will discuss in later chapters. The *Gorgias* establishes only *that there is* such a universal measure of goodness and beauty, and that virtue, education, philosophy, friendship, and inner harmony help humans imitate this measure as far as possible.

II.2. Ignorance of the Highest Human Goods as the Root of Vice

The conversation between Socrates and Polus about whether unjust rhetors and tyrants really have the power that they appear to have (*Grg.* 466b–481b) is especially relevant when it comes to understanding the *Gorgias'* insights about moral imperfection. My aim is not to assess the strength of Socrates' overall argument in this section of the dialogue, but rather to examine some of the important points about moral decision-making that Socrates makes in this context. Polus asserts that tyrants like Archelaus have power and happiness because they can do whatever appears best to them, but Socrates claims that nobody can be both unjust and happy (472d). To make his point, Socrates draws a distinction between what we "wish" (*boulesthai*) for—the good (468b)—and what "seems best" (*doxē beltiston einai*) to us (466e). People cannot help but wish for good things and the happiness they bring, such as "wisdom and health and wealth and the other such things" (467e), and in this sense everything we do is for the sake of the good (468b). Socrates later reminds Callicles of this point when he says that "the end of all actions is the good, and all other things must be done for the sake of it but not it for the sake of other things" (499e–500a). Polus admits that when someone without "intelligence" (*noun*) does what appears best, yet it "happens to be" bad (468d), it is neither good for that person nor a sign of power (466e, 468e). According to Socrates' argument, although the tyrant certainly does what appears best to him, it is possible for him to fail to attain what he wishes for, namely things that are good in reality and the happiness they bring. The tyrant (or any vicious person) therefore does not have real power, because real power is the ability to attain the highest human goods.

If Socrates is correct that all people seek goodness and happiness, then nobody commits injustice while knowing that it makes him "wretched" (470e). When Socrates later reminds Callicles of this point, he states that all injustice is committed involuntarily: "[Polus and I] agreed that no one does injustice wishing [*boulomenon*] to do so, but all doers of injustice do so involuntarily [*akontas*]" (509e). If living viciously really is harmful to oneself, as Socrates maintains, then it follows that the vicious person does not understand that his vice makes his own life worse, and it is in this sense that living viciously is involuntary. Socrates echoes this sentiment in reference to himself elsewhere in the dialogue: "For if I am doing something incorrectly in the course of my life, know well that I do not make this error voluntarily but through my lack of learning" (488a). Here again, the lack of knowledge about what one is really doing makes an action or choice involuntary. Hence, Callicles possesses neither knowledge nor an opinion that injustice, immoderation, or other such ways of behaving will harm him and make him miserable, otherwise he would not embrace them.

Several other passages in Socrates' conversation with Callicles further support the idea that the root of Callicles' vice is ignorance of the highest goods for humans. When Socrates explains the image of the leaking jar at 493a–d, he says that, according to what he has heard, a "thoughtless" (*anoētous*) person repeatedly carries water to a perforated jar with a perforated sieve in an attempt to fill it up. The jar symbolizes this person's "desires" (*epithumiai*), which are "insatiable" due to the large holes that result from "immoderation" (*akolaston*), while the sieve represents his "soul," which leaks because of "disbelief and forgetfulness." Such a person attempts to achieve happiness by filling the leaking jar as much as possible, but this is a Sisyphean task that makes him "wretched." Thoughtlessness, forgetfulness, and disbelief are all forms of ignorance; in the context of the image, the person would not persist in this way of life or regard it as best if he understood, first, its inherent futility, and second, that there was a better alternative available to him, such as the virtuous life. Later in the dialogue, Socrates remarks that the opposite of the moderate soul is the "foolish [*aphrōn*] and immoderate [*akolastos*] soul" (507a). The vicious soul lacks wisdom, as reflected in the literal meaning of the term *aphrōn*—"no wisdom." Moreover, Socrates points to Callicles' lack of understanding about the world, saying that it "escaped" Callicles' "notice" that "geometrical equality has great power among both gods and human beings," because Callicles has "no care [*ameleis*] for geometry" (508a). Callicles cannot properly appreciate the "orderliness" (*kosmiotēta*) in the world, nor does he comprehend the beauty and goodness of "the orderly life, sufficient and satisfied with the things that are ever at hand" (493c–d). In each case, Socrates shows us that Callicles would not be pleonexic, nor would he interpret the world in the way he does, if he had a better understanding of reality, the highest human goods, and the nature of genuine happiness.

Relatedly, Socrates claims several times throughout the dialogue that all humans agree with his view that it is worse to commit injustice than to suffer it (474b, 475e). These statements are puzzling, of course, given that people commit injustice all the time, and his interlocutors openly disagree with him. In light of the passages discussed above, though, we can understand Socrates as saying that if everyone *really understood* the truth about the matters they discuss in the dialogue, then we could not help but agree with it, because "what is true is never refuted" (473b). When Callicles asks Socrates whether he agrees with his claim that pleasure is the good, Socrates replies that he does not agree, adding, "nor do I think that Callicles will [agree] either, when he himself looks on himself correctly" (495d–e). As I indicated above, if Callicles understood the futility and misery inherent to the pleonexic way of life, he would neither praise nor pursue it. Callicles is "dissonant" with himself (482b) in that his views are inconsistent with each other, which is also a symptom of his ignorance. Socrates, by contrast, remains in tune with himself by always following philosophy, since "philosophy always says what you now hear from me" (482a). For Socrates, when we see the truth, we cannot help but accept it and live in conformity with it (or become "in tune" with it). In this way, the truth compels agreement from everyone.

The view that ignorance is the root of vice is also reflected in Socrates' myth of the afterlife at the end of the dialogue. Socrates describes the important characteristics of the vicious who are judged and punished fittingly:

> But often, laying hold of the great king or some other king or potentate, [Rhadamanthus] perceives that there is nothing healthy in the soul, but it has been severely whipped and is filled with scars from false oaths and injustice, which each action of his stamped upon his soul, and all things are crooked from lying and boasting, and there is nothing straight on account of his having been reared without truth; and he sees the soul full of asymmetry and ugliness from arrogant power, luxury, wanton insolence, and incontinence of actions; and having seen it he sends it away dishonorably, straight to the prison, having come to which it is going to endure fitting sufferings. (524e–525a)

The corrupt leader in this example was "reared without truth,"[46] which causes him to act unjustly, dishonorably, arrogantly, and so on. Without a proper

46. In the *Phaedrus*' palinode speech, Socrates says that souls who are "turned toward injustice by some company or other" do not easily "recall" sacred beauty or become virtuous (250a).

education to show us what goods are most important for happiness, we can easily make the mistake of caring only about conventional goods ("luxury") and using whatever means necessary—including vicious ones—to acquire them. If Socrates is right that virtue makes the soul beautiful, healthy, and harmonious, it follows that the corrupt leader's vicious action causes his soul to become ugly, unhealthy, and "asymmetrical." The "fitting sufferings" in the afterlife serve as the education that the unjust person never had, and they will purify his soul of its imperfections. Regardless of how literally one reads this myth of the afterlife, it confirms Socrates' point that lack of understanding about the human good is the source of vice.

Through these insights about moral decision-making, Plato shows us that humans are erotic beings who cannot help but desire what appears best to us. The fundamental problem, though, is that what *appears* best to some (or even most) people is not what is *really* best for them. We love what appears best to us regardless of whether we are virtuous, vicious, or somewhere in between. Callicles feels *erōs* and *epithumia* just like anybody else, but he has erroneous opinions about what is most important for human happiness (*eudaimonia*) and the nature of moral excellence. He has strong desires for goods that the majority of people regard as the highest goods in life, such as pleasure, wealth, political power, and good reputation. None of these things is inherently bad, but his view that these goods are the sole ingredients of the good life leads to his excessive desire for an unlimited amount of such goods. Further, Callicles is motivated by his fear and shame at the prospect of suffering injustice (another reason why he wants the political power to defend himself), and this too is a very common fear that is not vicious in its own right. He has misguided views that "the strong" (or, those capable of taking advantage of others) need not follow conventional laws and regulations that constrain the means we can use to procure these goods. His excessive, misdirected desire and his views about justice make him willing to commit vicious actions, which leads to destruction and misery for both himself and others, even though he does not see it that way. Under the right conditions, anyone in ancient Athens or the contemporary world could become like Callicles.

Finally, Socrates' view that the unjust person must pay the penalty follows logically from his perspective on the root of vice. If those who commit vicious actions are ignorant of what is best for them and others, then punishment should not simply be revenge or payback for vicious action. Rather, punishment should educate and rehabilitate the wrongdoer:

> It is fitting for everyone who is subject to retribution and is correctly visited with retribution by another either to become better and be profited or to become an example to others, so that others, seeing him suffer whatever he suffers, may be afraid and become better. And some there are who are benefited and pay the just penalty, by gods and human beings—those who err in making curable errors; nevertheless the benefit comes about for them through pains and griefs both here and in Hades, for it is not possible otherwise that they be released from injustice. (525b–c)

As I indicated above, punishments are a "cure" for ignorance and vice, which are afflictions of the soul that cause misery. If punishment can bring vicious individuals closer to wisdom and the rest of the virtues, they will be "released" from their vice and thereby "become better and be profited." Just as children need education, not revenge, when they behave badly, so also vicious adults need to learn the extent to which their vice is harmful to themselves and others. Unfortunately, Socrates does not give details about what punishments we should use or how exactly they will educate the person who is punished.[47] In any case, Socrates is at least clear that punishment must aim to serve as an effective moral education, which the vicious person, tragically, never received.

II.3. The Tyrannical Soul's Ignorance of the Good in *Republic*

To some extent, Callicles falls victim to "misology," the hatred of *logos*, which is a serious danger that Plato warns about in *Republic* VII and *Phaedo* 89a–91c. Socrates gives an account of one way that someone can become a misologue in *Republic* VII, and some of his descriptions are consistent with Callicles' views, actions, and tyrannical character. Socrates warns that "dialectic" (*R.* 537e) equips students with a powerful tool—the ability to use arguments—that they can easily abuse if they do not yet have "orderly and stable natures" (*R.* 539d). The person who tries and fails to engage in genuine dialectic while he is still immature soon loses the "convictions about what's just and fair" that he received from his parents and society

47. For more detailed studies of Plato's discussions of punishment, see Mackenzie (1981) and Shaw (2015).

(538c), because he is unable to adequately defend these convictions when arguing with someone more experienced in dialectic: "When a question is posed and comes to the man who is so disposed, 'What is the fair?'—and after answering what he heard from the lawgiver, the argument refutes him, and refuting him many times and in many ways, reduces him to the opinion that what the law says is no more fair than ugly, and similarly about the just and good and the things he held most in honor" (538d–e). If the young person cannot quickly find the "true" views about justice, goodness, beauty, and so on (538e), then he will give up on trying to seek truth about the world through reason or philosophy.[48] As Socrates puts it in the *Phaedo*, such a person will "finish out the rest of his life hating and reviling arguments" and will be "robbed of the truth and knowledge of the things that *are*" (*Phd.* 90d). Misology causes a seriously harmful form of ignorance, because it prevents us from using reason to understand the aspects of reality that are most important for living a good life, namely the true nature of goodness, beauty, and virtue.

Worse still, the sort of ignorance that stems from misology does not only prevent us from improving our lives—it also actively fosters vice. First, misologues "misuse" arguments "as though it were play" by not taking them seriously, "always using them to contradict" like "puppies enjoying pulling and tearing with argument at those who happen to be near" (*R.* 539b). Socrates emphasizes that the misologue's lack of respect for reason's potential makes him become hubristic and ignorant of his own ignorance. Misologues conclude that there are no real, stable objects of knowledge or real measure of goodness: "Those especially who've spent their days in debate-arguments end up thinking they've become the wisest of men and that they alone have detected that there's nothing sound or stable—not in the realm of either practical matters or arguments—but all the things that are simply toss to and fro, as happens in the Euripus, and don't stay put anywhere for any length of time" (*Phd.* 90b–c).[49] Instead of faulting his own "artless" use of

48. Relatedly, Callicles has little trust in philosophy's ability to lead us toward truth or goodness, saying that it is only beneficial if one studies it for a short time in his youth (485c–e).

49. Callicles is also similar to the person Socrates describes in *Republic* VII who is intelligent and has the capacity for wisdom but is "turned" toward Becoming rather than Being, and so "serves" the wrong ends: "Or haven't you yet reflected about the men who are said to be vicious but wise, how shrewdly their petty soul sees and how sharply it distinguishes those things toward which it is turned, showing that it doesn't

reason, the misologue erroneously concludes that there is no stable truth established by arguments or in the realm of practical affairs (*Phd.* 90b–d). Sophists, rhetoricians, and their young students are undoubtedly among those who inspired Socrates' warning against misology, and he adds that they "deserve much sympathy" (*R.* 539a), since they are the victims of misguided intellectual influence.

Callicles may not exactly fit Socrates' descriptions of the misologue in the *Republic* and the *Phaedo,* but we should note the key similarities and differences between the two. On the one hand, Callicles is different from the misologue insofar as he has theoretical commitments that he thinks accurately describe the world, even if they are inconsistent with each other and riddled with problems. This means that he at least appears to think that he has a correct, stable *logos* about the nature of reality, unlike the misologue who holds that "there's nothing sound or stable" in "the realm of either practical matters or arguments." On the other hand, Callicles is similar to the misologue in that he does not use *logos* primarily as a guide to truth (unlike Socrates), but rather as a servant to his own desires. He strongly criticizes philosophical activity, and he does not respect philosophers. When he engages in arguments or discussion with Socrates, it is not to search for knowledge, wisdom, and virtue but instead to formulate justifications for the commitment he has already made to *pleonexia* and to win a public debate. Without understanding the truth about the nature of goodness, beauty, or virtue, Callicles simply pursues the "sort of life" that "flatters him" and appears to offer the most "pleasures" (*R.* 538d–539a). In this way, he exemplifies how our views about ethics and the nature of reality shape our deeds and character, since his unsophisticated rejection of conventional morality directly contributes to his vice.[50]

In keeping with these remarks about the fate of the misologue, the *Republic* suggests that vice stems from ignorance of the good, and the tyrannical soul represents the most extreme version of such ignorance. The *Republic* affirms that all humans seek goodness and happiness (*R.* 505d–e),

have poor vision although it is compelled to serve vice; so that the sharper it sees, the more evil it accomplishes?" (518a–519a).

50. Only those who already have a good character or an "orderly and stable nature" can entertain ideas similar to the ones Callicles espouses without accepting them, as Glaucon and Adeimantus demonstrate in *Republic* II (358c–d, 367e–368a). Callicles is not at the level of Glaucon and Adeimantus in this respect in that he accepts what others say about the nature and origin of justice, even though he is confused and inconsistent with himself.

and we choose to pursue whatever appears best to us in any given scenario. More specifically, we cannot help but pursue what appears to us as the highest possible good, since to do otherwise would be to knowingly deprive ourselves of some good and thus contradict our unconditional desire for happiness. However, most people (some more than others) fail to understand what the highest goods *really are*, or what is in reality best for ourselves and for others, and therefore fail to understand what genuine happiness is. Socrates states: "[The good is] what every soul pursues and for the sake of which it does everything. The soul divines that it *is* something but is at a loss about it and unable to get a sufficient grasp of what it is" (505d–e). All people select the ends that appear best to them, but they fail to "get a sufficient grasp" of what is really good for them and others. Only the wise have an accurate understanding of the highest human goods.[51]

Socrates and company agree that most people erroneously think of pleasure as the highest human good (505a). Most people organize their lives around experiencing as much pleasure (whether mental or physical) and avoiding pain as much as possible. The tyrannical soul takes this to the extreme by regarding only *his* pleasure as the highest good, and as a result he develops exceptionally intense desires (and eventually a dependency) on an exceptionally wide range of pleasures, especially those associated with power, domination, violence, fame, wealth, and the body. So, the good appears to the tyrant not just as his own pleasure but also as the ability to avoid the pain of unfulfilled desire, which becomes an impossible task sooner or later. While Callicles has not yet had the opportunity to exercise and augment his vices as much as the tyrant, they are similar insofar they ignorantly regard unlimited amounts of pleasure, power, and other common goods as the key to happiness. This view leads to excessive desire for such goods and therefore the willingness to commit as much injustice as is needed to obtain them.

The inordinate, misdirected *epithumia* and *erōs* of the tyrannical soul inhibit its capacity to reason, which further entrenches him in ignorance and vice. Reason is reduced to a mere servant of desire. Socrates explains that this is already the case in the oligarchic soul, which is less vicious than the tyrannical soul. In the oligarchic soul, the "desiring and money-loving part" (*epithumētikon te kai philochrēmaton*) sits on the "throne" of the soul, and the "calculating [*logistikon*] and spirited parts sit by it on the ground on

51. In the context of the *Republic*, the highest human goods are intimately bound up with "The Good" itself that is "beyond being" (509b). Of course, Socrates never says what the Good *is*, but only what it is *like* through the image of the sun in books VI and VII.

either side [as] slaves, letting the one neither calculate about nor consider anything but where more money will come from less; and letting the other admire and honor nothing but wealth and the wealthy" (553c–d). This power relation between the soul's three parts is similar in the tyrannical soul, except that the desires ruling it are not solely for money—the tyrannical soul wants a plethora of different things in limitless quantities, including the violent destruction of anyone who opposes him. When reason is enslaved to desire, its only function is to calculate what means one should use to satisfy the ends set by desire. The severe limitation of reason in such souls causes them to remain ignorant about the goods that are most important for happiness, which further entrenches their vice and fuels their excessive pursuit of conventional goods.

III. Callicles' Ideology

This section analyzes the views that Callicles endorses throughout the dialogue to get a better sense of the ideological position he uses to challenge Socrates. I call Callicles' views "ideological" instead of philosophical, because unlike the philosopher, Callicles neither cares about fully developing and testing his theories about the nature of morality or reality, nor does he aim to be consistent with himself at all times. Instead, when defending his ideology to others, he says whatever he thinks will be most persuasive at the present moment. He expresses views that are of vital interest to philosophers, yet he hates philosophy. The views he expresses in his speeches aim to justify his commitment to *pleonexia,* and he uses *logos* primarily as an instrument for persuading and dominating others. In section II.1, I show that Callicles' speeches share common threads with the broader sophistic movement in fifth-century Athens. He uses the common sophistic distinction between nature (*physis*) and convention (*nomos*) to argue that virtues such as justice and moderation, as well as the laws of the city, are all invented by the weak majority for their own advantage, and that those who are strong enough to break free from the laws should do so. As I indicated above in section I, Callicles holds that real virtue and happiness come from letting one's desires grow as large as possible and having the power to fulfill them without limit, a view which is summed up in his endorsement of *pleonexia.* Then, in section II.2 I argue that although Callicles appears to claim that there is a real ethical standard that is universally true when he claims that it is just by nature for the strong to rule over the weak, his position really implies that there is no such standard at all. By claiming that virtue and happiness solely consist in the unlimited fulfillment of one's own desires, Callicles recognizes no real measure for goodness outside of each individual's personal desires. I conclude section II.2 by pointing out that Callicles' views have much in common with popular philosophical views and orientations today for the sake of making the contemporary relevance of the *Gorgias* more salient.

III.1. The Praise of Nature and *Pleonexia*

Callicles' views on ethics, politics, and the nature of reality are intimately linked with his character, so the following analysis of his views builds on many of the features of his character I discussed above in section I. Before examining his ideas in detail, I will briefly mention some important themes in the intellectual context that gave rise to them, namely the sophistic movement in fifth-century Athens.[52] Although Gorgias and his companions primarily regard themselves as rhetoricians, Socrates points out the close connection between rhetoric and sophistry early in the dialogue: "Inasmuch as they are closely related—sophists and rhetors are mixed together in the same place and about the same things, and they do not know what use to make of themselves nor do other human beings know what use to make of them" (465c). While Gorgias does not claim to teach virtue as other sophists do,[53] his students are concerned with the same subjects as the sophists (the nature of virtue, how to excel in the *polis*, and so on), and they use their public speaking skills to gain sociopolitical advantages.

52. The recently published *Cambridge Companion to the Sophists* (Billings and Moore 2023) devotes considerable attention to the historical context, multifarious ideas, and receptions of the Sophists. In the introduction to that book, Joshua Billings and Christopher Moore rightly claim that there is no core set of philosophical doctrines that all Sophists share (4–5), unlike, say, a philosophical school of the Hellenistic period. Other scholars who provide illuminating examinations of the sophistic movement's complexities, as well as Plato and Aristotle's relationship to the movement, include Kerferd (1981), De Romilly (1998), Munn (2000, 77–83), Barney (2006), and McCoy (2008), especially pages 1–22. Barney (2017) also briefly discusses Callicles' relationship to the sophistic movement.

53. Gorgias claims that he cannot be blamed if his students use rhetoric unjustly, since he teaches people only how to persuade, and this power can be used for good or bad ends just like any other craft that is potentially dangerous (456c–457b). However, Socrates gets him to admit that he would teach his students about justice, the good, and the noble if they did not understand such things before becoming his student (459d–460a).

Protagoras' famous dictum that "man is the measure of all things, as well as the commonly used distinction between nature (*physis*) and convention (*nomos*), are two important ideas that sophists sometimes adopt and use in various ways. These ideas encourage us to reject social norms or established ethical teachings in favor of independent thought, the creation of one's own values or assessment of reality, and the development of one's individuality (we might call this attitude "sophistic individualism").[54] However, the sophists are by no means uniform in the way that they use these ideas, nor is it clear that any individual sophist has a fully developed, systematic theory of ethics or metaphysics that remains consistent over time. Rather, they adapt the basic framework of these ideas to achieve whatever end they happen to be pursuing, and (as is especially clear in the case of Callicles) they have no qualms about contradicting the things they said in the past if they are no longer useful.

Plato depicts Callicles as a fairly inconsistent thinker and speaker in the *Gorgias*. At 481d–e, Socrates points out that Callicles is always saying different things at different times (see also 499b–c), since he aims only to appease the fickle whims of the Athenian *demos* or his boyfriend, Demos. When Socrates interrogates Callicles after his first speech, he changes his notions of "superiority" and "strength" from physical force (or "bodily might," 489c) to "intelligence" (489e) and then to "courage" (491b). Later, he alters his view that pleasure is the good after Socrates quickly refutes his initial endorsement of unfettered hedonism, saying that some pleasures are good while others are bad (499b–c). Further, Callicles sometimes does not express his views precisely, as Socrates points out: "Now then do you see that you yourself are saying words but making nothing clear?" (489e). Rather than carefully developing systematic theories, Callicles has a general commitment to the view that the strong are superior to the weak without examining all implications of his views or clearly defining key concepts such as "strength." When Socrates points out flaws in his views,. Callicles alters his arguments and responds in whatever way he thinks will be most persuasive at the moment.

54. Rachel Barney (2006) has an illuminating discussion on the relativistic views associated with Protagoras' statement that "man is the measure" as well as the distinction between nature and convention. She sees both of these concepts as essential aspects of the sophistic movement, even though individual sophists give several different versions of each view (77–97).

However, even though Callicles does not have a fully-fledged, consistent theory of ethics, politics, or the nature of reality, there are nonetheless some common threads in his speeches. One such thread is his view that virtue according to nature (*physis*) is opposed to human laws or conventional ideas about virtue, or virtue according to *nomos*.[55] For Callicles, it is "just" according to nature for the strong to oppress the weak however they please. He claims that all conventional laws and valuations of justice, moderation, equality, and fairness are lies that the weak herd uses to protect itself against exceptionally strong individuals (483b–484a). He disparages moderation in his speech from 491–492c, saying that people praise moderation and justice only "because of their unmanliness" (492b). Virtue and happiness consist in allowing our desires to "be as big as possible" and possessing the "power" to fulfill them at all times (492a). We can summarize Callicles' position as an endorsement of the life of *pleonexia*, that is, a life of greed that consists in striving for unlimited pleasure, power, wealth, or any other type of good that people commonly seek. For Callicles, the best men are those who overcome the constraints that others place on them through fictional *nomoi* and instead live naturally, following their desires wherever they might lead. He regards this outlook as true and superior to all others on the basis of *physis*.

By rejecting conventional views on morality, Callicles paints himself as a free-thinking, independent soul who does not fall prey to society's corruptive influences. However, rather than offering ideas born from his own reflection, his speeches express a version of the traditional Homeric, male-centric ideology that prizes strength and dominance. In other words, Callicles echoes the Homeric idea that the strong are entitled to whatever they can take, even if he uses this idea to justify his claim that one need not follow the laws of the city.[56] Unlike Socrates, he does not follow reason wherever it leads for the sake of wisdom and virtue, but instead appropriates whatever concepts or arguments he can find to justify the commitment he has already made to *pleonexia*. His arguments do not stem from an authentic love for wisdom or truth, and so he has more in common with an ideologue than

55. Callicles says that, in general, *physis* and *nomos* are "opposed to each other" (482e).

56. The idea that the truly strong and free person can violate laws with impunity is also mentioned in *Republic* IX. Socrates says that those who influence the tyrannical soul at a young age "introduce" him to the idea that "complete hostility to the law" is "complete freedom" (*R.* 572d).

a philosopher. He is therefore hypocritical in that he passively adopts this pleonexic ideology instead of thinking critically, independently, or creatively.

III.2. Callicles Recognizes No Universal Measure for the Good

While Callicles' account of morality clearly uses the common sophistic distinction between *physis* and *nomos*, a close inspection of his views reveals that his conception of "nature" does not serve as a universal moral standard or measure as we might expect. On the surface, he seems to be saying that his account of morality is universally or objectively true. As opposed to explicitly espousing Protagorean relativism (along the lines that Plato interprets it in *Theaetetus*) by saying "as each thing appears to me, so it is to me" (*Tht.* 152a), Callicles seems to posit a universal measure—nature—that serves as the ultimate standard for how everyone should live. However, to use the terms of the *Statesman* (283c–285c), the life of *pleonexia* aims only for a "relative measure" instead of a "due measure" (*metrion*). In the realm of morality (especially with regard to words and actions, 283e), reaching the due measure is to act or speak *well*, and it aims at a definite, real standard.[57] By contrast, perpetually seeking more is a goal that is relative only to what one currently possesses, which is never enough. In other words, the life of *pleonexia* does not posit a measure that serves as a limit that one can ever attain or live up to.[58] In effect, Callicles' speeches imply that there is no real measure for goodness or morality outside of the human soul, or, put another way, no universal ethical standard *in reality*. Instead, the individual's insatiable desires should be the only primary end that one

57. In the *Statesman*, to attain the due measure in the realm of morality or in any area of expertise (*technē*), one must consider factors such as "what is fitting, the right moment, [and] what is as it ought to be—everything that removes itself from the extremes to the middle" (*Plt.* 284e). According to the Visitor, it is by discerning the due measure that "those of us who are bad and those who are good most differ" (*Plt.* 283e). Further, he asserts that due measure must be real (not fabricated by humans) for expertise (*technē*) to be possible: "It is by preserving measure in this way that they produce all the good and fine things they do produce" (*Plt.* 284a–b).

58. Socrates gestures toward Callicles' inability to identify a universal measure for goodness when he says that Callicles does not see that "geometrical equality has great power among both gods and human beings," since it allows for "community, friendship, orderliness, moderation, and justness" or, more generally, the beautiful order of the cosmos (508a).

strives for throughout life. Even if Callicles thinks he identifies a universal moral standard in nature, his conception of it is incoherent, and he is likely blind to the fundamental inconsistencies in his arguments. As I indicated above, he is more concerned with producing a persuasive or probable account to defend his egoistic interests than with elaborating a sound theory. In any case, Callicles' endorsement of *pleonexia* is rooted in the Protagorean rejection of the idea that there is a real, universal human good. In section III.1 below and in chapter 2, section I.1, I will show that Socrates counters Callicles' Protagorean orientation by arguing that there is a real measure for goodness that one should seek and emulate.

One final important component of Callicles' speeches is his critique of philosophy and the philosophical way of life. He views the philosopher as someone who spends too much time pursuing what should merely be a preparatory exercise for his own way of life, namely the life spent engaging in political and other social affairs in the *polis* (485c–e). Callicles takes himself to have common roots with lifelong philosophers such as Socrates, as he evidently spent some time studying philosophical topics in his youth (Socrates says that Callicles has "been sufficiently educated, as many of the Athenians would say," 487b). Accordingly, Callicles states that one should study philosophy in "due measure" (*metriōs*) while he is young (484c), but spending too much time pursuing it will "corrupt" a man (484c). He sees the active life pursuing political power and wealth as more appropriate for a man. Philosophy, by contrast, is "unmanly" (485d), because the philosopher neither spends enough time preparing to defend himself in the law courts against others' injustices (486a–c), nor does he experience "human pleasures and desires" (484d). Callicles praises his own way of life, and he argues that the philosophical life is a waste of time.

To the extent that he is critical of socially established values, Callicles (and the sophists) share an important similarity with Socrates or genuine philosophers.[59] Callicles' vision of the good life critiques socially established values such as "having an equal share" (484a) with others in the *polis*. That is, he calls social values, laws, and customs into question and proposes an

59. Eric Sanday (2012) helpfully observes in the *Gorgias* that although Socrates and Callicles defend starkly contrasting views about the good life, Socrates nonetheless shares Callicles' view that it is necessary to "overthrow completely" socially established, "received wisdom." Rejecting conventional values is necessary to "shepherd the good into the world" through Socratic philosophy (197).

alternative view of social life that he considers true. Ironically, Callicles is performing an imperfect version of the very activity (philosophy) that he criticizes. However, we should notice that he defends wholesale rejection of social values, as opposed to Socrates' more nuanced assessment of them. As I will discuss in chapter 2, Socrates defends some important tenets of conventional Athenian morality even as he disagrees with common reasons that people use to support these views.

Returning to the issue of contemporary relevance, Callicles' ideology has much in common with contemporary worldviews common among both philosophers and nonphilosophers. As a particular instantiation or version of ideas that were common in the sophistic movement, Callicles' basic ideological orientation is alive and well. Rachel Barney rightly remarks that modern readers take interest in the sophists because of the similarities they share with many modern ideas and attitudes: "If there is any consensus to be found among their defenders (and their enemies as well), it is the constantly mutating view that the sophists are our contemporaries—whether that makes them Enlightenment rationalists, eminent Victorians, cynical *fin de siecle* perspectivists, analytic moral philosophers, or most recently of all, postmodernists."[60] She also points out that in the *The Will to Power Notebooks,* Friedrich Nietzsche agrees with Callicles' view that there is no universal measure for the good. He claims that the sophists "postulate the first truth that a 'morality-in-itself, a 'good-in-itself,' do not exist, that it is a swindle to talk of 'truth' in this field."[61] Due to all the difficulties that philosophers encounter in trying to establish the basic premise that there is a universal measure of goodness, many conclude that there is no such thing. Those who agree with Socrates that there is such a measure, and that his conception of virtue is necessary for the good life, should value interlocutors who pose serious challenges to these views. At 486d, Socrates says that Callicles is like the stone that people use to test whether something that looks like gold is authentic. That is, Callicles presents an excellent test for whether Socrates' views express true insights. As I will argue in chapter 2, Socrates' expression of Platonic virtue ethics in the *Gorgias* successfully critiques the Calliclean ideology and way of life, and it presents a more accurate portrait of the good life.

60. Barney 2006, 78.

61. Nietzsche 1967, 233.

Conclusion

Plato artfully portrays Callicles as a concrete and multidimensional individual but also such that many readers can see at least some resemblance between him and ourselves—in our moral character, our values, our ideas, or all of the above. Callicles is intelligent, precocious, and ambitious, yet deeply misled. Having hastily rejected all reasons to live justly and moderately, he lacks a healthy measure to guide him and instead follows his limitless desires to the point of viciousness and self-destruction. He is mistaken about what is truly good for his well-being and blindly disregards the well-being of others. Through his conversation with Socrates, readers have the opportunity to weigh the value of the superficially alluring way of life Callicles advocates against the atypical life of the philosopher who is in love with wisdom and the rest of the virtues. Socrates attempts to help Callicles rise out of his ignorance by giving an effective critique of his views and a persuasive defense of the virtuous life. Even if Socrates does not succeed in persuading Callicles, readers might learn from Callicles' mistakes and gain inspiration from Socrates. The next chapter focuses on the exemplary manner in which the *Gorgias*' account of virtue is tailored to people like Callicles.

Chapter 2

Socrates' Fitting Response to Callicles

Socrates formulates a response to Callicles that takes into account both his disordered soul and his pleonexic ideology, because this approach has the highest chance of motivating Callicles (and those like him) to pursue genuine virtue and a more philosophical life. Having established in chapter 1 that reason (*logos*), nonrational desire (*epithumia*), and love (*erōs*) are the three aspects of the soul most relevant to moral life in the *Gorgias*, I show in this chapter that Socrates' response is rooted in this moral psychology insofar as he aims to influence Callicles' reason *and* nonrational desires for the sake of redirecting his *erōs* toward virtue and the other higher goods. Addressing both of these aspects is the most effective way to pedagogically benefit another person, since both play crucial roles in defining our values and shaping our decision-making. Socrates believes the views he defends, but he tactically expresses them in a way that will be as persuasive as possible to Callicles. By making his account fitting with respect to Callicles for the sake of motivating him to pursue virtue, Socrates exhibits in deed both the "true art of rhetoric" (*Grg.* 517a) and "the work of the good citizen" (*Grg.* 517c) that he discusses later in the dialogue. While it is unclear whether Callicles will ever decide to take on the project of cultivating Socrates' conception of virtue, the latter's philosophical rhetoric aims to guide Callicles toward this end.

Rather than expounding a theory of the good life in a vacuum, Socrates focuses on the issues that Callicles cares about most. He supports views that are diametrically opposed to the ones Callicles holds, which ensures that Callicles will have a vested interest in the conversation. Specifically, Socrates criticizes Callicles' profession as an abuse of rhetoric, he highlights the flaws in Callicles' views on the nature of happiness and power, and he diminishes the role that desires (and their satisfaction) play in the good life, all of which are relevant to Callicles' most highly prized ambitions. In short, Socrates focuses on the ends toward which we should direct our love (*erōs*) or what we should care about most if we want to be happy. Socrates also argues that Callicles' conception of the good life leads to misery (*athlios*), and that real happiness (*eudaimonia*) comes from attaining the highest human goods, namely the virtues of moderation, justice, courage, and wisdom, as well as philosophical education, healthy friendships, and inner harmony. The highest goods are universal insofar as they are necessary for *any* person to experience happiness, and this is because there is a real measure for human virtue, contrary to Callicles' view. In other words, the human good is not whatever an individual happens to desire; instead, happiness consists in attaining that which is best in reality. In addition, Socrates points out some of the most important implications of his views on virtue, which include suggestions about gender equality, the value of just punishment, the importance of internal harmony, and the true nature of power.

The pedagogical context of the *Gorgias* is also particularly relevant for understanding its account of *sōphrosunē*. Since Callicles values immoderation and the pursuit of *pleonexia* as essential components of the best possible life, Socrates criticizes the flaws in Callicles' position and defends a notion of *sōphrosunē* that emphasizes the need to habitually restrain and bestow limit to one's desires for the sake of cultivating the internal harmony that is requisite for a complete and fulfilling life. Socrates characterizes *sōphrosunē* in this context as a sort of "political" or "civic" (*politikēn*) virtue,[1] which is an imperfect version of genuine *sōphrosunē*, but also a crucial step toward it. He uses this tactic because one must first recognize the futility of immoderation and cultivate the sort of shame (*aischos*) necessary to rein in his desires if he is eventually going to become open to cultivating genuine *sōphrosunē*. Socrates' defense of self-restraint in this context thus establishes a middle path between Callicles' unfettered hedonism and the genuine *sōphrosunē* that Plato discusses in the *Phaedrus*. This interpretation makes sense of the fact that the *Gorgias*' account of moderation differs substantially from those in other

1. This term "civic virtue" occurs in the *Republic* at 429d–430e as characters discuss the nature of courage. The *Republic* describes civic virtue as the type of virtue one acquires without practicing philosophy. In book X (*R.* 619c–d), Socrates says that civic virtue comes from living "in an orderly regime" and "participating in virtue by habit, without philosophy."

Platonic dialogues. The *Gorgias* aims to show why the virtues are desirable, which makes it well-suited to those who are questioning what goods they should care about most. In this way, the *Gorgias* is especially relevant for those who are critically engaging with competing conceptions of the good life that are held by various types of people in their society. For the same reasons, teachers interested in motivating students (who currently have no such motivation) to care more for moral self-cultivation and independent thinking can gain insight by working through these elements of the text. Dialogues such as the *Phaedrus*, on the other hand, are particularly helpful to those who are already interested in philosophy and virtue but need to develop a deeper understanding of the true nature of virtue.[2]

This chapter also carries forward the previous chapter's reflection on why this way of interpreting the *Gorgias* holds contemporary relevance. As I already mentioned, Socrates' critique of Calliclean ideology helps us to critically examine the characteristics, views, or inclinations we might share with Callicles. In addition, for those who attempt to motivate others to value moral self-cultivation in the context of philosophical pedagogy, there is much to learn from Socrates' approach to this task. Even though Callicles is either totally beyond reach or just short of this state due to his vicious character and misguided views, Socrates displays a method of appealing to such a person in a way that attempts to steer him away from the destructive path he is currently on. In this vein, the *Gorgias* can help us understand ways to use philosophical rhetoric to benefit others. Further, although Socrates' arguments about the value of virtue, friendship, self-harmony, philosophical education, and so on occur in this pedagogical context, they nonetheless express insights that are strong when taken on their own. That is, they offer strong reasons for why the Platonic conception of virtue reliably leads to a happier life and greater benefit to others. Socrates' critiques of Callicles convincingly explain why the pleonexic way of life inevitably leads to misery and unfulfillment, even if one successfully attains an enormous amount of conventional goods.

To better understand why Socrates' response to Callicles is fitting to the type of soul the latter represents, section I examines the core philosophical views and commitments that Socrates defends throughout the *Gorgias*, namely, that there is a real measure for human virtue that allows us to discern the highest human goods, which are necessary for happiness. The

2. The *Phaedrus* also adds to the *Gorgias*' treatment of how to use rhetoric virtuously and philosophically, as I will discuss in chapters 3 and 4.

highest human goods are the virtues, philosophical education and activity, friendship, and self-harmony. Section I also examines the important implications of these claims regarding gender equality, the ideal goals of discipline, and the true nature of power. Then, section II examines the dialogue's suggestions about the potential pedagogical benefit of rhetoric when it is subordinated to philosophy and virtue. Here I show that Socrates' goal is to "persuade" (*peithō*) Callicles that his current understanding of the good life is deeply flawed, and, in addition, he tries to help Callicles cultivate his sense of shame to help him keep his desires in check. Finally, section III shows that Socrates endorses a conception of *sōphrosunē* that emphasizes the need to "restrain" and limit one's desires for the sake of increasing one's own well-being, since Callicles must first understand the value of restraining desire if he is ever going to pursue genuine *sōphrosunē* or the philosophical life. Socrates' account is therefore fitting in the sense that it is meant to be as persuasive as possible to souls like Callicles who currently have no desire to cultivate genuine virtue.

I. Socrates' Core Views

Throughout the *Gorgias*, Socrates both critiques Callicles' ideology and elaborates his core views. Rejecting Callicles' view that there is no real measure for goodness apart from an individual's own desires, Socrates argues that there is a real measure or standard for human virtue that we must learn about in order to lead a good life, as I show in section I.1. In this context, he does not go into detail about *what* this measure is—there is no discussion of the Forms or the divine that we find in similar discussions of this issue in other dialogues. Nonetheless, Socrates clearly argues *that there is* such a measure, and that humans can ascertain important insights about it by observing the beauty, order, and structure of the world. Socrates' points about this real measure of goodness lead him to conclude that some goods are essential for human happiness (*eudaimonia*), which I call the highest goods, and some are nonessential, which I call the lower goods. So, in section I.2, I show that for Socrates, the highest human goods are the virtues, philosophical education, friendship, and self-harmony, while the lower goods are conventional goods such as wealth, pleasure, political power, fame or honor. Callicles holds that acquiring an unlimited amount of the lower goods by dominating others is what brings happiness, while Socrates, by contrast, claims that the higher goods are most essential for living well.[3] In section I.3, I explain three important implications of Socrates' core views that the *Gorgias* brings to light. First, Socrates' views have progressive implications in the realm of social justice, since they critique traditional Athenian misogyny and promote the idea that one's socioeconomic class does not solely determine his level of happiness. Second, it follows from his views about the virtues that just punishment should benefit (rather than pay simple retribution to) the wrongdoer. Third, Socrates' claims imply that genuine power is not simply social, political, or military power but rather the ability to attain happiness through the highest human goods.

I.1. There Is a Real Measure for Virtue

Against the claims of Callicles, Socrates argues that there is a real measure for human virtue. This measure is not made up by humans but is instead something that we must "look toward" (as he says in the passage below) and emulate in some way. By saying that we must look toward something other than ourselves, Socrates need not mean something that is literally external or an authority figure who gives commands. The important point is that the measure of moral goodness is not set by whatever we happen to desire, and it is a feature of reality with which we can harmonize by living virtuously. He presents an analogy comparing the measure of goodness to the ideal models that someone with a *technē* looks toward[4] when creating something excellently:

> Well then, won't the good man, who speaks with a view to the best, say what he says not at random but looking off toward something? Just as all the other craftsmen look toward their work when each chooses and applies what he applies, not at

3. This disagreement between Socrates and Callicles raises the question of whether having some minimum amount of the lower goods is necessary for happiness, a question that the Peripatetics and Stoics would later debate. Aristotle claims in the *Ethics* that we need "moderately supplied goods" to achieve *eudaimonia* (1099a31–b9), while the Stoics held that virtue alone is sufficient for the good life. For an account of this debate, see Cicero's *De Finibus*. Socrates does not explicitly address this question in the *Gorgias*.

4. In a similar way, the divine craftsman or demiurge in the *Timaeus* looks to a changeless "model" and "reproduces its form and character" in the visible cosmos (*Ti.* 28a–c).

> random, but in order that he can get this thing he is working on to have a certain form [*eidos*]. For example, if you wish to look at painters, house builders, shipwrights, all the other craftsmen—whomever of them you wish—see how each man puts down each thing that he puts down into a certain arrangement, and furthermore compels one thing to fit and harmonize with another, until he has composed the whole as an arranged and ordered thing. (503d–504a)

Craftsmen identify the patterns or standards that govern whether something is well-ordered, well-functioning, arranged, and harmonized, and then apply them to the raw material of their craft in order to produce something beautiful.[5] The harmony that the craftsman bestows allows each part of his object to fit and function well with the others. Just so, the virtuous person learns to discern the habits, character traits, and other goods that are most essential to a beautiful, well-ordered, happy way of life, and she chooses to make them her highest priority. The virtuous person imposes the real measure of goodness onto her own soul in order to make it well-arranged and well-ordered. The tyrannical soul, by contrast, is disordered and so constantly in a state of miserable conflict. This passage contains the only use of the term *eidos* in the *Gorgias*; Socrates does not propose a theory of Forms in the dialogue as he does in others such as the *Republic* or the *Phaedrus*; "form" in this passage indicates the structure given by a craftsman to his object that allows it to be beautiful or function well. Arrangement, well-structured form, and "harmony" give objects as well as souls the measure they need to fully realize their capacity for excellence, beauty, and (in the case of souls) happiness.

A passage from the *Theaetetus*, another dialogue that does not explicitly discuss Forms, sheds light on Socrates' claims in the *Gorgias* that there is a real, universal measure for goodness. In the famous "digression" passage, Socrates claims that there is a "pattern in reality" that sets the standard for human virtue and happiness:

---

5. In my view, Socrates' claims about goodness (*to agathon*) and beauty (*to kalon*) in the *Gorgias* are consistent with Diotima's claim in the *Symposium* that "good things are always beautiful as well" (*Smp.* 201c). The better something is, the more beautiful it is, and so the two terms work hand in hand to express different aspects of the same underlying reality.

> My friend, there are two patterns set up in reality. One is divine and supremely happy; the other has nothing of God in it, and is the pattern of the deepest unhappiness. [*paradeigmatōn, ō phile, en tōi onti estōtōn, tou men theiou eudaimonestatou, tou de atheou athliōtatou.*] This truth the evildoer does not see; blinded by folly and utter lack of understanding, he fails to perceive that the effect of his unjust practices is to make him grow more and more like the one, and less and less like the other. For this he pays the penalty of living the life that corresponds to the pattern he is coming to resemble. (*Tht.* 176e–177a)

Reality is constituted such that the way of life one leads determines whether one is happy or miserable. In this context, Socrates says that it is "God" who sets the patterns and serves as the ultimate measure for good and evil. He associates God with the virtues of justice and piety, and we "become like God" (*homoiōsis theoi*) by becoming just and pious (*Tht.* 176b).[6] Thus, the way of life that is patterned after God's nature is best and happiest, and the more one's life deviates from this pattern, the more miserable it is. Again, these patterns are established in reality, and not by humans—just as only a certain set of foods universally promote bodily health, so also certain traits, habits, and actions make us happy, and others make us miserable. Although Socrates does not say explicitly in the *Gorgias* that God or some kind of divinity sets the measure of goodness (though he gestures toward this view in his myth of the afterlife, as I discuss below), he at least claims that this measure is "set up in reality," as the *Theaetetus* puts it.

Socrates also mythologically represents his view that there is a real measure for virtue in his description of the afterlife at the end of the *Gorgias*. At the very beginning of the myth, Socrates claims that there is an eternal "law" that determines whether humans will receive reward or punishment in the afterlife in accordance with the virtue or vice they cultivated in their earthly lives:

> Now in the time of Cronos there was the following law [*nomos*] concerning human beings and it exists always and still to this day among the gods, that he among human beings who went through life justly and piously, when he came to his end, would

6. David Sedley (1999) insightfully explores the theme of "becoming like God" as it appears in Plato.

> go away to the islands of the blessed to dwell in total happiness apart from evils, while he who lived unjustly and godlessly would go to the prison of retribution and judgment, which they call Tartarus. (*Grg.* 523a–b)

Socrates' use of the term *nomos* is likely a deliberate counter to Callicles' rejection of *nomoi* in favor of "nature." In the context of the myth, *nomos* is not a product of the human imagination. Rather, the real *nomos* "exists always" "among the gods," and it applies to all human beings. The "law" that the gods enforce on people could symbolize the measure for goodness that Socrates discusses throughout the dialogue—those who discern and live in accord with the measure (or "law") by acquiring the higher goods earn the "reward" of happiness, while those who fail to do so "punish" themselves with misery. In other words, the rewards and punishments doled out from an external source (the gods) in the myth of the afterlife mirror the internal consequences that follow from virtue and vice during one's lifetime. Similarly, Socrates' claim that those who lack virtue in life require rehabilitative and purificatory punishment (*Grg.* 525b–c) extends to the afterlife in the myth. Since it is a myth,[7] it is difficult to tell how literally we should understand Socrates' point about gods and the law, but we can at least see that it supports his view discussed elsewhere in the dialogue that humans are not the measure of all things, and we instead must learn reality's measure of justice and injustice, beauty and ugliness, and so on.

Socrates claims that goodness and beauty are present in the cosmos and not simply in our minds, another indication that human desire or imagination is not the source of the measure for virtue. Moreover, the order that the virtues give to the soul mirrors the beautiful order of the cosmos.[8] Rachel Barney (2017) helpfully summarizes the contrast between Socrates'

7. Socrates makes a puzzling claim at the beginning of this myth: "Hear then, as they say, a very fine rational account [*kalou logou*], which you consider a myth, as I think, but I consider it a rational account; for I shall tell you the things I am going to tell you as being true" (523a). Perhaps he means that Callicles might see the myth as fictional nonsense, whereas Socrates sees it as a mythological expression of true philosophical points.

8. In the *Timaeus,* Plato makes a similar point (though in a different context) by suggesting that the soul should "conform" to the beauty and harmony of the cosmos: "We should redirect the revolutions in our heads that were thrown off course at our birth, by coming to learn the harmonies and revolutions of the universe, and so bring into conformity with its objects our faculty of understanding, as it was in its original condition. And when this conformity is complete, we shall have achieved our goal: that most excellent life offered to humankind by the gods, both now and forevermore" (90d).

and Callicles' understanding of the human's place in the cosmos: "Socrates insists later on, 'partnership and friendship, orderliness, self-control, and justice hold together heaven and earth, and gods and men, and that is why they call this universe a world order, my friend, and not an undisciplined world-disorder' (507e–508a). Callicles advocates *pleonexia* only because he 'neglects geometry' (508a): instead of being predatory animals, we should observe and emulate the orderly structure of the cosmos as a whole." As I discussed in the previous chapter, Callicles sees no measure or standard for goodness outside of fulfilling his desires—like a predator, he only calls "good" whatever satisfies his appetites. He sees no shred of truth in conventions or laws that seek to establish peace, and concludes that the strong excel by following their appetites and oppressing the weak (e.g., 483b–484c). Socrates calls attention to the beautiful order of the cosmos as an indication that goodness and beauty are not human fantasies or labels we place on things because we desire them. Beauty and goodness, as well as particular instances of beauty such as virtue, order, arrangement, and friendship, come from a source outside of the human mind that we must learn about and instantiate so far as possible if we want to attain the effect of goodness, namely happiness. As I will discuss below, we need a well-ordered soul to achieve the internal states of completeness and sufficiency, both of which bring fulfillment. The well-ordered soul also experiences pleasure that is not harmful, even though pleasure is not its primary aim. A well-ordered soul is a healthy soul, and living with a healthy soul allows for happiness, while living with an unhealthy soul does not.

I.2. The Highest Human Goods Are Necessary for Happiness

Before analyzing Socrates' view that the highest human goods are necessary for happiness, it is worth noting that the *Gorgias* repeatedly reminds the reader that happiness is a primary focus of the dialogue. The debate between Socrates and Callicles (481b–527e) concerns a choice between two fundamentally different ways of life, and each argues that his own is happiest. The characters explicitly compare the value of well-known ways of life in ancient Athens,[9] with Socrates defending the philosophical

9. Andrea Wilson Nightingale (1992) explores how the *Gorgias* mirrors the debate between brothers Zephus and Amphion in Euripides' (lost) *Antiope* about whether the active life or the contemplative life is superior. Socrates and Callicles reprise and deepen this debate in their own context.

life[10] in pursuit of the virtues, on the one hand, and Callicles defending the life of the rhetorician, sophist, or politician in pursuit of power and *pleonexia*, on the other. Throughout the conversation, Socrates repeats that the topics they are discussing are the most important ones in human life (458a–b, 472c–d, 487b, 487e–488a, 500c–e). For example, he states: "For indeed these things that we are disagreeing about do not happen to be at all small, but are more or less those things that it is most fine to know about and most shameful not to know about; for the chief point of them is either to know or to ignore who is happy and who is not" (472c–d). If we all naturally strive for happiness for ourselves and others as our ultimate goal,[11] then identifying the best methods for achieving this end is perhaps the most urgent and vital task that each of us faces. To regard questions about the value of justice, injustice, power, and other core ethical topics as "small matters" (as Callicles calls them at 486c–d) is a serious mistake. Socrates is aware that the conversation of the *Gorgias* might have drastic ramifications not only for the participants but also for the listeners; their

10. Or, as Socrates puts it at *Gorgias* 500c, his own "life in philosophy" (*ton bion ton en philosophia*). Socrates emphasizes throughout the text that philosophy is not just a theoretical discipline but rather a way of life organized around the pursuit of wisdom and the rest of the virtues. In his analysis of the *Symposium*, Pierre Hadot (2002) argues that Socrates is Plato's depiction of the ideal philosopher: "We may suppose that wisdom represents the perfection of knowledge, which is identified with virtue; yet as we have seen, knowledge or *sophia* in the Greek tradition is less a purely theoretical wisdom than know-how, or knowing-how-to-live. We can recognize traces of this know-how not in the theoretical knowledge of Socrates the philosopher, but in his way of life, which is precisely what Plato evokes in the *Symposium*" (44). I agree with Hadot, and in my view, Plato also depicts Socrates as an exemplar of the philosophical life in the *Gorgias* and the *Phaedrus*.

11. In *Symposium* 204c–205b, Diotima argues that happiness is the ultimate goal of all of our desires. She points out that, almost all of the time, we want particular things for the sake of something else, but this "chain" of desires ends when we get to happiness. We do not want happiness for the sake of something else, but as an end in itself. Desire for happiness, and therefore desire for good things, is common to everyone. Aristotle makes a similar argument in *Ethics* I: "Happiness above all seems to be [complete], for we always choose it on account of itself and never on account of something else. Yet honor, pleasure, intellect, and every virtue we choose on their own account—for even if nothing resulted from them, we would choose each of them—but we choose them also for the sake of happiness, because we suppose that, through them, we will be happy. But nobody chooses happiness for the sake of these things, or, more generally, on account of anything else" (*EN* 1097b1–6).

discussion takes place in a public place (perhaps outside a gymnasium)[12] in front of other young men who are tempted to adopt the same way of life as Callicles and company, as are many of Plato's readers.

Socrates makes several definite claims about virtue throughout the *Gorgias* that are consistent with the socially accepted, "conventional" morality that Callicles criticizes, but he disagrees with popular notions about *why* one should follow these ethical standards. In other dialogues, Plato discusses the common reasons that motivate people to behave justly. In the *Theaetetus*, for example, Socrates points out that most people are motivated to avoid committing common injustices or breaking laws for the sake of their own reputation: "It is not at all an easy matter, my good friend, to persuade men that it is not for the reasons commonly alleged that one should try to escape from wickedness and pursue virtue. It is not in order to avoid a bad reputation and obtain a good one that virtue should be practiced and not vice" (*Tht.* 176b–c).[13] Put another way, external rewards or punishments are what usually prevent people from committing injustice. Aside from having a bad reputation, there is also the threat of legal punishment, damaging one's career, or putting one's own friends or family in danger. Of course, we are punished for behaving unjustly only when we are caught doing so by others. This fact prompts Glaucon to tell the myth of Gyges in *Republic* II, after which he claims that nobody who could reliably escape punishment would choose to behave justly (*R.* 359d–360d). Hence, in the *Gorgias*, Socrates agrees with the basic principle of Athenian *nomos* that one should not commit injustice, but not because of any external reward or punishment, as most people think. Rather, he shifts our focus to the internal effects of virtue and vice.

Indeed, Socrates emphasizes that virtue and vice are intimately tied to the ultimate internal reward, happiness (*eudaimonia*). His ethical arguments throughout the dialogue suggest that the virtues are preeminent among the highest goods, because they are the most crucial for leading a morally good, happy life. When Polus claims that tyrants such as Archeleus and

12. Debra Nails (2002) points out that the *Gorgias*' discussion must take place somewhere public, since Gorgias has just finished giving a display speech when Socrates and Chaerephon arrive on the scene at the beginning of the dialogue (326).

13. Glaucon makes a similar observation in *Republic* II, claiming that "the opinion of the many" is that justice belongs to the class of goods that are a kind of "drudgery, which should be practiced for the sake of the wages and the reputation that comes from opinion [of other people], but by itself should be fled from as something hard" (*R.* 358a).

the king of Persia are happy, Socrates makes his first major ethical claim in the dialogue: "For I assert that the noble and good man and woman are happy [*kalon kai agathon andra kai gunaika eudaimona einai*]; the unjust and base, wretched [*athlion*]" (470e). For Socrates, one achieves *eudaimonia* by becoming noble and good, and this holds true for every human. Again, just as none of us decides what makes our bodies healthy or sick, so also we do not choose what improves the soul and gives rise to *eudaimonia*—the virtues are necessary for happiness, even if we disagree or seek our happiness solely in other types of goods. Likewise, the opposite of *eudaimonia*, being wretched (*athlios*) or miserable, is a consequence of lacking virtue, regardless of one's possessions or external conditions. Without virtue, we will not use the lower goods well; ignorance and vice inevitably lead us to cause detriment to ourselves and others with whatever wealth, power, or other lower goods we might have. While Socrates does not specify what qualifies a person as "noble and good" in the statement above, the rest of the conversation makes clear that he means the virtues of justice, moderation, courage, and wisdom (e.g., see 507a–c). Among the highest human goods that Socrates discusses in the dialogue, the virtues are his primary focus. As I will show below, the other highest goods are closely connected to virtue in various ways, either as promoters of virtue, effects of virtue, or some other such relation.

There are several reasons why the virtues bring happiness according to the *Gorgias*. First, as I discussed in chapter 1 (section III.1), the virtues more than any other goods contribute to an individual's sense of completeness and self-sufficiency. "Completeness" denotes a state of perfection or full development, and "sufficiency" is the absence of need for, or dependency on, other things to be happy (*Phlb.* 20d). In my view, the *Gorgias* does not explicitly address the question of whether the virtues *alone* are sufficient for happiness, but it is at least clear that they are more essential than anything else. It is possible that sufficiency requires a minimum threshold of external goods, including healthy relationships, as Aristotle argues in *Nicomachean Ethics* I:

> The complete good [*teleion agathon*] is held to be self-sufficient [*autarkes*]. We do not mean by self-sufficient what suffices for someone by himself, living a solitary life, but what is sufficient also with respect to parents, offspring, a wife, and, in general, one's friends and fellow citizens, since by nature a human being is political. [. . .] As for the self-sufficient, we posit it as that

> which by itself makes life choiceworthy and in need of nothing, and such is what we suppose happiness to be. (*EN* 1097b8–16)

The person who has achieved the amount of completeness and self-sufficiency that is attainable for humans leads a "choiceworthy" life, or, in other words, a life that anyone would feel fortunate to live. When it comes to one's own desires, Socrates says that the virtuous, self-restrained person leads an "orderly life, sufficient and satisfied [*ikanōs kai exarkountōs*] with the things that are ever at hand" (*Grg.* 493c–d). This person is psychologically "at rest" and does not feel a painful lack of external goods (493e). When the virtuous person interacts with others, her virtue enables her to function well within her professional, interpersonal, and social spheres. The virtuous person creates commitments that are beneficial to both herself and others, and she effectively lives up to those commitments. In sum, the virtues are those qualities of the soul that allow us to live a flourishing, satisfied, healthy, frequently pleasant life (in other words, to experience *eudaimonia*), and virtuous behavior provides various types of benefit to the people whose lives we affect.

The education that philosophical inquiry promotes is also a necessary step in attaining *eudaimonia.* I use the term "philosophical education" in a broad sense as the education that takes place through dialogue and independent reflection, and which is not simply for the sake of gaining craft knowledge or expertise (*technē*) in practical tasks. This sort of education can help us attain knowledge or wisdom that is valuable for its own sake and not simply as a means to completing a given project. As I argued in chapter 1, "philosophy" in the *Gorgias* is a way of life that involves constant learning and the cultivation of virtue. Socrates demonstrates that philosophical inquiry helps us discern what we should care about most; through it we can, for example, perceive the value of the virtues and the inherent futility of a life spent solely in pursuit of the lower goods. In the same passage quoted above, after Polus asks Socrates if the king of Persia is happy, Socrates replies that he cannot answer, since he does not "know how he stands in regard to education [*paideias*] and justice" (*Grg.* 470e). Philosophical education is essential for happiness, because it dispels ignorance about what is most essential for living a morally good, happy life. In this way, philosophical education can steer us away from the viciousness and misery that result from having inordinate, misguided desires for limitless pleasure, power, wealth, and so on.

Although there is not a substantial discussion devoted exclusively to friendship in the *Gorgias*, Socrates states in key passages that it is indispensable for a happy life. Throughout the conversation, he implies what Aristotle later makes explicit, namely, that "without friends, no one would choose to live, even if he possessed all other goods" (*EN* VIII, 1155a3). If we have nobody to share our lives with, to support us in times of trouble, to trust, or to serve, we cannot help but feel emptiness and loneliness. Socrates states that the vicious person "would be unable to share in common, and he in whom there is no community [*koinōnian*] would not have friendship [*philia*]" (507d–e). In a genuine friendship, each person seriously cares for and promotes the other's well-being so far as possible, and the vicious person has no such relationship. In the passage already quoted at *Gorgias* 507e–508a, friendship (along with "community, orderliness, moderation, and justness") "holds" people "together" in a peaceful and harmonious way, preventing painful isolation and chaotic strife. Virtue and self-harmony make real friendship possible, since we must have some level of virtue to consider the well-being of others to be as important as our own. The person who lacks virtue, by contrast, tends to care only about satisfying his own desires and uses others merely as means for this satisfaction. Finally, friends enhance our philosophical education and increase our self-knowledge. We rely on others to share their insights with us, to bring our own imperfections or ignorance to our attention, to guide us toward self-improvement, and to act as partners in the search for truth.[14] For the reasons stated above, all of these important projects are requisite steps on the path toward *eudaimonia*.

Another one of the highest goods according to the *Gorgias* is inner harmony. The meaning of Socrates' harmony metaphor is multifaceted. One important aspect of remaining in harmony with ourselves is to ensure that we do not hold views that contradict one another. Socrates' love for philosophy and virtue leads him to have a much stronger commitment to rational consistency than he does to agreeing with the majority of people: "It is superior that my lyre be out of tune and dissonant, and the chorus I might provide for the public, and that most human beings disagree with me and say contradictory things, rather than that I, being one man, should be discordant with myself and say contradictory things" (482b–c). Socrates

14. In chapters 3 and 4 I will discuss the important link between self-knowledge and intimate relationships according to the *Phaedrus*. In *Alcibiades* I, Socrates claims that a close friend is like a mirror in which we can better see ourselves, just as getting physically close to someone allows us to see our reflection in his or her pupils (132a–133c).

does not care about saying what the majority of people want to hear or agreeing with their views for the sake of being accepted by them. Socrates' self-examination and his discussions with others contribute to his goal of remaining "in tune" with himself, or, put another way, ensuring that his views are rationally supported and do not conflict with one another. This harmony increases our self-understanding by helping us clarify what we know and what we do not know. As most of Plato's dialogues show, Socrates' interlocutors are often not aware that they hold contradictory views until Socrates shows them. Their erroneous opinions are thus connected with a lack of knowledge about themselves and what will bring them happiness, as Socrates indicates when he says that Callicles will not think that pleasure is the good when he "looks on himself correctly" (495d–e). If we gain a clearer view of ourselves in this way, we will be more likely to seek the true goods.

Likewise, the virtues help us to achieve another sense of inner harmony that Socrates alludes to in the *Gorgias*. This other sense of self-harmony has to do with reforming those desires that are inordinate and misguided, such that they do not cause painful conflict with one another or with reason. The person with this sort of self-harmony is the opposite of Callicles insofar as her desires are capable of being satisfied simultaneously (i.e., fulfilling one desire does not necessarily detract from fulfilling others), and the primary objects of her desire are the same ones that her reason deems most valuable. For example, the person with inner harmony desires the amount of wealth, bodily health, and external goods that she (correctly) thinks are necessary to live well. Her nonrational desires are not in conflict with what she thinks best, and so she does not experience inner conflict about how much wealth, for example, she should pursue. Since she desires a limited and appropriate amount of such goods, her acquisition of wealth does not interfere with, say, her ability to care for her bodily health. By contrast, someone like Callicles would, for instance, destroy his health and deplete his wealth (both of which he desires to maintain) by pursuing his other intense desire for excessive bodily pleasure. The soul necessarily experiences inner conflict when it has competing, unlimited desires.

Hence, we can also understand self-harmony as self-friendship. The *Gorgias* shows that another important pitfall of Callicles' unfettered hedonism is that it does not account for the role that self-friendship plays in one's happiness. For Socrates, the flaws in Callicles' character and ideology are signs that the way of life he pursues causes him to lack self-friendship. Plato states this insight succinctly in the *Lysis*: "The bad [*tous kakous*]—as another saying goes—are never alike, not even to themselves. They are out of kilter and unstable [*emplēktous te kai astathmētous*]. And when something is not like itself and is inconsistent with itself, it can hardly be like something else and be a friend to it" (*Ly.* 214c–d). By only caring about satisfying his nonrational desires, Callicles neglects education, the development of his reason, and the self-improvement that would allow him to thrive in other areas of his life. One must have at least some level of self-friendship before he can be friends with others, which is another point that Aristotle adopts and expands:

> But the marks of friendship in relation to those around us, and by which friendships are defined, seem to have arisen from things pertaining to oneself. For people set down as a friend someone who wishes for and does things that are (or appear to be) good, for the other person's sake, or as someone who wishes for his friend, for the friend's own sake, to exist and to live. [. . .] But each of these criteria is present in the decent person in relation to himself. [. . .] For this decent person is of like mind with himself and longs for the same things with his whole soul. Indeed, he both wishes for the good things for himself, that is, the things that appear such to him, and he does them (since it belongs to a good person to work at what is good); and he does them for his own sake, since he acts for the sake of the thinking part of himself, which is in fact what each person seems to be.[15] (*EN* 1166a1–18)

15. The rest of this passage gives more detail about the similarity between self-friendship and friendship with others: "[The decent person] also wishes that he himself live and be preserved, and especially that [part of himself] with which he is prudent. For existence is a good to the serious person, and each wishes for the good things for himself. Yet no one chooses to possess every good by becoming another—for even now, the god possesses the good—but rather by being whatever sort he is; and it would seem that it is the thinking part that each person is or is most of all. Such a person also wishes to go through life with himself, since he does so pleasantly: the memories of what he has done are delightful, his hopes for the future are good, and such things are pleasant. His thought is also well supplied with objects of contemplation. He shares pains as well as pleasures with himself above all, since what is painful as well as pleasant is always the same for him and not different at different times. Hence he is without regret, so to speak. And so, because each of these belongs to the decent person in relation to himself, and because he stands in relation to a friend as he does to himself—for the friend is another self—friendship too seems to be a certain one of these qualities and friends, those to whom these belong" (*EN* 1166a18–33). He adds that each person is "two or

The person who has achieved self-friendship is at peace with himself; he is not preoccupied with internal strife or the constant pursuit of lower goods, and there is no conflict between the different aspects of his own soul ("longs for the same things with his whole soul"). This inner peace frees him to genuinely care for others and to spend time and effort promoting their well-being. As Aristotle famously puts it, "The friend is another self" (*EN* 1166a33). The person who takes good care of his entire soul will be a true friend to another.

I.3. Important Implications of Socrates' Claims about Virtue

First, Socrates' claim that there is a universal human good has important implications in the realm of social justice. His view that happiness comes from moral excellence and that misery results from moral depravity applies to everyone regardless of social class, gender, or other such features of one's identity. Regarding the passage quoted above where Socrates states that "the noble and good man and woman are happy" (*kalon kai agathon andra kai gunaika eudaimona einai*) (*Grg.* 470e), Dodds states that "*kalos kagathos*" is a standard phrase used by Athenian aristocrats to set themselves apart from common people, but that Socrates repurposes the phrase here for his own views on gender and the good life. This phrase is not applied to women anywhere else in Greek literature.[16] Plato's deliberate application of this term to all men and women emphasizes the natural equality between men and women that he points out in other dialogues such as the *Republic*, where Socrates and company agree that men and women differ only with respect to their bodies, not their souls (454d–456a). By highlighting the similarity between the souls of men and women, Socrates seriously challenges traditional Athenian misogyny. Further, his statement makes virtue and vice the measure of happiness, not one's wealth or social class, putting the nobility on a level playing field with everyone else when it comes to the most precious good in human life. Modern readers searching for contemporary value in ethical and political discussions of the *Gorgias* might say that the absence of discussions about social justice is a shortcoming of the dialogue, especially regarding hugely important issues of gender, slavery, and a strictly hierarchical society. While it is true that these issues are not the main focus

---

more, on the basis of the points stated, and the peak of friendship is like friendship toward oneself" (*EN* 1166a35–1166b1).

16. Dodds 1959, 242–243.

of the text, Plato still builds progressive suggestions into the core ethical claims that Socrates defends.

Second, if virtue is among the most important goods for happiness, then we should also value anything that helps to promote virtue, as Socrates makes clear in his second major claim in the dialogue. In his conversation with Polus, he states: "But according to my opinion [*doxan*], at least, Polus, the one who does injustice and is unjust is altogether wretched, but more wretched if he does not pay the just penalty nor meet with retribution when he does injustice, and less wretched if he pays the just penalty and meets with just judgment from gods and human beings" (472e). Socrates conceives of "penalty" as rehabilitation rather than revenge. Criminal justice (ideally) improves the condition of the person who is punished by making him more capable of cultivating virtue. Socrates frequently uses a medical metaphor to make his point—receiving a just penalty is the only way to be cured of the soul's most serious illnesses, vice and misery. Just as bodily illnesses harm the body, so also vices such as injustice and immoderation harm the soul: "How much more wretched a thing than an unhealthy body it is to dwell with a soul that is not healthy but rotten, unjust, and impious" (479b–c).[17] We should be eager to pay the penalty "lest the disease of injustice, become chronic, should make his soul fester with sores underneath and be incurable" (480b), a comment that prefigures the passage about incurable souls in Socrates' myth of the afterlife at the end of the dialogue (525c). Punishment prepares for the development of virtue in the same way that medicine prepares for healing. That is, medicine puts the body's elements in a position from which the body can take over in order to spontaneously heal itself. Similarly, properly administered penalties help people begin the process toward developing the virtues, especially moderation and justice: "For justice doubtless moderates [*sōphronizei*] men and makes them more just and comes to be the medicine for baseness" (478d). Socrates' view that it is better to pay the penalty than to get away with injustice is perfectly consistent with his first claim about the necessity of virtue for happiness; if virtue is one of the highest human goods, then we should embrace punishment whenever it can foster virtue.

Third, Socrates' account of virtue refutes the rhetors' notion of power (*dunamis*) and offers a new conception of it. Gorgias, Polus, and Callicles conceive of power as having the ability to get what one wants at any given time (452e, 466b–c, 491e–492c), as well as the ability to protect oneself

17. Plato's *Timaeus* also characterizes vice as an illness of the soul at 86a–90e.

against suffering injustice (486a–c). They also regard the inability to protect oneself against suffering injustice as deeply "shameful" (486a). As I discussed in the previous chapter, Socrates' critique of Polus and Callicles entails (among other things) that even the tyrant does not have the power to get what he really "wishes" for (467d), namely "the good" (468b) and happiness, and so is not powerful at all. For Socrates, real power is instead the ability to obtain the higher goods and the happiness that arises from them. Happiness is what everybody naturally aims for, and so those who can attain it are those who are most powerful. Only the virtuous person has the power to properly cultivate his soul and thereby attain satisfaction, rest, and inner harmony, all of which are essential for human happiness. If this is true, then it follows that one must "procure a power [*dunamin*]" for avoiding injustice (509d–e), and that "the most shameful help not to be able to provide for oneself or for one's friends or relatives" is the protection against committing injustice (509b).

After concluding his myth of the afterlife at the end of the dialogue, Socrates sums up the core views he has elaborated throughout the dialogue. He states:

> You are not able to prove that one should live any other life than this one, which is manifestly advantageous in that place [the afterlife] too. But among so many speeches, the others are refuted and this speech alone remains fixed: that one must beware of doing injustice more than of suffering injustice, and more than everything, a man must take care not to seem to be good but to be so, both in private and in public; and if someone becomes bad in some respect, he must be punished, and this is the second good after being just—becoming so and paying the just penalty by being punished; and one must flee from all flattery, concerning both oneself and others, and concerning both few men and many; and one must use rhetoric thus, always aiming at what is just, and so for every other action. (527b–c)

Socrates restates that committing injustice is worse than suffering injustice because of the internal effects (happiness or misery) of virtue and vice. The benefits and dangers of having a certain moral character do not at all depend on whether others notice it, which means that we should care for virtue "both in private and in public," and we should care not about "seeming" but rather *being* good. Given these views, it follows that helping others to cultivate virtue should be the primary aim of punishment, and successful punishment is therefore a serious benefit. Likewise, activities or professions such as rhetoric should not aim to "flatter" for the sake of producing pleasure and political advantage, which are ultimately aimed at indulging one's own nonrational desires. Instead, rhetoric and "every other action" should be used justly and for the sake of promoting virtue in others, a goal that sometimes must be reached by causing others discomfort (as Socrates causes his interlocutors discomfort). These views are diametrically opposed to the ones that Polus and Callicles stated earlier in the dialogue, which shows that Socrates addresses the issues that Callicles and company care about most, and he seeks to persuade them that his own ethical views and practices constitute the real route to the happiness for which they already strive.

Importantly, while Socrates thinks that these core ethical views are true, he does not go so far as to say that he *knows* they are true.[18] Given several key remarks in the dialogue, it is more precise to say that Socrates regards them as true, well-supported opinions or judgments (*doxai*) rather than knowledge. At 472e he explicitly calls his view about punishment an "opinion" (*doxan*), and at 486e he collectively refers to the views he has been defending as opinions using the same term. Socrates' *doxai* have strong accounts that he has repeatedly tested, but they do not have the precision and stability of, say, mathematical knowledge. For this reason, they need to be repeatedly tested to ensure that the *logoi* supporting them stand up to rational scrutiny. Socrates denies that he has knowledge of the ethical matters at issue, saying instead that he is still "seeking" it: "For I, at any rate, do not say what I say with knowledge [*eidōs*], but I am seeking in common with you" (506a).[19] He is keenly aware of his own mortal limitations when it comes to gaining knowledge, so he holds himself accountable by repeatedly reexamining his views in common with others, and he encourages them to do the same. However, he emphasizes the strength of the accounts that support his opinions when he says that they are "held down and bound" by "iron and adamantine arguments," and that "no one who says something different is able not to be ridiculous" (508e–509a). Socrates has enough awareness of his own human limitations to stop short of claiming that he has perfect, infallible knowledge, yet he also maintains

18. Socrates does not use terms that would be translated into English as "knowledge," such as *gnōsis, epistēmē,* or *oida,* to describe the views he defends.

19. At 509a Socrates repeats that he "does not know" (*ouk oida*) the answers to the ethical questions at issue.

that philosophical inquiry continually supports these views and no others. In contrast to Callicles' misology, Socrates trusts the *logoi* about virtue and therefore lives in accord with them. Thus, when it comes to making the inevitable choice of how to live, his way of life harmonizes with the views he defends throughout the dialogue.

II. Socrates' Pedagogical Aims

Plato does not depict Socrates reciting his own views to a generic audience. Rather, Socrates customizes his discourse to ethically and pedagogically benefit the individuals with whom he speaks. In section II.1, I argue that Socrates' primary aim in his conversation with Callicles is to *persuade* him to pursue a more virtuous life, and so his account of virtue is shaped by (what I call) his philosophical rhetoric. While Socrates makes strong points relating to virtue that he believes are true, he unfolds only the arguments that will have the most potential to benefit Callicles. If Socrates were to give a one-size-fits-all response to Callicles, then Callicles would miss Socrates' insights either partially or entirely. I expand on the theme of philosophical rhetoric in the *Gorgias* in II.2, where I argue that Socrates' goal is not to give a comprehensive, exhaustive, strictly rational demonstration of the topics discussed; instead, he says all that is necessary to persuade Callicles to pursue moral self-cultivation.[20] Further evidence for this view is that Socrates gives a different, fuller account of virtue (and especially *sōphrosunē*) when talking to a different interlocutor who is more capable of receiving such an account, as he does in the *Phaedrus*, which I will discuss in chapters 3 and 4. In section II.3, I show that Socrates' philosophical rhetoric also aims to help Callicles cultivate his sense of shame, and to do so I first examine the meaning of the term shame (*aischos*) in Plato. I argue that if Socrates succeeds at this goal, then it would help Callicles to understand what is truly shameful, feel shame about his own moral imperfection, and seek to remedy this imperfection. Section II also lays the groundwork for section III, where I will argue that one of Socrates' key tactics is to persuade Callicles that self-restraint (a civic virtue) is a valuable characteristic, since Callicles must first take steps toward self-restraint before he is ready to pursue genuine Platonic virtue. As I argued in chapter 1, Callicles is not only Plato's depiction

20. I thank Ronald Polansky for sharing his unpublished notes on the *Gorgias*, where he makes a similar point.

of an individual but also a moral type who represents a common type of person and a commonly held ideology. By having Socrates refute Calliclean ideology using his philosophical rhetoric, Plato gives us an exemplary case of how the philosopher can turn someone who has no interest in Platonic virtue toward a more philosophical and virtuous life.

II.1. Philosophical Rhetoric in the *Gorgias*

At the beginning of the *Gorgias,* Socrates strongly criticizes the common use of rhetoric throughout Greece. During his conversation with Gorgias (*Grg.* 447a–461b), Socrates draws a distinction between craft (*technē*) and "experience" (*empeiria*, 462c), and he places rhetoric in the latter category along with pastry baking, cosmetics, and sophistry (463b).[21] Socrates argues that an *empeiria* does not qualify as a craft because, unlike craftsmen, those who possess an *empeiria* simply aim to "flatter" (463b) or pander to others by causing them as much pleasure and gratification as possible (462d, 501b–c). Craftsmen, on the other hand, do what is *best* for the people or objects they affect, which is not always the same as what is most pleasant (464d). As I discussed above, a *technē* promotes the good of its object by "looking off toward" a certain measure and applying it to the object (503d–504a). Later, Socrates tells Callicles that the prominent rhetoricians in Greece[22] mostly aim to "please citizens for the sake of their own private

21. Socrates says that each of these four "experiences" have corresponding arts: pastry baking corresponds to medicine, cosmetics corresponds to gymnastics, rhetoric corresponds to the judge's art (*dikaiosunē*), and sophistry corresponds to legislation (464b–466a). The first two pairs are related to the body, and the latter two, to the soul. To illustrate the difference between craft and experience with an example, Socrates explains the difference between medicine and pastry baking: "I was saying, I suppose, that cookery does not seem to me to be an art, but experience; whereas medicine, I said, examines the nature of him of whom it takes care and the cause of the things that it does, and it has a reasoned account [*logon*] to give of each of these things, medicine does. But the other—its care is wholly with pleasure, and it proceeds altogether artlessly toward pleasure, without having examined to any degree the nature of pleasure or the cause, all in all irrationally [*alogōs*], making virtually no distinct enumeration, but by routine and experience saying only the memory of what usually comes about, by which then it also provides pleasures" (500e–501b).

22. Socrates' critical comments about rhetoric are explicitly addressed to the common way of using rhetoric in Greece during his lifetime: "Now what about the rhetoric directed toward the Athenian people and the other peoples of free men in the cities—what in the world is it, in our view?" (502d). This is consistent with Socrates' criticisms of rhetoric

benefit" instead of trying to do what is best for the people and the city. Conventional rhetoricians talk to their audience without "a view to the best [*to beltiston*]" or caring about whether "the citizens shall be as good as possible" as a result of their speeches. Instead, they "strive for gratifying the citizens and, for the sake of their own private interest, make light of the common interest, and associate with the peoples as if with children, trying only to gratify them, and giving no heed to whether they will be better or worse because of these things" (502e). Unlike the philosopher, the average rhetorician cares nothing for virtue, the truth, or the well-being of others, and he will say anything his audience wants to hear so long as it brings him pleasure, political power, or some other perceived advantage.

However, Socrates' criticisms of rhetoric in the *Gorgias* do not apply to all forms of rhetorical practice. While he criticizes the conventional uses of rhetoric during his lifetime, he also suggests that we can use rhetoric for genuine ethical and pedagogical benefit. The person who practices the "true art of rhetoric" (*tē alēthinē rhētorikē*) (517a) "makes preparations for the citizens' souls to be as good as possible and [fights] to say the best things, whether they will be more pleasant or more unpleasant to the hearers," and Socrates adds that people "have never yet seen" this kind of rhetoric (503a–b). Toward the end of the dialogue, Socrates says that "rhetoric, and every other action, must be used always for what is just" (527c), such as for prosecuting "oneself and his son and his friend, if he acts unjustly" (508b), since receiving proper penalties for injustice benefits the wrongdoer's soul. We educate others through using spoken and written *logos*, and since rhetorical skill makes *logos* as effective as possible, we can use rhetoric "for what is just" by persuading others to care for their souls and to promote social well-being.[23] As I will

---

in the *Phaedrus*, where he targets the way people *use* rhetoric instead of rhetoric itself (see especially 260c–d). The *Gorgias* and the *Phaedrus* both suggest it is easy to abuse rhetoric if one does not have adequate knowledge of reality and the intent to promote the well-being of others. In this way, rhetoric is not a self-sufficient craft—it must be paired with philosophy in order to be used well. For more analysis of the accounts of rhetoric in the *Gorgias* and the *Phaedrus*, see Yunis (1996).

23. I agree with Marina McCoy (2008), who argues that although the philosopher and the "sophistical rhetorician" each use rhetoric according to the *Gorgias*, there are two important differences between them. First, philosophers (exemplified by Socrates) "possess the character traits of goodwill (*eunoia*), responsibility for one's own speech (*parrēsia*), and a commitment to knowledge (*epistēmē*)." Second, the philosopher is "willing to be self-critical about his own practice in ways that the others, when faced with the challenge of philosophy to their worldviews, are not" (87).

discuss further in the next section, Plato depicts Socrates not only *discussing* how to use rhetoric virtuously but also *demonstrating* throughout the entire dialogue how to use rhetoric in an attempt to turn his interlocutors toward philosophy and virtue. By criticizing the common use of rhetoric, Socrates aims to minimize his interlocutors' obsession with using rhetoric simply as a means for acquiring conventional goods, and he gets them to consider a life dedicated to virtue as a more valuable alternative. Rather than wholly rejecting rhetoric, Socrates criticizes the abuse of rhetoric and offers a guide for how to use it justly and pedagogically.

Moreover, Socrates suggests that rhetoric can benefit not only individuals but also the entire *polis*. He claims that ideal politicians persuade citizens in order to promote their well-being, and that doing so constitutes both the true art of rhetoric and the "work of a good citizen." He objects to Callicles' assertion that former Athenian politicians such as Pericles, Cimon, Miltiades, and Themistocles were good leaders. While these older leaders were better at gratifying the desires of the Athenian people than the contemporary politicians, it does not follow that they improved the city:

> Indeed in my opinion [Pericles, Cimon, Miltiades, and Themistocles] became more skilled in service than those of today, at any rate, and more capable of supplying the city with the things it desired. But as to leading desires in a different direction [*metabibazein tas epithumias*] and not yielding, persuading [*peithontes*] and forcing them toward the condition in which the citizens were to be better, those earlier men excelled these in nothing, one might almost say; yet this is the one work of a good citizen [*monon ergon estin agathou politou*]. (517b–c)

Just as the rhetoric that Gorgias, Polus, and Callicles practice aims at saying only what the audience wants to hear, and, as a result, gaining the rewards that follow from popularity, so also democratic politicians traditionally aim at gratifying the populace for the sake of their personal gain. This popular way of using rhetoric does not attempt to improve the city in the way that the doctor improves the body, which may often involve denying the patient what he wants, or even causing the patient temporary pain. For Socrates, the virtuous use of rhetoric, or the true art of rhetoric, aims at promoting virtue, education, friendship, and the other goods that are most crucial for a well-functioning society. Rhetoric must serve the virtuous ends set by philosophy and proper statesmanship. In addition to practicing the true art of rhetoric, Socrates exemplifies the work of a good citizen through his very conversation with the interlocutors throughout the *Gorgias,* as he tries to persuade them to care for virtue more than they care for conventional goods. His rhetoric is politically responsible, because he tries to prevent his interlocutors (and those listening) from misusing rhetoric to simply gratify the majority's desires, a practice that is often detrimental to the health of the *polis.*[24]

II.2. Socrates Aims to Persuade Callicles

While we might expect Socrates to say that he is trying to teach Callicles the truth about justice, moderation, happiness, and so on, he repeatedly claims that he is trying to "persuade" (*peithō*) his interlocutors (*Grg.* 493d, 494a, 527c). Just after telling the myth of the afterlife, his final plea to Callicles is the following: "Be persuaded, then, and follow me there where, having arrived, you will be happy both living and when you have come to your end, as the argument indicates" (527c). However, Socrates' aim of persuading his interlocutors to accept the views discussed above is fitting, because he recognizes that he cannot simply transmit all of his wisdom about the good life in one conversation. As he says in the *Symposium*, wisdom is not "like water, which always flows from a full cup into an empty one when we connect them with a piece of yarn" (175d). Instead, Socrates displays how we can use rhetoric to promote justice (527c), or, put another way, to use rhetoric in service of philosophical education.

In addition to using his usual *elenchus* to show the flaws in his interlocutors' misguided views, Socrates gives speeches of varying length that display his rhetorical skill and contain arguments defending the value of virtue and philosophy. His speeches are finely crafted in terms of style and structure, are often charged with feeling (they provoke the emotions of Callicles), quote poetry, and use images and myths to help make the philosophical arguments more vivid. The rhetorical elements of these speeches work in tandem with the philosophical arguments to affect both the rational and nonrational aspects of his listeners' souls. Socrates' account of virtue, then, is shaped by his philosophical rhetoric and his goal of persuading Callicles to pursue virtue. Rather than a complete, exhaustive, strictly rational analysis

24. At another level, the text of the *Gorgias* itself can be seen as an example of Plato practicing the true art of rhetoric and the work of a good citizen, insofar as the text can help its readers in the ways discussed above.

of virtue, it is the account that is most fitting and persuasive to Callicles and those like him, and we must understand this account in light of its pedagogical function. If Socrates were to successfully persuade Callicles to take up the pursuit of wisdom and virtue, it would be a valuable step in Callicles' pedagogical development.

More evidence that Socrates rhetorically tailors his *logos* to the needs of his interlocutors is the fact the views he endorses are often the opposites of those his interlocutors hold.[25] Socrates speaks to the issues about which his interlocutors have strong opinions and care deeply, such as their profession, their ambitions, the nature of power, and their aspirations for happiness and prosperity. They take it that their views about these topics are obviously true. By seriously defending the opposite of these views, Socrates aims to send them into a state of puzzlement and wonder, which might lead them to inquire further about these views in the future and eventually cultivate their own souls. Callicles explicitly calls attention to Socrates' stark opposition to commonly held opinions concerning rhetoric, justice, power, punishment, and so on: "For if you are serious and these things you are saying happen to be true, wouldn't the life of us human beings have been turned upside down and don't we do, as it would appear, all the opposite things to what we ought?" (481c). In response, Socrates points out that insofar as he and Callicles are human, they have similar traits, such as reason, desire, and love, as well as similar concerns, such as justice and injustice, the nature of power, the best way of to live, and the goods that are most important for happiness. They differ, however, when it comes to the degree to which each understands (or misunderstands) reality and the objects that they prioritize. Socrates says that both he and Callicles are "lovers," but they have different objects of love—Callicles loves the Athenian *demos* and the young Demos,

25. This is not to say that Socrates and Callicles have no common ground. They share an important similarity in their critical attitude toward socially established ethical views, but the manner of their critiques differ—Callicles wholly rejects common social values as mere fictions meant to stifle those who are strong by nature, while Socrates gives a more nuanced assessment, as I discussed above. Eric Sanday (2012) helpfully explains their similarity: "Callicles has an important and potentially philosophical point [. . . namely,] that the reception of norms and practices as one's own demands that we be prepared to win release from received norms and standards. A norm is received as one's own only if it can be subject to critique. The proper reception of norms that are central to our identity and way of taking up the world demands that we be prepared to release ourselves from what we and others take to be most real and good, from the familiar as such, and ready ourselves to discover the unexpected" (210).

while Socrates loves philosophy and Alcibiades. Throughout the rest of the dialogue, Socrates argues that Callicles needs to change the objects of his love to become virtuous and happy. Callicles currently has a misdirected, distorted form of love that Socrates aims to positively influence through his philosophical rhetoric.[26] In this way, Socrates shapes his account of virtue as a critical response to the views and values that Callicles already possesses.

Socrates' persuasion could catalyze Callicles into a gradual transition toward self-cultivation by influencing not only his reason but also his *epithumia* and *erōs*—his whole soul, as it were. Importantly, Socrates says that desire is the most persuadable aspect of the soul: "And this part[27] of the soul in which the desires [*epithumiai*] exist happens to be such as to be persuaded [*anapeithesthai*] and to change around up and down" (493a). Socrates tries to redirect[28] Callicles' intense nonrational desire away from his current primary goal (excessive amounts of pleasure, power, etc.) and toward the highest human goods. His account of virtue appeals to all aspects of Callicles' soul in order to have the greatest possible chance at being persuasive, since all aspects of the soul play a role in deciding one's values and priorities. This is especially important for souls such as Callicles who are already ruled by their nonrational desire.

Socrates also makes an important remark about *erōs* near the end of their conversation. Callicles says that although Socrates' words "seem good" to him, he "suffers the experience of the many" and is "not altogether persuaded [*peithomai*]." Socrates' response sheds further light on his aims: "Yes, for love [*erōs*] of the people, Callicles, which is present in your soul, opposes me. But if we investigate these same things often and better, perhaps you will be persuaded" (513c–d). Callicles' love for rhetoric and the rewards it brings prevent him from truly considering the philosophical life

26. Robert Metcalf (2018) also notes the significance of the difference between the objects of Socrates' and Callicles' love: "Callicles cannot contradict what his beloved says, just as Socrates cannot contradict his beloved philosophy (481d–482a). The unmistakable suggestion here is that there is an erotic ground to their disagreement, an erotic explanation of what has occurred in the *logos* and *elenchos* thus far" (109).

27. The word "part" does not appear in the Greek text. Socrates simply uses the word "this" (*touto*) to refer to whatever aspect of the soul has nonrational desires.

28. As Charles H. Kahn (1987) explains, Plato often discusses desire and *erōs* as if they were bodies of water that can be redirected through *logos* and habituation (77–103). For example, Plato uses this simile in *Republic* VI: "When someone's desires incline strongly to some one thing, they are therefore weaker with respect to the rest, like a stream that has been channeled off in that other direction" (485d).

as a better alternative to his current ways of life. Socrates' *logos* must also influence Callicles' *erōs* if it will have any impact on him. As I argued in chapter 1, we feel *erōs* toward the goods that we think are the best and will make us happiest. So if, by the end of their conversation, the primary object of Callicles' *erōs* is still the people of Athens (and everything he gets by pleasing them), he will persist in his current way of life no matter how well Socrates refuted his arguments. Socrates aims to (at least) incite in Callicles the desire to examine the matters they discussed often and in a better way, because only by doing so will he learn to see the truth of Socrates' views for himself, which will in turn lead him to develop the desire to leave behind his current way of life and cultivate virtue instead.

A passage in *Republic* VII helps to illuminate the pedagogical potential of Socrates' philosophical rhetoric, especially as it pertains to the way he aims to influence both the reason and the nonrational aspects of his interlocutors' souls. In the context of Plato's famous image of the cave, Socrates says that the freed prisoner must help to "turn" the "whole soul" (*holē tē psuchē*) of the prisoners who are still in chains in order to free them:

> "But the present argument, on the other hand," I said, "indicates that this power is in the soul of each, and that the instrument with which each learns—just as an eye is not able to turn toward the light from the dark without the whole body—must be turned around from that which is coming into being together with the whole soul until it is able to endure looking at that which is and the brightest part of that which is. And we affirm that this is the good, don't we?" (*R.* 518c–d)

Rather than "putting sight into blind eyes" (*R.* 518c), protreptic education involves the "turning" or transformation of the student's "whole" soul such that he can see reality for himself. If turning the whole soul symbolizes the process we must undergo to acquire wisdom, then this process requires a reorientation of one's reason and nonrational desires such that wisdom and the rest of the virtues become one's top priorities. Just after this passage, Socrates says that moderation, courage, and justice are "produced by habits and exercises" (*R.* 518d). Virtuous habits and exercises help nonrational desires become more harmonious with (the correct use of) reason by lowering their intensity and redirecting them from conventional goods toward the Good itself. Getting adjusted to the sun's light—or, approaching an understanding of the Good—through education and rehabituation is a gradual process

(*R.* 516a–c), and turning the whole soul will take further effort on the student's part (with the help of others). The soul must have moderation, courage, and justice to at least some extent in order for its reason to be turned toward Being and endure the sight of it.[29] Philosophical rhetoric can help to motivate this change in the soul by helping the listener to become aware of his own ignorance, the flaws in his conception of the good life, and the benefit of higher goods such as wisdom and friendship, which in turn could lead him to invest himself in the search for these higher goods.

II.3. Socrates Aims to Help Callicles Cultivate His Sense of Shame

Socrates' philosophical rhetoric also attempts to help Callicles cultivate his sense of shame (*aischos*), since it is an important step in the process of cultivating virtue for someone like Callicles.[30] Plato associates the term *aischos* with constructive activities such as critical self-reflection, examination, and cultivation. He does not associate the term with other senses of the English word "shame," such as the feeling of inferiority or embarrassment about certain aspects of ourselves we cannot change, such as our economic class, family history, and so on. Both Plato and Aristotle see shame as crucial for learning and developing virtue. As Mark Brouwer and Ronald Polansky[31] point out, the Stranger in the *Sophist* claims that shame is a necessary step in philosophical education: "The people who cleanse the soul, my young friend, likewise think the soul, too, won't get any advantage from any learning that's offered to it until someone shames it by refuting it, removes the opinions

29. Socrates suggests that the virtues of moderation, courage, and justice (as they are defined in the *Republic*) are intimately linked to the body, while wisdom is "somehow more divine": "Therefore, the other virtues of a soul, as they are called, are probably somewhat close to those of the body. For they are really not there beforehand and are later produced by habits and exercises, while the virtue of exercising prudence is more than anything somehow more divine, it seems; it never loses its power, but according to the way it is turned, it becomes useful and helpful or, again, useless and harmful" (*R.* 518d–e).

30. Hannah Arendt associates this Platonic sense of shame with the modern notion of conscience in her brilliant text "Thinking and Moral Considerations: A Lecture" (1971). In her discussion of the meaning of self-harmony in the *Gorgias*, she argues that we must learn to engage in self-dialogue through philosophical reflection in order to actualize our potential to have a conscience and engage in critical self-reflection (439–446).

31. Brouwer and Polansky 2004, 233.

that interfere with learning, and exhibits it cleansed, believing that it only knows those things that it does know, and nothing more" (*Sph.* 230c–d). If wisdom and the rest of the virtues require one to learn certain things, then anything that "interferes" with this learning—such as the false opinion that one already possesses virtue—must be "cleansed" from the soul, and shame is an effective cleanser. According to the sense in which Plato uses the term, experiencing shame about our own imperfections motivates us to rectify those imperfections.[32] Similarly, in *Nicomachean Ethics* X.9, Aristotle claims that people must have an "underlying character" that "feels affection for the noble and disgust at the shameful" before "speech and teaching" can have any impact on the formation of their character (*EN* 1179b5–32).[33] Aristotle likewise sees that shame is an important factor in motivating one to care about living in accord with the virtues. Shame allows us to feel disgust toward vicious behavior, and therefore avoid it, rather than avoiding it only due to the threat of some external penalty. Without a sense of shame, one will not feel pain at the thought of one's own immoral behavior and will therefore not seek moral improvement with the help of others.

Plato sometimes depicts Socrates helping his interlocutors cultivate their sense of shame to show us the substantial positive influence that shame can have on an individual. Besides the *Gorgias*, another important dialogue where we see an example of this is the *Symposium,* where Alcibiades confesses that Socrates sometimes makes him feel shame:

> Socrates is the only man in the world who has made me feel shame [*aischunesthai*]—ah, you didn't think I had it in me, did you? Yes, he makes me feel ashamed: I know perfectly well that I can't prove he's wrong when he tells me what I should do; yet, the moment I leave his side, I go back to my old ways: I cave in to my desire to please the crowd. My whole life has become one constant effort to escape from him and keep away, but when I see him, I feel deeply ashamed, because I'm doing

32. Bernard Williams (1993) likewise observes that "shame may be expressed in attempts to reconstruct or improve oneself" (90). In the *Phaedrus* 242c–243d, Socrates uses the term "shame" four times to describe how he feels about his first speech, and he calls his first speech "shameless." He shows how shame can lead to moral purification, since he "cleanses" himself of the impiety (toward Erōs) of his first speech by giving the palinode speech (243a).

33. For more on the importance of shame in Plato, see Rod Jenks (2012) and Christina Tarnopolsky (2010). See also Protagoras' speech about shame in *Protagoras* (322c).

> nothing about my way of life, though I have already agreed with him that I should. Sometimes, believe me, I think I would be happier if he were dead. And yet I know that if he dies I'll be even more miserable. (*Smp.* 216b–c)

Socrates tries to help Alcibiades improve his character by seeing the baseness of his own desires and "way of life" such that he will feel shame about them. The discussions they have together make it clear to Alcibiades that he should lead a more virtuous and philosophical way of life. When he feels ashamed of his inordinate, misguided "desire" for conventional goods (such as "pleasing the crowd") and the depraved way of life they lead to, he gains the motivation to reign them in and control them through virtuous rehabituation. Unfortunately, Alcibiades does not maintain the consistent effort needed to effectively cultivate himself, and so he constantly reverts to his "old ways" and pursues the life of the corrupt politician. Still, Socrates' way of making Alcibiades experience shame gives Alcibiades the opportunity and motivation to change his life for the better. Socrates does as much as he can to motivate Alcibiades to cultivate himself, but Alcibiades tragically fails to successfully cooperate in this project.

Shame is an important and ubiquitous theme in the *Gorgias*, and Socrates' remarks about it have much in common with the *Sophist* and *Nicomachean Ethics* passages discussed above. In their exchange about whether committing injustice is more shameful than suffering it, Socrates and Polus define the term "shameful" in the following way: "Whatever is most shameful is most shameful by providing the greatest pain or harm or both" (477c). Callicles regards suffering injustice as the most shameful thing that humans can experience, especially when we lack the power to defend ourselves (483a, 486a–c, 492a). By contrast, Socrates says that we should be most ashamed of committing injustice (522d), on the grounds that our own vice causes the most serious harm to ourselves (477a–c, 511a). Being unjustly killed or having our possessions confiscated is not shameful in his view, since "no man may escape his destiny" (512e), or, put another way, it does not make sense to feel shame about things that are out of our control.[34] For Socrates, having a properly cultivated sense of shame means

34. Socrates has a similar view in the *Apology*, where he says that the Athenians will not harm him if they kill him unjustly, but they will harm themselves (30c–d). Since it is more harmful to commit a vicious act than to suffer one, we should care more about avoiding vice than avoiding death (39a). In a similar vein, he says that we should

that we feel the most shame about the things that are, in reality, the most detrimental to human virtue and happiness.[35] So, Callicles' problem is not a complete lack of shame. Rather, his flaw is that he feels shame about things that are only apparently bad, yet he feels no shame about that which is *actually* bad, namely his own vice.

Cultivating our sense of shame also leads to greater self-knowledge, a good that is closely tied to moral virtue. Shame helps us to adopt a critical, unbiased perspective on our character, knowledge, habits, desires, and so on. From this perspective, we gain a clearer understanding of our strengths as well as the aspects of ourselves we need to improve. To motivate Callicles to take a clearer view of himself, Socrates says that Callicles' views share similarities with certain images and are consistent with behaviors that very few people would want to be associated with. He compares the immoderate way of life that Callicles advocates to the activity of trying to fill a jar that has many large holes (*Grg.* 493a–c), the life of a "stone-curlew," a bird that proverbially eats and defecates at the same time (494b), and the life of a "catamite" (494e).[36] Socrates claims that if Callicles is right to say that we should seek as much pleasure as often as possible, then it follows that we should adopt such behaviors:

> Is this the case if he should scratch only his head—or what more shall I ask you? See, Callicles, what you will answer if someone

value living virtuously more than living as long as possible in *Gorgias* 512e–513a: "For the true man, at any rate, must reject living any amount of time whatsoever, and must not be a lover of life. Rather, turning over what concerns these things to the god and believing the women's saying that no man may escape his destiny, he must investigate what comes after this: In what way may he who is going to live for a time live best?"

35. At 477d, Socrates refers to immoderation (*akolasia*) and injustice as forms of "baseness of soul" (*psuchēs ponēria*), and, according to his argument, "baseness of soul is most shameful of all" since it is "the greatest harm." Therefore, it is "the greatest evil among the things that are" (477e).

36. Socrates may rely on homophobic and misogynistic attitudes to support his argument when he references "catamites" (*kinaidoi*), but a full treatment of this question lies outside the scope of this book. The term *kinaidos* in classical Athens was commonly used to describe the passive, penetrated partner in a male homerotic relationship, and men or boys who were considered catamites faced various types of discrimination for being perceived as feminine. Andreas Serafim (2016) surveys the scholarly literature about the term *kinaidos.* He emphasizes that it had negative moral connotations and was often used as an insult for a man who was perceived as "unmanly" (3–5). I thank Marina McCoy for making me aware of this point.

> asks you in succession all the things that follow on these. And the culmination of such things as these, the life of catamites, is this not terrible and shameful and wretched? Or will you dare to say that these men are happy, if they have an ungrudging amount of what they want? (494e)

Socrates points out that badness, misery, and shamefulness all go hand in hand. He holds up a mirror to Callicles so that the latter can see the futile misery inherent in the way of life he aspires toward. The unfettered hedonist who argues that we should experience as many intense pleasures as possible appears unable to deny (without contradicting himself) that a life of, say, constantly scratching an itch would be best. If Callicles truly perceives the similarity he has to the leaking jar or the stone-curlew, he might begin to see the life of *pleonexia* as fundamentally flawed and become aware of his own ignorance. By feeling shame at these imperfections in himself and in his own views, he may develop a desire to change for the better. Callicles' new experience of shame about his own imperfections helps to refine his sense of shame in that he will start to see vice or ignorance as truly bad and shameful, and he may feel less shame at the prospect of suffering injustice.

When Socrates helps Callicles cultivate his sense of shame, he enacts a form of "punishment" or discipline that aims to influence Callicles' non-rational desires. As I mentioned in chapter 1, Socrates *demonstrates* the sort of punishment he talks about in the very discussion he has with Polus and Callicles. He explicitly points out that his *logos* is a type of just punishment. When Callicles attempts to exit the conversation, telling Socrates to "ask someone else" about the nature of punishment, Socrates replies: "This man here does not abide being benefited and suffering for himself this thing that the argument is about, being punished" (505c). According to Socrates, an important aim of just punishment is to reform the inordinate, misdirected desires of the person being punished.[37] Our nonrational desires will be attached to an object no matter how virtuous or vicious we are. Shame can motivate us to build more virtuous habits, and such habits influence *what* we desire as well as the intensity of those desires. The noble form of shame that Socrates tries to produce in Callicles contributes to making his desires align with virtuous living and a healthy soul. Socrates puts his conception of discipline

37. I agree with Jessica Moss (2005), who argues that "Socrates uses shame" in the *Gorgias* "as a tool for undermining the attraction" that his interlocutors feel for "ethically harmful pleasures" (138).

as rehabilitation into practice when he gives a fitting "punishment" to Polus and Callicles by refuting and persuading them. If Socrates succeeds in helping Callicles experience noble shame, then Callicles will also genuinely investigate questions about the nature of virtue more often and in a better way (513c–d).

Further, Socrates' and Callicles' disagreement over what is most shameful is bound up with their debate about whether there is a real measure that serves as a universal human good. Socrates wants us to recognize that there is a real universal human good as opposed to merely conventional ones or the relative measure of *pleonexia*. If this is true, then the opposite of the universal human good, namely vice and the wrongdoings it leads us to commit, are similarly bad in reality and not just according to *nomos*. Cultivating our sense of shame therefore involves learning that there is real measure for morality. Just as Socrates argues that there is a universal human good that promotes happiness, so too he argues that vice is universally harmful, and therefore we should be ashamed about committing it. The person who does not feel shame about his own vice completely misidentifies what brings humans happiness and what brings us misery. If we recognize that good and evil are not merely conventional, and we learn to appreciate that others have inherent value, we will feel ashamed when we commit vicious actions, even if there is nobody around to observe us.

Of course, Callicles may never even begin the transition toward a better way of life, but Socrates makes the most effective attempt possible to help him do so. Plato shows us that Socrates goes to the greatest possible lengths to help his interlocutors improve themselves, yet he simultaneously helps us to see that the interlocutor—just like every individual—must independently decide to learn, think philosophically, and transform himself if Socrates' guidance is going to have any benefit. We certainly need others to assist us throughout the educational process, but we must also contribute our own effort and resolve, especially when it comes to moral transformation. After being refuted several times and ceasing to cooperate in the discussion, Callicles says that he does not "care [*melei*] at all" about Socrates' arguments (505c). If this is an honest remark, then it is unlikely that Callicles will be persuaded that his views are misguided, feel ashamed of his vice, or cultivate virtue after his conversation with Socrates. Callicles may be an example of the "incurable" sort of soul mentioned in Socrates' myth of the afterlife (525c).[38] Just as the incurable souls serve as an warning

38. Raphael Woolf (2000) plausibly argues that Callicles is "the hard case" that "reveals the limit of the Socratic method" (1).

to others in the context of the myth, so also Callicles' vice and unwillingness to learn (clearly put on display during his conversation with Socrates) serve as a warning, or an example of what not to do, to the young men who observe their conversation as well as to the readers of the *Gorgias*.

III. Socrates Tactically Equates *Sōphrosunē* with Self-Restraint

Throughout his discussion of the virtues in the *Gorgias*, Socrates devotes substantial attention to *sōphrosunē.* His focus on this virtue is appropriate, since a fundamental tenet of Callicles' ideology is the view that immoderation (*akolasia*), defined as letting one's desires grow as large as possible while constantly satisfying them, is key to the good life. Against Callicles' view, Socrates defends *sōphrosunē*, but the conception of this virtue that he employs in the *Gorgias* is distinctive among the accounts of *sōphrosunē* we find in other dialogues. In the *Gorgias*, his account of *sōphrosunē* emphasizes that restraining desires is necessary for happiness, but not solely because restraining some desires will help us to fulfill other desires. In section III.1, I show that Socrates tactically equates the term *sōphrosunē* with the characteristic of self-restraint, which is the ability to lessen the intensity of one's desires and to fulfill only the ones that truly promote the well-being of oneself and others. The limit and harmony that self-restraint gives to the soul is importantly related to *sōphrosunē*, and we could see it as a civic virtue that acts as a helpful transition toward genuine moderation. In section III.2, I show that Socrates' concept of self-restraint is bound up with his view that there is a real measure for virtue, in that self-restraint gives limit and measure to the soul's desires. Without imposing a limit on our desires, we cannot lead a virtuous and happy life, since we will inevitably fall into the trap of seeking to constantly satisfy limitless desires, which brings nothing but misery and unfulfillment. Again, this account of moderation as self-restraint has the most potential to benefit Callicles—Callicles is already familiar with the notion of limit insofar as he endorses the violation of interpersonal and social limitations, so Socrates aims to show him the value of the limit that self-restraint gives to the soul. Moreover, cultivating self-restraint is an important transition toward a fully virtuous life. Individuals such as Callicles must first recognize the value of self-restraint and cultivate this characteristic before they are ready to understand and pursue the more genuine, fully developed conception of moderation that we find in the *Phaedrus*.

III.1. Sōphrosunē as Self-Restraint in the *Gorgias*

Socrates' discussion of *sōphrosunē* in the *Gorgias* is not as thorough or as multifaceted as those we find in other dialogues such as the *Phaedrus*. However, the *Gorgias* offers a significant development of a common conception of *sōphrosunē* that Plato identifies in other dialogues, namely the practice of restraining some desires solely for the sake of fulfilling others. In the *Phaedo*, Socrates describes the nonphilosopher's view of *sōphrosunē*, which he calls "simple-minded moderation" (*Phd.* 68e), as the practice of "exchanging pleasures for pleasures," since it amounts to restraining some desires for the sake of fulfilling others: "Nevertheless, as it turns out, [those with simple-minded moderation] master some pleasures only because they're mastered by other pleasures. And this is similar to what I was saying just now, that they've been, after a fashion, moderated by self-indulgence" (*Phd.* 69a). Like the immoderate person, the individual with simple-minded moderation prioritizes fulfilling his own desires, but he indulges only certain desires and restrains others under the impression that this is the best way to maximize his own pleasure over an extended period of time. Similarly, the oligarchic soul in *Republic* VIII "forcibly holds down" his desires for luxuries and other expensive pleasures, but only because he values money above all else and wants to accumulate as much of it is possible (553e–554e). Another version of this flawed conception of *sōphrosunē*, which Plato calls "mortal moderation," appears in the *Phaedrus*. I will discuss it in detail in the next chapter (section II.2).

I will use the term "self-restraint" to refer to the notion of *sōphrosunē* uses throughout the *Gorgias*, and it is distinct from the "simple-minded," oligarchic, or "mortal" versions of moderation in the *Phaedo*, the *Republic*, and the *Phaedrus*, as well as (what I call) the genuine moderation of the *Phaedrus*. When Socrates asks Callicles if those who rule others should also rule over themselves, Callicles asks Socrates what he means by "ruling himself." Socrates replies: "Nothing complicated, but just what the many [*hoi polloi*] mean: being moderate and in control of oneself [*sōphrona onta kai egkratē auton heautou*], ruling the pleasures and desires [*epithumiōn*] that are in oneself" (491d–e).[39] Socrates initially aligns his notion of *sōphrosunē*

39. The characteristic of self-restraint that Socrates advocates in the *Gorgias* is similar to Aristotle's notion of *enkrateia,* though the two accounts are not identical. I point out only that both focus on controlling one's desires. For Aristotle's discussion of *enkrateia,* see *Ethics* VII. He claims that the self-restrained person successfully quells his desire for

with common notions of restraining desire and self-rule in order to begin with a conception of *sōphrosunē* that is accessible to Callicles.

Later, though, Socrates refines this initial statement about ruling desires by saying that we should fulfill only the desires that truly improve our souls. Here Socrates introduces the key idea that sets the *Gorgias'* account of self-restraint apart from the accounts of the popular notion of moderation discussed above. The self-restrained person understands the difference between the desires that make her "better," or promote virtue, and those that make her "worse" or more vicious, and she fulfills only the former (*Grg.* 503c–d). In other words, the person with self-restraint manages her desires with a view to self-cultivation by satisfying solely those desires that are conducive to *eudaimonia* and virtuous behavior. At 505a–b, Socrates compares the vicious soul to a sick body. Just as the sick person should not fulfill the desires that worsen his condition, so also the vicious person should "restrain" (*eirgein*) those desires that will further entrench him in vice. Socrates then shows at 506c–507e that the person with this conception of *sōphrosunē* becomes able to act justly, courageously, and piously and live an overall good life, an argument that is meant to bolster this characteristic's value in the eyes of Callicles. The person who practices self-restraint may often experience painful internal strife as he forcibly prevents himself from acting on harmful desires, but the more he does so, the more he resembles the recovering patient who diligently follows the doctor's unpleasant yet beneficial treatments.

Another important feature of Socrates' defense of *sōphrosunē* is to show Callicles that two of its opposites, immoderation (*akolasia*) and *pleonexia*, inevitably lead to misery, as I have already shown. Socrates calls the immoderate life in pursuit of unlimited pleasure "the most wretched," since such a person never attains lasting satisfaction or peaceful inner harmony. No matter how frequently he manages to feed his desires, their insatiability would cause him to suffer the pain of unfulfilled desire for the majority of his life (*Grg.* 493a–494a).[40] The immoderate person will always have large

the nonvirtuous action in favor of the choice he rationally identifies as virtuous, while the akratic person gives in to his desire (*EN* 1146b19–25). Further, Plato highlights self-rule as a key component of *sōphrosunē* in *Republic* IV, where Socrates defines this virtue as the unanimous agreement between the three parts of the city or soul about which one should "rule" (432a). I take it that self-rule in this sense is built into the notion of self-restraint in the *Gorgias*.

40. Aristotle similarly observes that the immoderate or "licentious" life is necessarily full of pain: "Hence [the licentious person] is pained both by failing to obtain his desire and by desiring itself. For desire is accompanied by pain" (*Ethics* III.12, 1119a3–5).

holes in his jar, to use the language of the leaking jar image, and can never attain the peace of having a full jar, even if he succeeds at constantly pouring "water" or lower goods into it (which is, of course, a highly improbable achievement). Socrates' critique of immoderation thus implicitly highlights an important facet of self-restraint, namely, that it helps one to avoid the destructive irrationality and pain of *akolasia* and *pleonexia*.

In effect, Socrates' critique of immoderation suggests that Callicles should abandon his pleonexic way of life and acquire self-restraint as a necessary developmental or transitional step toward genuine moderation. As I argue in chapter 4, although the genuine virtue of moderation includes the ability to set one's desires in order, restraining one's desires alone does not make one moderate. Nonetheless, Socrates tries to persuade Callicles to value self-restraint, because he will have no hope of ever becoming genuinely moderate if he does not first adopt the habit of restraining his inordinate desires. Throughout the dialogue, Callicles shows no inclination toward restraining himself for the reasons discussed in chapter 1, and Socrates subtly draws attention to this when he remarks that Callicles "asserts without restraint [*anedēn*]" the view that pleasure is the good (494e–495a). Using concepts already familiar to Callicles in order to have the deepest possible pedagogical impact, Socrates' rhetoric thus tries to make self-restraint as appealing as possible to Callicles, since self-restraint needs to become Callicles' most immediate concern at this stage of his life.

III.2. *Sōphrosunē* as Limit

In the context of his discussion of *sōphrosunē*, Socrates associates this characteristic with limit. Limit is the best concept for Socrates to use in his discussion with Callicles, because Callicles already has a concept of limit insofar as he endorses the limitlessness of *pleonexia*. Callicles thinks there is no real measure for the good apart from one's own desires, and one should therefore seek to fulfill these desires without limit. To counter Callicles' opinion, Socrates argues that a benefit of self-restraint is that it actually increases the soul's overall experience of satisfaction by imposing limits on its nonrational desires. If we habitually restrain our desires, they eventually adopt limits by growing less intense, which in turn quells the pangs of inordinate desire. The less intense an individual's desires become, the less he experiences the pain of unfulfilled desires, and he remains satisfied for a longer period of time. In other words, if we reign in our desires for lower goods and thereby decrease their intensity, then we require a lower quantity of such goods (or we need them less frequently) to feel satisfied, which means that the soul can remain in a peaceful state of rest for a greater length of time. Relatedly, self-restraint steers us away from the destructive consequences of excess, both for ourselves and others. The person who rules his desires is less likely to feel compelled to use other people as means for his own satisfaction, as Callicles aims to do, and contributes less to his own misery.

For these reasons, the limit and measure that self-restraint instills in the soul brings it closer to the state of completeness and self-sufficiency (discussed above) that one needs for happiness. The person who places a limit on her desires makes them more satiable, and she therefore minimizes her dependency on external goods and her experience of unfulfillment, escaping its inherent pain. Socrates states:

> Now probably these things are somewhat strange, but they make clear what I wish to point out to you—if I am somehow able—so as to persuade you to change your position, and instead of the insatiable and intemperate [*akolastōs*] life to choose the orderly life, sufficient and satisfied [*ikanōs kai exarkountōs*] with the things that are ever at hand. Well, am I persuading you somewhat and do you change to the position that the orderly are happier than the intemperate? (*Grg.* 493c–d)

Bringing one's own soul closer to a state of completeness and sufficiency causes one to need less and therefore suffer less. Thanks to the limit in her soul, the self-restrained person is no longer "insatiable" but instead "sufficient and satisfied with the things that are ever at hand." If a relatively limited amount of external goods is available, the self-restrained person remains satisfied and is much less perturbed by this than the average person, because she requires much less to feel satisfied. Correlatively, when there is an abundance of external goods available, the self-restrained person will not habitually overindulge and become immoderate. In this sense, self-restraint makes one more powerful—if power includes the ability to acquire everything one needs and be without lack, then becoming more complete and sufficient through self-restraint is indispensable for attaining a valuable kind of power. In a related sense, self-restraint brings power to the individual by making him the ruler of his own desires instead of their slave. As a result, the self-restrained person is free to care for and cultivate good relationships with others, since he does not feel compelled to commit injustice against others for the sake of fulfilling his inordinate desire.

Furthermore, self-restraint begins the process of imposing the beautiful harmony that we observe in the cosmos onto the soul. In the context of the *Gorgias*, this means cultivating the soul such that it has the order, beauty, harmony, and symmetry that we find in the world around us:

> The wise say, Callicles, that heaven, earth, gods, and human beings are held together by community, friendship, orderliness, moderation, and justness; and on account of these things, comrade, they call this whole an order, not disorder and intemperance [. . .] it has escaped your notice that geometrical equality [*hē isotēs hē geōmetrikē*] has great power among both gods and human beings, whereas you think one must practice taking more [*pleonexian*]; for you have no care for geometry [*geōmetrias*]. (508a)

Recognizing the beauty and harmony of the cosmos helps us learn that there is goodness or value outside of our own desires. Such a realization can motivate one to care for and imitate the beauty that is external and common insofar as others can recognize it as well. The geometrical symmetry that is physically manifest in the patterns of nature, animal bodies, plants, the movement of the heavenly bodies, and so on shares an important similarity to the inner harmony and beauty that the virtues give to the soul. In both cases, limits give definite order, arrangement, and the ability to function well.[41] Just as the craftsman looks toward a model and then instills the model's order onto the object of his craft (503d–504a), so also the virtuous person gives beneficial organization to his soul by properly cultivating his reason and nonrational desires. The limit that self-restraint gives to the soul counteracts the toxic misery that results from pursuing an unlimited amount of lower goods or *pleonexia*; for Socrates, instilling the best limits in our soul should be our top concern, not the accumulation of an unlimited amount of lower goods. Humans are limited beings, and we must avoid the hubris of seeking an unlimited amount of lower goods through domination. Instead, our desires must be in harmony with our own limits in order for us to be virtuous and happy. Through reason we can identify what goods are most essential for happiness (the higher goods) and the amount of lower goods we need, which may turn out to be very little. Again, self-restraint is only the beginning of the process of making the soul as harmonious as

41. Woolf (2000) rightly argues that for Socrates, internal harmony is a "necessary condition for harmonious relations with others" (7).

possible. The person who has fully developed moderation (and the other virtues) has instantiated the real measure of virtue in his soul so far as is possible for humans.

Finally, cultivating self-restraint and limit in the soul can also begin the process of enhancing one's understanding of the world. Self-restraint prevents vice and improperly directed desires from skewing our apprehension of reality. As I showed in chapter 1, Callicles has misconceptions about the nature of reality in that he thinks there is no real measure for justice or virtue and that one should therefore simply gratify himself as much as possible. Importantly, Plato suggests that one's moral character and values influence the extent to which we can apprehend (or misapprehend) reality.[42] Callicles' vicious pursuit of conventional goods leads him to see the world as a measureless resource for his own satisfaction. So, he tries to manipulate and pillage the world and those who inhabit it without restraint, which further entrenches his misguided understanding of reality. Socrates' virtue, by contrast, allows him to fully appreciate the beautiful order of the cosmos, and he imposes a similar order and beauty in his own soul. Self-restraint does not provide the same insight about the nature of the world as the genuine moderation that Socrates possesses, but it will at least prevent improperly directed desires from obscuring our view of reality, and it can facilitate the development of genuine moderation.

Conclusion

In the *Gorgias*, Plato has Socrates defend the value of virtue, friendship, self-harmony, and philosophical education in a way that aims to benefit the sort of individual who has no interest in pursuing such things. Although Callicles is committed to the pleonexic way of life, Socrates tries to steer him away from it by showing him that the goal he cares about most—his own happiness—depends on caring for the higher goods, as it does for every individual. In doing so, Socrates demonstrates how to practice the sort of rhetoric that truly benefits others and promotes the well-being of one's

42. Hadot (2002) elucidates the ancient view that our manner of living affects our ability to gain insight about the nature of reality, and he rightly observes how important this idea is to the Platonic tradition (64–70). Michel Foucault (2001) also explores this idea, and he agrees that "there cannot be knowledge without a profound modification of the subject's being" (27).

society. Far from being a text that we should see as a product of immaturity in Plato's thinking, the *Gorgias* combines profound reflections on morality, rhetoric, and philosophical pedagogy, as we can see by considering its crucial formal and contextual features. In chapters 3 and 4, I explore the *Phaedrus* from a similar perspective. These latter chapters will complement this reading of the *Gorgias* in several ways thanks to similarities in the content of these dialogues as well as their key contextual differences, the most important of which is the type of soul that Phaedrus typifies.

Chapter 3

Pedagogy, *Erōs* Without Virtue, and Mortal Moderation in *Phaedrus*

I argued in the previous chapter that, in the *Gorgias,* Socrates characterizes the virtue of *sōphrosunē* as the ability to habitually restrain and manage desires in a way that benefits one's own soul. Socrates suggests to Callicles that *sōphrosunē* is the virtue one needs to instill limit in his desires and give order to the whole soul, which prevents the pointless misery that results from inordinate, misguided desires and the constant pursuit of more and more conventional goods. However, the *Phaedrus* calls our attention to the fact that the ability to restrain desire can also be used for bad or vicious ends.[1] As I have suggested, one can certainly develop self-restraint as a civic virtue that makes the soul more well-ordered and satisfied, a goal that Socrates tries to lead Callicles toward in the *Gorgias.* However, one can also restrain desires for the sake of cleverly and selfishly acquiring more pleasure or other goods over a long period of time—we often restrain some desires in the present so that we can indulge others in the future, a practice that

1. Immanuel Kant makes a similar point in his *Groundwork for the Metaphysics of Morals* when discussing his concept of the good will. Conceiving of moderation as self-control, he claims that one can be both self-controlled and villainous: "Moderation in affects and passions, self-control, and sober reflection not only are good for many aims, but seem even to constitute a part of the inner worth of a person; yet they lack much in order to be declared good without limitation (however unconditionally they were praised by the ancients). For without the principles of a good will they can become extremely evil, and the cold-bloodedness of a villain makes him not only far more dangerous but also immediately more abominable in our eyes than he would have been held without it" (Ak 4:394).

Socrates in the *Phaedrus* criticizes, calling it mere "mortal moderation" and "slavish economizing" (256e). Indeed, there is an important point of continuity between the *Gorgias*' account of *sōphrosunē* as self-restraint and mortal moderation in the *Phaedrus* (though they are not identical, as I explain at the end of section II.2 below). That is, the characteristic of self-restraint in the *Gorgias* and mortal moderation in the *Phaedrus* highlight how managing one's desires is better than living as a slave to them. Crucially, though, the *Phaedrus* identifies the limitations and potential abuses of mortal moderation and offers significant insights about the true nature of *sōphrosunē*. Following the language of the *Phaedrus*, I refer to Lysias' notion of *sōphrosunē* as "mortal moderation," and I call Socrates' contrasting notion of this virtue as "genuine *sōphrosunē*" throughout the remainder of this book for the sake of clarity.

A primary reason why the *Phaedrus* contains more suggestions about the rich and multifaceted Platonic conception of *sōphrosunē* than the *Gorgias* is the significantly different pedagogical context in which Socrates speaks. Unlike Callicles, Phaedrus is not completely committed to a particular ideology or way of life; while he is clearly interested in the conventional use of rhetoric and the way of life that accompanies it, he also shows the potential and the openness necessary for leading a philosophical way of life in pursuit of the virtues. The *Phaedrus* is thus an example of how to properly guide those inexperienced in practicing philosophy and cultivating virtue but who nonetheless have the potential or inclination for pursuing these endeavors. At the beginning of the dialogue, Phaedrus is enamored with both the style and the content of Lysias' speech, which one can use to seduce "nonlovers" and thus maximize one's own sexual pleasure (*Phdr.* 230e–234c). In response, Socrates emphasizes that true virtue, and especially the virtue of *sōphrosunē*, does not simply amount to restraining some desires for the sake of fulfilling others (i.e., mortal moderation), nor can it be reduced to obeying a set of predetermined rules, such as the rule Lysias proposes to always have sex with nonlovers instead of lovers. As I will argue in chapter 4, Socrates shows Phaedrus how to move past common notions of *sōphrosunē* and toward genuine *sōphrosunē*, through which we actualize our own potential to acquire self-knowledge, to participate in healthy and happy (or "eudaimonic") relationships, and to gain insight about the true nature of reality.

Given the extent to which Socrates' pedagogical aims influence his account of virtue, I analyze the important pedagogical elements of the *Phaedrus* in section I of this chapter, including the type of soul Phaedrus represents as well as the pedagogical methods and goals Socrates exemplifies throughout the dialogue. Then, section II argues that the first two speeches lay a crucial groundwork for the dialogue's insights about *erōs* and *sōphrosunē*.[2] I show that the first two speeches contribute to the dialogue's overall examination of *erōs* by depicting the ways that those who lack virtue handle the *erōs* they experience. Similarly, I analyze the first two speeches' depiction of mortal moderation, which is a common yet misguided notion of *sōphrosunē*. Both sections of this chapter prepare the way for chapter 4, where I examine Socrates' sophisticated reflection on genuine *sōphrosunē*, the philosophical erotic relationship, and virtuous life more broadly, all of which are best understood as a response to the depiction of *erōs* without virtue and mortal moderation in the first two speeches.

Scholars often interpret the *Phaedrus*' discussions of *erōs*, rhetoric, and virtue from the perspective of Plato's own philosophical development. Some argue that Plato must have written the *Phaedrus* when he was either young and naive or old and senile, using as evidence the apparent foolishness of criticizing writing in a written text. Such interpretations led Jacques Derrida (1981) to remark that the *Phaedrus* "was obliged to wait almost twenty-five centuries before anyone gave up the idea that it was a badly composed dialogue" (66–67). Further, Charles Kahn (1996) claims the *Phaedrus* lacks "argumentative structure" (371).[3] Of course, many twentieth- and twenty-first-century scholars have recognized the brilliance of the *Phaedrus*, but developmental approaches to interpreting the text have remained predominant. Scholars such as Martha Nussbaum (1986) argue that the *Phaedrus*' praise of *erōs* is a sign of Plato's maturity. She contends that Plato grew to

2. By "the first two speeches," I mean Lysias' speech (read aloud by Phaedrus) and Socrates' first speech. Socrates' first speech makes the same argument as Lysias' speech, namely that one should give his sexual favors to a nonlover instead of a lover. Assigning the *Phaedrus*' three speeches to particular speakers might be more difficult than it appears, though, given Socrates' comment that his first speech really "belonged to Phaedrus" (244a) because Socrates was "drugged" and under Phaedrus' "spell" (242e). For the sake of clarity, I will refer to the three speeches (which occur in the dialogue in the following order) as "Lysias' speech," "Socrates' first speech," and "the palinode."

3. As I mentioned in chapter 1, many point to the *Republic* or the *Philebus* as Plato's more mature, philosophically rigorous accounts of virtue or the good life. The *Republic*, for example, bases its account of virtue on an accompanying account of the soul, and it gives a thorough treatment of the relationship between each of the virtues. While the *Phaedrus* has much in common with the *Republic* regarding virtue and the soul, it explores these topics using a significantly different approach, especially in the heavily mythological, image-laden palinode speech.

recognize the importance of *erōs* in human life, which he had previously neglected in dialogues such as the *Republic* and the *Phaedo*.[4] Some scholars appreciate the pedagogical elements of the text, and I pay close attention to the ways in which Socrates' discussion of virtue is pedagogically tailored to Phaedrus (and souls like him) for the sake of helping him advance on the path to virtue.[5] In my view, reading the dialogue from the perspective of its own pedagogical context instead of the biographical perspective of Plato's own development provides valuable insight into its discussions of virtue (especially *sōphrosunē*), love, and rhetoric. Far from being the product of an immature stage of Plato's thinking about virtue or a dialogue that lacks a substantial reflection on virtue, the *Phaedrus* presents a paradigmatic example of philosophical and ethical pedagogy. Socrates, who represents the mature philosopher, uses (what I call) philosophical rhetoric to guide a common type of soul or moral persona, represented by the character Phaedrus, toward a deeper understanding of the nature of moral virtue and the ways in which it is beneficial. In other words, Socrates aims to show Phaedrus how *erōs* and philosophical activity can lead to a "divine upheaval of customary beliefs" (*theias exallagēs tōn eiōthotōn nomimōn*) (265a), including customary beliefs about *sōphrosunē*, which may in turn lead to a better understanding genuine *sōphrosunē* and the decision to pursue it.

When read together, then, I argue that the *Gorgias* and the *Phaedrus* show us that we must begin the process of cultivating *sōphrosunē* by restraining

4. Martha Nussbaum (1986) claims that the first two speeches of the *Phaedrus* contain "important features of [Plato's] own earlier view" of *erōs* that he expressed in earlier dialogues, which he then "criticizes" through the palinode speech (202). Against her view, I argue that the first two speeches accurately assess *erōs,* but only *erōs* as it is handled by those who lack virtue. Socrates' palinode points out that *erōs* need not be handled this way, and it shows us how to handle *erōs* virtuously and philosophically.

5. Harvey Yunis (2011, 6–7) and Jessica Moss (2012, 1–23) highlight the dramatic and pedagogical context of the *Phaedrus*—specifically, Socrates' goal of guiding Phaedrus toward a better way of life—in their interpretation of its content and the unity of its various themes. Marina McCoy (2008) also rightly emphasizes that Socrates' rhetoric aims to direct Phaedrus' love toward the Forms, so that he will continue to try to understand them in the future. My analysis aims to expand on and provide more detail to the approach these scholars use to understand Socrates' pedagogical goals and tactics with Phaedrus. In particular, I demonstrate how Socrates shows Phaedrus the limitations in Lysias' analysis of *erōs* and his conception of *sōphrosunē,* and I also show how Socrates leads Phaedrus toward a better understanding of and appreciation for genuine *sōphrosunē* and the virtuous handling of *erōs.*

or placing a limit on our desires for pleasure, power, fame, wealth, and other conventional goods in order to avoid the destructive irrationality of overly intense desire or greed (*pleonexia*); however, when we turn our attention to fully actualizing our potential for virtue, we should transcend self-restraint in order to achieve genuine *sōphrosunē*. The *Phaedrus* primarily speaks to those at a higher state of pedagogical and ethical development than the *Gorgias* does, since it focuses on transcending conventional ways of limiting ourselves through the transformative power of *erōs*, philosophy, and virtue. The soul inclined toward vice and tyranny, represented by Callicles, primarily needs to see the dangers of *pleonexia* and the value of self-restraint, but the much more open, responsible, and philosophically inclined individual, represented by Phaedrus, needs to see the transformative power of properly directing *erōs* by cultivating virtue and living philosophically. Instead of examining all claims about virtue in the *Gorgias* and the *Phaedrus* in a vacuum, I emphasize the way in which they are aimed at helping Socrates' interlocutors advance on the path to virtue.

As was the case with Callicles in the *Gorgias*, many readers may see something of themselves in Phaedrus, or they may feel the same lure toward the way of life that Lysias represents as Phaedrus does at the beginning of the dialogue. Modern individuals who have something in common with Phaedrus might be those who have genuine curiosity about philosophical questions, take an interest in the fine arts, have interests in the sciences that are not purely instrumental, and so on, but who are also enticed to pursue more conventional goods and occupations. For example, one could picture a talented young philosophy student at a modern university who is tempted to pursue a lucrative career as a lawyer for a self-interested corporation. Similarly, readers who have more in common with Socrates can learn from the exemplary way in which he guides a soul like Phaedrus toward virtue and philosophy. Socrates practices what he says the artful rhetorician should do at 271d–272b by speaking about his subjects (erotic love, virtue, and so on) in a way that best fits the type of soul Phaedrus instantiates, since doing so will have the highest likelihood of persuading him to pursue a more philosophical and virtuous life. As I argued in the previous chapter, those who aim to help others cultivate themselves through philosophical pedagogy have much to learn from the ways in which Socrates' philosophical rhetoric aims to benefit his interlocutors. Socrates focuses on the topics that are most interesting to Phaedrus and engages with him in a way that has the most potential to benefit him given the level of development he currently occupies.

The *Phaedrus*' insightful reflections on virtuous and vicious ways of handling the erotic love we experience are also relevant to contemporary life. Although the dialogue primarily focuses on ancient Athenian pederastic relationships, most (if not all) points about *erōs* also apply to modern intimate relationships between consenting adults regardless of their sexuality, especially the points about how we can respond to the love we feel in ways that are either beneficial or harmful to those we love. Erotic love is an extremely common and impactful component of our interpersonal lives, and how we choose to act on the love we feel has serious, real-world consequences. Erotic love can easily lead to harm when it motivates us to pursue only our own selfish ends at a cost to those we love, but we need not handle our experience of erotic love in this way. Many readers may share the limited view of *erōs* described in Lysias' speech and fail to see it as a powerful experience of the soul that can lead toward a more virtuous, fulfilling life if we channel it virtuously. Similarly, if we conceive of moderation or moral excellence in general simply as the ability to control ourselves and effectively calculate the best ways to maximize pleasure, then we run the risk of treating others as instruments and closing ourselves off to the possibilities that the rich Platonic view of virtue can help us to achieve in our own lives.

I. The Pedagogical Context of the *Phaedrus*

Phaedrus represents the type of person who is interested in and open to the possibilities of philosophy, but who is also tempted to pursue a more customary way of life in pursuit of goods such as wealth, pleasure, and fame. In Phaedrus' case, the latter is represented by Lysias, who exemplifies the life of the conventional rhetorician. In section I.1, I argue that Phaedrus' philosophical potential is signaled by his enthusiasm for *logos* (especially speeches, but also dialogue), his interests in philosophical topics, and his propensity for wonder, but his desire to lead the life of a conventional rhetorician currently prevents him from committing himself to a philosophical life. In this sense, he is "going in two directions," as Socrates says at the end of the palinode (257b). Due to his young age and Lysias' poor influence on him, Phaedrus is not fully aware of the tremendous possibilities of *erōs* and of all the benefits that genuine virtue brings. Section 1.2 aims to show that Socrates' primary aim in the conversation is to make these possibilities clear to Phaedrus and to help him see their value. If Socrates succeeds, Phaedrus will begin to direct his very own *erōs* toward wisdom and the rest of the virtues. Then, section I.3 argues that Socrates attempts to pedagogically benefit Phaedrus by "guiding his soul" through philosophical rhetoric over the course of the entire dialogue. Philosophical rhetoric takes various forms at different points in the conversation, including speeches, dialogue, myth, poetry, and flirtation. While chapter 2 already discussed philosophical rhetoric as Plato depicts it in the *Gorgias*, I return to this topic as it appears in the *Phaedrus*, since the two depictions of philosophical rhetoric are not exactly the same and occur in different contexts. The second half of the *Phaedrus* is an especially insightful meditation on ways rhetoric can be used to help or harm others, and it sheds light on how to use rhetoric philosophically, virtuously, and pedagogically.

I.1. Phaedrus' Soul

Though my primary focus is on Plato's depiction of Phaedrus the literary character, details about the historical Phaedrus and information about him from other Platonic dialogues provide helpful context. Born in roughly 444 BCE, he was from a wealthy Athenian family, received an education, and was a member of the Socratic circle.[6] He likely had the opportunity to pursue a career relating to political life, though it is unclear if he did so. The dramatic date of the *Phaedrus* is likely between 418 and 416 BCE, which means that Phaedrus is in his midtwenties at the time of the conversation, a time when aristocratic young men in ancient Athens began their careers.[7] Of course, Plato includes him as one of the characters present in the *Symposium*, the dramatic date for which is very near that of the *Phaedrus* (February 416). At the start of the *Symposium*, he proposes that Agathon and company should spend the evening giving speeches in praise of *erōs*

6. Nails 2002, 232.

7. The dramatic date of the *Phaedrus* is unclear, and there are two primary dates that scholars propose. Harvey Yunis (2011) claims that the dramatic date must be 403 or later, which would make Phaedrus around forty-one years old at the time of the conversation, due to several "historical indications" in the dialogue's references to Polemarchus, Lysias, and Isocrates (7–10). However, I do not think any of these historical indications necessarily entail a dramatic date of 403, and I agree with Nails (2002), who claims that it must be 418–416 (314). This date is before Phaedrus' exile in 415, an event that none of the characters reference in the text, and it fits with Socrates' comments about Phaedrus being a beautiful young man throughout the dialogue. For comments on the vocative addresses that Socrates frequently uses for Phaedrus, which include "young man" (*neania*) and "darling boy" (*pai*), see Stephen Scully's glossary to the *Phaedrus* (2003, 133–134).

(*Smp.* 177a–e), and Plato suggests that he is the beloved of Eryximachus. He delivers a speech arguing that we pursue virtue for the sake of not appearing ignoble to the person for whom we feel *erōs,* and in this context he mentions the famous army of lovers (*Smp.* 178a–180c). Socrates remarks in the *Gorgias* that Callicles is a friend to Andron (*Grg.* 487c), a member of the oligarchy of the Four Hundred in 411,[8] which means that there is at least a superficial link between Callicles and Phaedrus. Significantly, he was among the accused in the infamous profanation of the Eleusinian mysteries in 415 along with Alcibiades. After the accusation, Phaedrus fled Athens and lived in exile. These events happened shortly after the dramatic date of the *Phaedrus.*[9] Phaedrus died in 393 at the age of roughly fifty-one. Little else is known about the historical Phaedrus.[10] In any case, details about the historical Phaedrus are much less important for my purposes than Plato's careful depiction of Phaedrus as a literary character. In my view, Phaedrus the character represents a universal type of person insofar as he has important characteristics that are shared by many people, especially young adults, in both ancient and contemporary society. I examine each of these important characteristics below.

First, Phaedrus is a lover of spoken and written speeches (*logoi*), but not simply as a means for attaining other ends such as wealth and political power. At the beginning of the dialogue, he is obsessed with Lysias' speech about why one should grant sexual favors to a nonlover instead of a lover (*erastes*). Socrates finds Phaedrus carrying a copy of the speech with him into the country so he can memorize it and practice delivering it himself (227b–228e). Later, Socrates says he is impressed with Phaedrus' love for speeches: "You're truly divine when it comes to speeches, Phaedrus, simply astonishing. Of all the speeches that have been made during your lifetime, I'd say no one has produced more of them than you, whether you were the one speaking, or in one way or another you forced others to speak" (242a–b).[11] Many people, such as Socrates' three interlocutors in the *Gorgias*, are attracted to rhetoric and speechmaking because they are powerful tools for manipulating and dominating others, as I discussed in the previous

8. Nails 2002, 29.

9. Nails 2002, 314.

10. Nails (2002) also mentions that "Diogenes (3.29, 3.31) identifies Phaedrus as 'Plato's favorite' " (234).

11. As I mentioned above, Phaedrus lives up to this reputation for inspiring speeches in the *Symposium.*

chapters. Phaedrus' love for speeches, by contrast, appears less self-serving; unlike someone such as Callicles, Phaedrus does not see spoken and written *logos* solely as means for gratifying his own desires for pleasure, wealth, or political power. Instead, Phaedrus loves speeches *as* speeches. That is, he is keenly interested in their form and style, to the point that he does not care about their content as much as he should. This attitude toward speeches is dangerous, because he could fall asleep due to the beautiful "singing" of the "cicadas," as Socrates says at 258e–259a. That is, he could become so fixated on the outward, stylistic beauty of a speech that he would be easily persuaded by its arguments, and so would fail to examine the content of the speeches critically for the sake of finding the truth.

When Socrates suggests that they examine what counts as good speech writing (or writing "with measure," 258d), Phaedrus replies: "Are you asking if we ought to do this? What would anyone possibly live for—so to speak—if not for such pleasures? It is not, I suppose, for those pleasures which necessarily cause pain before pleasure or else no pleasure at all, and so are rightly called slavish" (258e). He already understands the difference between "pure pleasures" and "mixed pleasures," as Socrates calls them in the *Philebus* (46a–53c)—pure pleasures do not cause pain beforehand, while mixed pleasures do—and he clearly values the former over the latter. He spends his leisure time seeking the "pure" pleasures of hearing and delivering speeches, since he loves the beauty of written and spoken words. Importantly, although Phaedrus' relationship to rhetoric is not the same as the philosopher's (as I will discuss further below), it indicates that he is much more open to seeing *logos* as the philosopher does and caring for "wisdom-loving speeches" (257b).

Indeed, Phaedrus' love of *logos* is closely tied to the second characteristic of his soul that is important for my purposes, namely his potential to become the sort of person who loves wisdom and the rest of the virtues above all else; for Socrates, this sort of person most deserves the name "philosopher."[12] Socrates suggests several times in his palinode speech that Phaedrus is a philosophic soul, or in other words, the sort of person who has incipient philosophical qualities and propensities. He states that "few

12. In Pierre Hadot's chapter "The Definition of Philosopher in Plato's *Symposium*" in *What Is Ancient Philosophy?* (2002), he compellingly argues that the *Symposium* sheds especially clear light on Plato's conception of philosophy. Socrates, as the ideal philosopher, shares crucial similarities with Diotima's depiction of the *daimōn* Eros: "Socrates, or the philosopher, is thus Eros: although deprived of wisdom, beauty, and the good, he desires and loves wisdom, beauty, and the good" (45).

souls" can recognize (or "recall") "images" of divine beauty in the material world, such as the beauty of bodies and the beauty of words, but Phaedrus is one such soul. When someone like Phaedrus looks at "earthly beauty and is reminded of true beauty" (249d), this experience may in turn lead to a love of wisdom and the rest of the virtues (249c–251d). In Socrates' myth about souls as they were before they descended into bodies, he says that both Phaedrus' soul and his own traveled in "Zeus' entourage," which places them in the class of souls that have philosophical natures in earthly lives (250b–c). Those who were in Zeus' entourage frequently experience *erōs* for "beautiful people and beautiful things" (249e), as all people do, but philosophic souls are most likely to direct this *erōs* virtuously and "with a good deal of dignity" (252c), as I will discuss further in chapter 4.

Besides Socrates' claims about Phaedrus, there are several more indications that he has the potential to lead a philosophical life. In addition to loving rhetorical speeches, he is also eager to inquire with Socrates through philosophical dialogue and to assess arguments with him, even if rhetorical style is still his primary interest at this point. When Socrates suggests that they discuss arguments about whether rhetoric is an art (260e), Phaedrus replies: "We must hear these arguments, Socrates. Lead them out so we can review what they say and how they say it" (261a). Phaedrus enthusiastically cooperates with Socrates in the second half of the dialogue by answering his questions honestly and commenting about what he has heard from others regarding their topics of discussion. Another indication of Phaedrus' philosophical potential is that he experiences "wonder" at Socrates' philosophical insight; Phaedrus remarks that he is "astonished" (*thaumasas*) by Socrates' palinode speech (257c), and calls Socrates an "astonishing man" (*thaumasie*). As Socrates says in the *Theaetetus*, "wondering" (*to thaumazein*) is "an experience which is characteristic of a philosopher," and that wondering "is where philosophy begins and nowhere else" (*Tht.* 155d). Aristotle echoes this point in *Metaphysics* I.2 when he says that "it is owing to their wonder [*thaumazōn*] that men both now begin and at first began to philosophize" (982b13). Phaedrus' wonder at Socrates' palinode therefore indicates that he already has some degree of curiosity about the wisdom that the true philosopher regards as his top priority, and as I will show in section I.2, Socrates aims to lead Phaedrus to a fully-fledged love of wisdom.

Further, Phaedrus has a number of interests related to philosophy that can lead to a deeper love of wisdom, including myth and poetry, as well as the topics of love, sex, and friendship. Socrates, a mature philosopher, shares these interests, though from a more developed, educated point of view. Phaedrus sees and appreciates the beauty in many different things, such as bodies, stories, natural beauty (229b), speeches, and poetry. Socrates associates philosophy with being a lover of beauty in the palinode when giving the myth of the soul's descent into the body: "The soul which has witnessed Being the most in heaven shall be planted into the seed of someone who will become a lover of wisdom, or a lover of beauty, or of something musical and erotic" (248d). While Socrates may be associating lovers of beauty and philosophers to help him convince Phaedrus to care for philosophy, it is clear that philosophers and "lovers of beauty" in this sense have much in common. Regarding those who love myths, Aristotle in *Metaphysics* I remarks: "Now he who wonders and is perplexed feels that he is ignorant (thus the myth-lover is in a sense a philosopher, since myths are composed of wonders)" (982b19). When discussing what we can tell about Phaedrus based on his interests, John Sallis (1975) constructs a helpful picture of *Phaedrus*' interests: "Phaedrus is one who associates with physicians and sophists, who has some interest in investigations of nature, and who draws heavily upon mythical things." (106). Phaedrus' question about whether the "mythical story" (*muthologēma*) Boreas and Oreithuia is "true" (*alēthēs*), implying that there might be a more naturalistic explanation for the incident (229c–d), indicates that he is interested in truth and understanding the real causes of things, even if he has not so far spent much time or effort rigorously devoting himself to truth. As I will discuss further in sections I.2 and I.3, Socrates covers all of these topics that Phaedrus already cares about to capture his attention and reveal to him the value of the virtuous and philosophical life.[13]

A third important quality of Phaedrus' soul that Plato calls our attention to is the significant attraction he feels toward the way of life led by many rhetoricians in Athens at this time. Although Phaedrus has incipient philosophical qualities, he also idolizes Lysias and the sort of person Lysias represents, that is, the person who uses rhetoric for the sake of gaining conventional goods such as wealth, pleasure, and renown. Phaedrus is obviously enamored with Lysias and his rhetorical ability at the beginning of the dialogue (227c–228a, 234c). Socrates refers to Lysias as Phaedrus' "darling" at 236b, and remarks that Phaedrus is getting excited, defensive, and competitive when Socrates criticizes Lysias' speech and says

13. Socrates says that the palinode is "poetical" because of Phaedrus. Addressing a prayer to the god Eros at the end of his palinode, he says: "If my phrasing and other things have been rather poetical, understand that Phaedrus has forced them upon me" (*Phdr.* 257a).

he can deliver a better version of the same speech. If Phaedrus decides to become more similar to Lysias, then it is likely that he will adopt some of the qualities that Socrates often associates with the sophists. Although a rhetorician such as Lysias may not be a sophist per se, his speech shows influence from common ideas in the sophistic movement.[14] Specifically, the distinction between nature and convention is implicitly at play in Lysias' speech when it rejects the *nomoi* surrounding erotic relationships by arguing that one should give his sexual favors to lovers rather than nonlovers (230e–234c). His speech also aims to subvert socially accepted views about erotic relationships in favor of his own self-serving ends, arguing that a beautiful young man should give sexual favors to him, a nonlover, rather than an intimate partner by way of the traditional Athenian homoerotic relationship. When discussing the nature of rhetoric, Phaedrus voices the following view that is common among rhetoricians and sophists, and he may be in danger of adopting it himself: "I've heard people say that a student studying to become an orator need not learn what justice really is but merely what it seems to be to the masses who are in a position to pass judgment. Nor does he have to learn what is truly good and beautiful, but only what seems so; persuading comes from this, not from the truth" (260a). Socrates associates this way of using rhetoric with Lysias and Thrasymachus at 266c, and Phaedrus calls this crowd of famous rhetoricians "kingly." This way of practicing rhetoric is concerned only with learning about popular opinions as well as rhetorical techniques and styles that are most effective for persuading the majority of people (which Socrates calls the "prerequisites" of rhetoric, 268e), but it has little regard for understanding the "truth" about beauty, goodness, and justice.

Another reason the figure of Lysias is attractive to Phaedrus is the wealth and reputation he attains by practicing rhetoric. Phaedrus mentions at the beginning of the dialogue that Lysias is staying at the house of a rich man, Morukhas (227b),[15] and according to Nails, Lysias and his brother Polemarchus "were, by 404, among the wealthiest people Attica" thanks to the family shield-making business run by their father, Cephalus, the host

14. Due to this influence from the sophists on rhetoricians such as Lysias and Gorgias, many consider rhetoricians such as Lysias as very similar to the sophists. In a recent article, Jenny Bryan (2021) offers convincing support of this point. See also Barney (2006, 77, 77n1).

15. In Stephen Scully's translation of the *Phaedrus*, he notes that Aristophanes "singles out Morukhas for his lavish living" (2n5).

of Socrates and company in the *Republic* (191a–e). After Phaedrus recites Lysias' speech, Socrates identifies Lysias' real motivation for composing it:

> There once was a darling boy, a young man really, a very beautiful young man, and he had a great number of lovers. One of them was wily and persuaded the young man that he was not in love with him at all when in fact he loved him no less than the others. When he was making his case, he tried to persuade the young lad that he ought to grant his favors to someone who didn't love him rather than to one who did. (237b)

The "young man" Socrates refers to is Phaedrus, of course, and while Lysias is actually in love with Phaedrus, he "persuaded" Phaedrus that he is not in love with him and that Phaedrus should have sex with a nonlover such as himself. Assuming Socrates is correct in his assessment of Lysias' real motivation, Lysias' tactic reveals one of his key characteristics—he is one who always aims to maximize his own profit, though in this case, the profit is sexual pleasure. He cleverly uses his intellectual and rhetorical gifts to deceive and manipulate Phaedrus into having a sexual relationship with him. Like the oligarchic soul in the *Republic*, he restrains some of his desires for the sake of fulfilling others (553e–554e). In this way, he is a good example of someone who practices mortal moderation, a characteristic I will examine closely in section II.2 below. Should Phaedrus decide to identify with people such as Lysias, he would adopt their goal of using intellectual and moral talent in a highly calculated way for the sake of accumulating as many conventional goods as possible.

Thus, these three important characteristics of Phaedrus' soul that Plato brings to our attention reveal that he is at an important crossroad in his life—he can either take up the common, conventional way of practicing rhetoric and adopt the lifestyle associated with it, or he could choose to actualize his potential to live a more philosophical life in pursuit of wisdom and the rest of the virtues. He stands at a crucial juncture in his life, and he has not yet committed himself to either path, as Socrates makes explicit at the end of his palinode speech:

> If in the former speech Phaedrus and I said anything that shocked you, find fault with Lysias, father of the speech, and stop him from making such speeches; rather turn him toward [*trepson*] a love of wisdom [*philosophian*] just as his brother

> Polemarchus has already been turned. Do this so that this lover [*ho erastēs*] here, Phaedrus, may also stop going in two directions as now [*mēketi epamphoterizē kathaper nun*], but devote his life solely to Love and wisdom-loving speeches [*philosophōn logōn*]. (257b)

One of the two "directions" that Phaedrus could pursue is the way of life Lysias represents, and the other is the philosophical, virtuous life exemplified by Socrates.[16] Unlike someone such as Callicles, Phaedrus does not reject the value of the "higher goods," as I called them in the previous chapters—the virtues, philosophical education, healthy relationships, and so on—but has not yet fully embraced them either. Socrates, of course, aims to "turn" Phaedrus toward the second "direction" by showing Phaedrus that the higher goods are superior and more conducive to happiness than the conventional goods that Lysias prioritizes, and I will examine how he attempts to do so in the next two sections.

I.2. Socrates' Pedagogical Aims

In the first line of the *Phaedrus*, Socrates asks Phaedrus where he has been and where he is going (227a). This question has several layers of meaning. Obviously, there is the literal meaning—it expresses Socrates' curiosity about where Phaedrus has spent his day so far and where he is headed as he now leaves the city. The question also prefigures Socrates' myths about where the soul comes from before we are born and where it will go when we die (e.g., 246b–249d, 256a–e). In my view, the content of the dialogue adds a further layer of meaning to this question: what sort of pedagogical and ethical influence has Phaedrus undergone so far in his life, and what way of life is he going to pursue (i.e., "Where is he going")? In other words, the rest of the dialogue will prompt us to ask what sort of person Phaedrus is at this point in his life and what sort of person he is going to become.

16. Because of Phaedrus' intellectual interests and his young age, he resembles the young men Socrates discusses in *Republic* VII (537d–539d) that I discussed in chapter 1, section III.3, in connection with Callicles. There Socrates explains how young men who could potentially become virtuous philosophers can become horribly corrupt if they receive poor intellectual influence—when such youths see the flaws in the "convictions about what is just and fair" that their parents taught them (538c) and fail to discover what is truly just and fair (538e), they will simply decide to spend their time pursuing any goods that happen to "flatter" them (539a).

His ensuing conversation with Socrates will prompt him to consider this question deeply, since Socrates' speeches and questions about love, virtue, and the practice of rhetoric will bring to Phaedrus' attention the serious decisions he must make about these spheres of his life.

Several key passages give us insight into the type of pedagogical influence Socrates aims to have on Phaedrus. One striking example is when Socrates discusses the myth of the cicadas. He tells Phaedrus that they should spend their leisure time under the plane tree in philosophical conversation, pursuing the truth about rhetoric, writing, and related questions, which will prevent the cicadas from lulling them to sleep. They must avoid becoming "bewitched" by the cicadas, just as Odysseus avoided the spell of the sirens (258e–259b). If they succeed, then in the future the souls of the dead cicadas will give a good report about Socrates and Phaedrus to the Muses: "But [the cicadas] report to Kalliope with the beautiful voice, the oldest of the Muses, and to heavenly Qurania, the second oldest, those who have gone through life loving wisdom and honoring their musical art; for of all the Muses these two send out the most beautiful voices and are especially fond of heaven and of speeches, both divine and human. For many reasons, then, we must say something and not fall asleep at the noon-hour" (259d). Although Phaedrus likely does not take this myth literally, Socrates makes his point clear that philosophy is a noble and valuable pursuit, and Phaedrus happily agrees to continue engaging in dialogue. Later, just before they investigate the question of whether rhetoric is an art, Socrates gives another clear indication that his goal is to persuade Phaedrus to pursue a more philosophical life: "Approach, my noble creatures [i.e., arguments about whether rhetoric is an art]; persuade Phaedrus, this beautiful boy, that unless he loves wisdom sufficiently [*hikanōs philosophēsē*], he will never become a competent speaker about anything" (261a). Here Socrates nearly makes explicit one of the tactics he uses throughout the entire dialogue; knowing that Phaedrus already has vested interest in becoming an excellent rhetorician, Socrates aims to "persuade" him that he cannot achieve this goal without philosophy. If Phaedrus becomes persuaded of this view, then he may decide to commit himself to philosophy in the future.

Another key passage is a less explicit, yet very revealing, indication of Socrates' pedagogical intentions. In the palinode, Socrates describes how a virtuous lover should foster his beloved's philosophical education, and this description accurately captures the way he pedagogically benefits Phaedrus throughout the dialogue, even if Socrates and Phaedrus are not a couple. Socrates says that lovers seek a beloved who has a soul that is similar to their own, and they share these similarities with the god whose "entourage" they were members of before their souls became embodied:

> Followers of Apollo and each of the other gods proceed in the manner of their god and search for a boyfriend whose nature resembles their god; when they acquire him they themselves imitate the god and persuade and discipline the darling, leading him into the service and ways of the god, according to each one's ability. They do so without envy or stingy ill-will toward the darling but in the hope that, trying as hard as they can, they may lead the loved one wholly and entirely to resemble both themselves and the god whom they honor. The eagerness of those truly in love and the initiation rite, if lovers obtain what they are eager for in the way I have outlined, become both beautiful and blessed. It is a blessedness which derives from the love-crazed friend but also benefits the boy who is befriended, provided, that is, the boy is captured. (253b–c)

Socrates' treatment of Phaedrus mirrors this description of the lover and beloved insofar as he "leads" and "persuades" Phaedrus to prioritize wisdom, virtue, and the philosophical use of rhetoric. By doing so, he is trying to make Phaedrus more similar to himself, since Socrates already cares more for wisdom and virtue than anything else. Unlike the disguised lover of Lysias' speech, Socrates does not try to manipulate Phaedrus for the sake of satisfying his own desires, but instead "benefits the boy" and leads him "into the service and ways of the god," which makes them "resemble" the "god whom they honor."[17] In the next chapter, I will discuss in detail what such benefit entails and what it means to resemble the divine. For the present context, though, the important point is that Socrates, just like the philosophic lover he describes in his palinode, attempts to persuade Phaedrus to cultivate his own soul through the pursuit of wisdom and virtue.

In a word, Socrates aims to "guide the soul" (*psuchagōgia*) of Phaedrus toward a more virtuous and philosophical life.[18] In doing so, he gives special

17. At *Symposium* 209b–d, Socrates gives another description of what a lover does when he finds a beautiful young man full of philosophical potential.

18. Scully's translation of the *Phaedrus* (2003) notes that Socrates' use of the term *psychagōgia* must have been "shocking" for Plato's ancient readers, because this term had "a negative connotation at this time, suggesting for the dead a conjuring up of souls from

attention to how one must virtuously direct his *erōs,* on the one hand, and virtuously use his rhetorical abilities, on the other. Jessica Moss argues that *psuchagōgia* is *the* primary topic of the *Phaedrus*, and that it helps to explain the unity of the dialogue, a question to which I will return below.[19] While readers are often puzzled about why close examinations of love and rhetoric appear in the same dialogue, the two are importantly similar in that they are both guides of the soul. A closely related term that appears ubiquitously in the dialogue is *proagō*, translated as "guide" or "lead" (see 227c, 230a, and 261a as just a few examples). Plato's frequent use of this term and his focus on *psuchagōgia* signal that it is a key thread that ties together much of the dialogue's content and drama. As I will discuss further below, *erōs* is a guide of the soul in that we experience erotic attraction toward the goods that appear best to us, but we also have the ability to change what we regard as best through philosophical education and rehabituation. Similarly, Socrates says explicitly at 271d that "the capacity of speech" (*logou dunamis*) is to "guide the soul [*psuchagōgia*]." Spoken and written *logoi* guide the soul in that they influence how people think and act both publicly and privately, whether it be in political settings such as the Assembly, educational settings, or everyday social interactions.

If rhetoric is that which makes *logos* persuasive (260d), and hence, an especially powerful guide of the soul, then the art of rhetoric is of vital importance to a discussion of spoken and written *logos*. Socrates goes to great lengths to show Phaedrus that neither love nor rhetoric are always good or bad—rather, it is our response to the love we feel, or the way we direct it, that makes it good or bad, and likewise, rhetoric can be used for noble or base ends. He is clear that rhetoric, writing, and speaking are tools that can be used for good or bad purposes when he says writing speeches "is not in itself shameful." Rather, "speaking and writing" are shameful only when they are done "shamefully or badly" (258d). Moreover, to make these points clear to Phaedrus, Socrates uses philosophical rhetoric, a practice I will discuss in detail in the next section (I.3). Hence, Plato depicts Socrates guiding Phaedrus' soul, and the discussion through which he does so focuses on two powerful guides of the soul, *erōs* and rhetoric. At another level, the discussion and dramatization of soul-guiding can also guide the souls of Plato's readers toward a deeper understanding of the topics discussed and

---

the underworld (as in Aristophanes' *Birds* 1555) and for the living persuasion through witchcraft and enchantment" (45n106).

19. Moss 2012, 3.

a greater love of wisdom.[20] If Phaedrus is receptive to these insights about love and rhetoric, he will be in a better, more educated position to decide whether he will respond to the love he feels in a virtuous way and whether he will use his rhetorical capabilities for noble ends.

Although my primary aim is not to fully answer the frequently discussed question of the unity of the *Phaedrus*, my interpretation of the type of soul Phaedrus typifies, Socrates' pedagogical aims, and the method Socrates uses to pedagogically benefit Phaedrus (philosophical rhetoric) supports points that others have already made in explaining that unity. Specifically, I agree with Harvey Yunis and Jessica Moss[21] in holding that the pedagogical context of the dialogue helps to explain why such a wide variety of topics fit together such that it makes sense for them to appear in a single dialogue. Scholars have been particularly interested in how the first half of the dialogue's focus on *erōs*, sex, virtue, interpersonal relationships, the soul, happiness, the nature of reality, and so on relate to the second half of the text's discussion about rhetoric, dialectic, and writing.[22] As I discussed above, Phaedrus has a wide range of interests—some relating to the first half of the dialogue, some to the second—and Socrates artfully weaves all of these topics together in a way that has the most potential to persuade Phaedrus to pursue philosophy, to cultivate virtue, and to use rhetoric in the service of these two ends. In short, Phaedrus has interests that could lead him to pursue either a philosophical life or the life of the conventional rhetorician (he is "going in two directions"), so Socrates covers the topics most relevant to Phaedrus with a view to pulling Phaedrus away from the path laid out before him by rhetoricians such as Lysias, who use rhetoric in the traditional, self-serving

20. Jill Gordon (1999) rightly argues that the effect Socrates aims to achieve with his interlocutor mirrors the effect that a Platonic dialogue can have on its reader: "What transpires when Socrates engages an interlocutor? What do we experience when we read one of Plato's dialogues? The answers to these questions are parallel: by understanding the desired effect of Socrates' dialectic on his interlocutors, we can also understand that of Plato's dialogues on his readers" (43).

21. Yunis (2011, 6–7) and Moss (2012, 3) highlight the dramatic and pedagogical context of the dialogue—specifically, Socrates' goal of guiding Phaedrus toward a better way of life—in their interpretation of its content and the unity of its various themes. Marina McCoy (2008) also correctly emphasizes that Socrates' rhetoric aims to direct Phaedrus' love toward the Forms, so that he will continue to try to understand them in the future (167).

22. Publications on the unity of the *Phaedrus* that deal with this question thoroughly include Moss (20121–23), Yunis (2011), Daniel Werner (2007), Franco Trivigno (2009), Tushar Irani (2017), and Charles Griswold Jr. (1986).

manner. Of course, this is not an exhaustive explanation of the dialogue's unity; rather, my interpretation of the dialogue's pedagogical context simply emphasizes that Socrates unites the various themes of the dialogue through his performance of philosophical rhetoric and his goal of helping Phaedrus take a crucial step in his ethical development.

Naturally, we must wonder whether Socrates achieves his pedagogical goals by successfully guiding Phaedrus toward a better way of life. At the end of the dialogue, Phaedrus appears to be persuaded by Socrates that philosophy and the cultivation of virtue are worthy pursuits (279c). However, we also know that he was accused of profaning the Eleusinian mysteries in 415, and the dramatic date of the *Phaedrus* is probably only a few years before this accusation, a fact that may suggest that Phaedrus never became a virtuous person. In my view, however, the dialogue ultimately leaves it unclear whether Socrates succeeds or fails in his goal of turning Phaedrus toward philosophy and virtue, since it does not give enough indication about Phaedrus' future to give a definitive answer. When considering Phaedrus from the point of view I have adopted—that is, as a symbol for a universal type of soul or moral persona with whom many of Plato's readers share some similarity—the fate of Phaedrus as an individual is not terribly important. Plato's most important concern in writing the *Phaedrus* is not to tell us whether Socrates succeeded or failed to benefit the historical Phaedrus. Rather, one of the dialogue's primary functions is to help readers who are like Phaedrus better understand the topics discussed and motivate them to pursue wisdom and virtue. In a similar way, the dialogue also functions to help those who are more advanced in their philosophical development learn to guide others toward wisdom and the rest of the virtues. The carefully crafted discussion between Socrates and Phaedrus that Plato depicts in the *Phaedrus* is a powerful means for achieving both of these ends.

I.3. Philosophical Rhetoric in the *Phaedrus*

The *Phaedrus* presents a pedagogically valuable type of rhetoric[23] through a combination of its analysis of the "art" (*technē*) of rhetoric (*Phdr*. 257b–274b) and Socrates' exemplary *performance* of this rhetoric throughout the entire

23. I began working on this topic in a paper titled "Philosophical Rhetoric as *Paideia* in Plato's *Phaedrus*," which was published by Parnassos Press in a volume titled *Paideia and Performance*, edited by Heather Reid, Henry Curcio, and Mark Ralkowski (2023). Here I substantially adapt and expand on some sections of that paper to fit the context of the present analysis.

dialogue.[24] Precisely determining the difference between education and persuasion in Plato is a complicated issue. In passages such as *Republic* 518b–d, *Timaeus* 51d–e, and *Phaedrus* 277b, Plato clearly distinguishes education (*paideia* and related terms) from persuasion (*peithō*). Although I do not comprehensively explore the similarities and differences between education and persuasion in this book, I claim that philosophical rhetoric has the potential to foster the education of the person who hears it. The goal of Socrates' philosophical rhetoric[25] is to guide the soul (*psuchagōgia*) of Phaedrus toward a virtuous, philosophical way of life, and it uses a combination of speeches, myth, philosophical dialogue, and flirtation to guide Phaedrus toward this end.[26] While other scholars have provided illuminating discussions of *psuchagōgia* and the pedagogical context of the *Phaedrus*, I show in this section that, over the course of the entire text, Socrates performs philosophical rhetoric with the aim of guiding Phaedrus toward the project of moral self-cultivation. The kind of persuasion that Socrates tries to produce is therefore a crucial step in Phaedrus' ethical and pedagogical development.

The *Phaedrus* and the *Gorgias* contain the two most substantial, nuanced assessments of rhetoric in Plato's corpus. Importantly, Socrates refers to rhetoric as a *technē* in the *Phaedrus*, even though he argues that it is not a *technē* in the *Gorgias* (462b–466a).[27] Shortly after the palinode, Socrates

24. Daniel Werner (2007) points out that it is possible to view rhetoric as "enacted" only in the first half of the *Phaedrus* through the three speeches and "expounded" in the second half through the characters' dialogue (99). In a similar vein, Christopher Rowe (1986) argues that the palinode speech alone is Socrates' demonstration of the true art of rhetoric (106–125). Against this view, I argue that Socrates performs philosophical rhetoric throughout the entirety of the *Phaedrus*.

25. McCoy (2008) describes Socrates' rhetoric as "Socratic rhetoric" or simply "good rhetoric," though she also uses the term "philosophical rhetoric" at times (167–196). All three labels are certainly appropriate, but I think the term "philosophical" best captures the point I aim to make in the context of this book's analysis.

26. As Pierre Hadot (2002) shows, philosophy for Plato (and for other ancient philosophers) is "a certain way of life and existential option which demands from the individual a total change lifestyle, a conversion of one's entire being, and ultimately a certain desire to be and live in a certain way" (3). Plato's Socrates exemplifies the philosophical life through his love of wisdom, his moral virtue, and his lifelong search for the truth about the nature of reality.

27. The question of whether rhetoric really is a *technē* according to the *Phaedrus* is complicated by the fact that Socrates takes this up as an open question with Phaedrus starting at 260e, and Socrates ends this discussion with an ambiguous remark: "Let

gives a concise definition of rhetoric: "Isn't the art [*technē*] of rhetoric, taken as a whole, a certain guiding of souls through words [*psuchagōgia tis dia logōn*] not only in the law courts and other places of public assembly, but also in private?" (*Phdr.* 261a–b). If rhetoric is a *technē*, one can develop some degree of precision in classifying different rhetorical techniques (265d), the kinds of effects they produce on certain kinds of people, and so on, as Socrates and Phaedrus do later in the dialogue (266c–271c), which I will discuss further below. The concept of "guiding" or leading contained in this definition is also important, because it suggests that rhetoric can *influence*, but not *force*, others to act or think a certain way. Phaedrus at first doubts that rhetoric can be practiced privately, saying that it is typically used only in law courts and the public assembly "in speech form," and that he has "not heard the term used more widely" (261b). Like most people, Phaedrus conceives of rhetoric as a public performance that is given in front of many people. However, Socrates demonstrates how to perform rhetoric privately in his very conversation with Phaedrus, even if Phaedrus does not realize it. Rhetoric is, most essentially, the guidance of another person's soul, so all the types of *logos* Socrates uses to guide Phaedrus toward philosophy and virtue, including speeches, myth, and philosophical dialogue, are important components of philosophical rhetoric. By using these different types of *logos* in a private setting to guide Phaedrus toward genuine self-cultivation, Socrates displays a rhetorical *technē* (for Phaedrus as well as the reader) that is new to the intellectual sphere of ancient Greece.

Indeed, Socrates' philosophical rhetoric in the *Phaedrus* uses several different genres of spoken *logos*, because, given Phaedrus' interests, this approach will make the conversation as engaging as possible to him. While Socrates spends a substantial amount of time having his characteristic dialogue that

---

this then be enough about the art and artlessness of speeches" (*Phdr.* 273b). I interpret the discussion in this section of the dialogue to show that rhetoric is an art when it is practiced dialectically and philosophically, as I describe in this section, but that even then, rhetoric does not have the same level of precision as some other arts. Other people who claim to practice the art of rhetoric do not have the art at all, as Socrates says at 269d: "But to the extent that there is art in this whole business, you're not likely to find the method or right approach, I'd say, where Lysias or Thrasymachos go." These conventional rhetoricians know only the "prerequisites" of the art of rhetoric, not the art itself (268a–269d). Socrates' summary of their discussion of rhetoric at 277b–c supports this interpretation, where he lists all of the requirements one must meet to "manage the class of speeches artfully, to the degree that it is within its nature to be artful, either with respect to teaching or persuading something, as the entire earlier discussion revealed to us" (277c).

is based around questioning and answering with Phaedrus, he uses rhetorical speeches, myths, and quotations of poetry because Phaedrus is so enamored with the spoken and written word, and especially with rhetorical speeches. If Phaedrus takes interest in the style or packaging of Socrates' *logoi*, this may in turn lead him to have more of a vested interest in their philosophical content. Of course, Socrates sometimes provides arguments to support his points, but he recognizes that rational argumentation is not the only way to influence another person's thinking and values. Although Phaedrus shows signs of philosophical potential, he has little experience with philosophical discussion, so Socrates engages in argument with him as far as possible given his abilities, but his use of argument is more limited than it would be with an interlocutor who has more training in philosophical argumentation. He tells many myths in their conversations, not only because Phaedrus is already interested in mythology (229c–230a) but also because it is easier for someone like Phaedrus to digest Socrates' philosophical points if they are expressed through images and stories. For these reasons, Socrates in the *Phaedrus* does not provide a comprehensive, strictly rational demonstration of the topics the characters discuss. Rather, Socrates shapes his accounts of virtue, love, the soul, and so on through his philosophical rhetoric with the aim of helping Phaedrus make progress on the path to the virtuous life.

To distinguish philosophical rhetoric as a new kind of *technē* even more clearly, Socrates identifies the ways that conventional rhetoricians abuse *logos* to fulfill their own desires and thus fall short of practicing a *technē*. Phaedrus says he has "heard people say" that to practice rhetoric, one "need not learn what justice really is but merely what it seems to be to the masses who are in a position to pass judgment," and, likewise, one does not have to "learn what is truly good and beautiful, but only what seems so; persuading comes from this, not from the truth" (260a). This passage describes the sort of persuasion that Socrates is *not* performing, and he later argues that those who persuade without knowledge of justice, goodness, and so on do not really practice the art of rhetoric at all, but only the art's "prerequisites," as I will discuss below. Socrates then gives his own description of how people commonly abuse rhetoric in political matters: "So, when a rhetorician who is mindless of good and evil encounters a city in the same condition and attempts to persuade it, not by praising a mere shadow of an ass as if it were a horse, but by praising evil as good, and by carefully studying public opinion, he persuades the city to do evil things rather than good ones" (260c). The average rhetorician lacks knowledge of the difference between what is really best for a city and what merely appears best for it, and persuading the *polis* to pursue the latter often brings the rhetorician some material reward. By persuading his audience to go after what merely appears best to them (and to himself) without knowledge of what is really best, the person who abuses rhetoric causes many kinds of "evil" in the political realm.[28]

However, one need not use persuasive power in this destructive way, a point that Socrates makes by personifying rhetoric. He states: "Lady Rhetoric might reply perhaps: 'Astonishing fellows, what nonsense you speak. I never required anyone to be ignorant of the truth when he learns to speak, but—if my counsel means something—to master the truth and then take me up. But I do make one major claim: without me, in no way will a man who knows the truth be able to persuade with art" (260d). The ultimate goal of philosophical rhetoric is the promotion of wisdom and the rest of the virtues, while common uses of rhetoric (in most cases, at least) aim for popular acceptance, and, consequently, power and pleasure for the orator. Ideally, the philosopher learns the truth regarding the matters about which he wishes to speak before using rhetoric to influence the lives of others. In this case, the philosopher's knowledge of the truth (and what is truly good) sets the ends toward which he tries to persuade others. For these reasons, Socrates tries to persuade Phaedrus that "unless he loves wisdom [*philosophēsē*] sufficiently, he will never become a competent speaker about anything" (261a). At the same time, Socrates emphasizes how necessary it is for the philosopher to learn the art of rhetoric—if the philosopher wishes to "persuade with art," he must understand rhetoric and learn to use it for philosophical ends.

To practice philosophical rhetoric in a way that is rightly called "artful," one needs to practice it "dialectically." This dialectical element requires one to know more than just the "prerequisites" of rhetoric, or the various rhetorical techniques that rhetoricians write down in "rhetorical textbooks" (266d) to teach their students (Socrates and Phaedrus list each of these rhetorical techniques from 266d–268a). In addition to these techniques, the philosophic rhetorician knows who needs to be persuaded, the

28. Compare this point to *Gorgias* 517a–c, where Socrates says that Athenian politicians traditionally give the city only what it "desires," and the popularity they gain from doing so brings them political power and other conventional rewards. By contrast, he claims, the "true [*alēthinos*] art of rhetoric" consists in "leading desires in a different direction and not yielding, persuading and forcing them toward a condition in which the citizens were to be better" (*Grg.* 517a).

sort of speech that will be most persuasive, the time at which one should be persuaded, the most beneficial views or actions she must persuade her audience to accept. Socrates claims that conventional rhetoricians lack all of this crucial knowledge, supposing that the prerequisites are all one needs to practice rhetoric:

> [We] shouldn't be harsh but forgiving if some people don't know how to think dialectically and are unable therefore to define what rhetoric is. On this account, they think that they have discovered the rhetorical art when they know only its prerequisites; and teaching others these things they believe that they have taught the art perfectly and that their students themselves must on their own come up with a way of saying each of the parts persuasively and with a way of fitting the parts appropriately into the whole, thinking that this is no work at all. (269b–c)

Just as a doctor must know what sort of patient needs certain "drugs" (*pharmakiois*), when the drugs are needed, the length of time the patients need the drugs, and so on (268a–c), so also the rhetorician must take all of these relevant considerations into account before persuading someone. Socrates uses two other examples to illustrate his point about the prerequisites of an art and the art itself—one is the art of writing tragedies, where knowledge of how to compose speeches, laments, and various plot devices are only the prerequisites of understanding how to make beautiful tragedy (268c–d), and the other is music or "harmonics," where learning to play musical notes and understanding the laws of harmony are the prerequisites for understanding "harmonics itself" (268e). In all four cases—medicine, music, tragedy, and rhetoric—one must know "the proper arrangement of parts, each fitted appropriately in relation to the other and the whole" (268d) in order to truly possess the art. In the cases of rhetoric and medicine, this also requires that one understand when to apply one's knowledge, what person(s) need it, the appropriate length of time required to apply it, and so on. Socrates' emphasis on the need to know these specificities in any given situation when practicing rhetoric is consistent with Plato and Aristotle's virtue-based approach to ethics—rather than simply follow a rigid set of rules or some universal formula, the virtuous person is sensitive to all of the complexities of each unique circumstance and makes her decisions accordingly.

Another reason why Socrates calls philosophical rhetoric "dialectical" is that it requires the philosopher to understand the similarities and differences between all kinds of speeches and souls, so that she can match the kind of speech to the kind of soul that will find it most persuasive (271b). Or, to use the butcher analogy, dialectic allows us to divide speeches and souls according to their "natural joints" (265e). After the philosopher has "classified" each kind of speech and soul, she must match the appropriate speech to a given soul and be able to explain "the reason why one soul is necessarily persuaded by speeches of a certain sort and another is not" (271b). Thus, if the philosopher understands what kind of speech causes each kind of soul to become persuaded of a given view (and she can explain why), then she possesses the "dialectical art" of rhetoric (276e). I use the term "philosophical" instead of "dialectical" to describe the genuine philosopher's kind of rhetoric according to the *Phaedrus*, because it is possible that a person could possess a dialectical understanding of speeches and souls (i.e., an understanding of the important similarities and differences of each) *without* having the philosopher's characteristic love for wisdom and virtue. This sort of rhetorician could lead her listeners toward self-serving ends that do not improve their souls. The philosophic rhetorician, on the other hand, knows what is most beneficial to her listener as well as the most effective means for facilitating such benefit. Again, Socrates demonstrates philosophical rhetoric through his words and deeds throughout the whole dialogue by using the sort of *logoi* that Phaedrus will most likely be persuaded by to guide his soul toward that which is truly beneficial for him, namely wisdom and the rest of the virtues.

In the context of the *Phaedrus*, flirtation is also a part of Socrates' philosophical rhetoric, though this need not be so in every case. Although Socrates and Phaedrus are not in a committed erotic relationship with one another, Socrates frequently flirts with Phaedrus, and Phaedrus reciprocates (see especially at 228a–e, 236b–237a, and 243e.) For example, Socrates frequently addresses Phaedrus with phrases like "my dear," my "darling boy," "excellent fellow," and so on. Plato is not simply adding superfluous dramatic details by depicting Socrates flirting with Phaedrus as they trade speeches and leisurely recline in a picturesque natural setting. Rather, the dialogue shows us that Socrates' flirting contributes to his efforts to persuade Phaedrus to see the value of virtue and philosophy (in this instance, at least).[29] Although it is not a rhetorical technique strictly speaking, flirting in this context is

29. McCoy (2022) also argues that Socrates flirts not for the sake of physically seducing Phaedrus but rather to "turn Phaedrus' soul away from the rhetorical approach of Lysias and towards philosophy" (50).

a pedagogical technique that increases the persuasive power of Socrates' arguments, and so is a component of philosophical rhetoric's project of influencing both rational and nonrational aspects of the interlocutor's soul. Given that Phaedrus is an amorous young man who is interested in the topics of love and sex, Socrates' flirting will ideally capture his attention and help him grow more interested in the topics they discuss together. As Charles Kahn points out, Plato often discusses desire and *erōs* as if they were bodies of water that can be redirected through reason, habit, or persuasion.[30] Moreover, as we know from Alcibiades' speech in the *Symposium* (218b), those who grow erotically interested in Socrates often grow interested in philosophy as well (even if Alcibiades ultimately does not commit himself to wisdom), so it is likely that Socrates' purpose in flirting with young men in general is to get them interested in philosophy. Socrates' flirting works in tandem with the content of the conversation to show Phaedrus the goods (especially happiness and a rewarding relationship) toward which the *erōs* he already feels can lead him if he channels it in a way that will help him pursue wisdom.

Toward the end of their discussion of rhetoric, Socrates uses an analogy about planting seeds to explain the ways in which philosophical rhetoric has the potential to be pedagogically and ethically beneficial. Regarding the speeches of those using philosophical rhetoric, he states: "These speeches are not fruitless but bear seed from which other speeches, planted in other fields, have the means to pass this seed on, forever immortal, and to make the person possessing them as blessed as is humanly possible" (276e–277a). The person using philosophical rhetoric uses his knowledge of his speech's subject matter (such as love or virtue), as well as his dialectical art of rhetoric, to "plant" a speech in the soul of someone else. Ideally, the person who hears the speech will continue to think about the speech he hears (i.e., it will "grow" in his mind) until he gains true insight into whatever subject the speaker discussed. Once the person who hears the speech gains such insight, it helps to improve his life (it makes him "blessed"), and he may even learn to use philosophical rhetoric to cause the same effect in others. Put another way, Socrates' philosophical rhetoric can inspire Phaedrus to examine the important philosophical issues they discussed more often and more thoroughly in the future (as he says explicitly in *Gorgias* 513c–d),

30. Kahn 1987, 77–103. For example, Plato uses this simile in *Republic* VI: "When someone's desires incline strongly to some one thing, they are therefore weaker with respect to the rest, like a stream that has been channeled off in that other direction" (*R.* 485d).

which can lead him to eventually become a virtuous philosopher who sees the truth for himself. By performing this very task with Phaedrus throughout the entire dialogue, Socrates sets a concrete example of philosophical rhetoric in practice. Socrates plants *logoi* in Phaedrus' soul in an attempt to guide him toward a devotion to philosophy, virtue, and "wisdom-loving speeches" (257b). Although the fate of the historical Phaedrus is uncertain, the philosophical pedagogy that Plato presents through Socrates can open the door to highly valuable ends for readers who take it to heart.

II. *Erōs* Without Virtue and "Mortal Moderation" in the First Two Speeches

Readers of the *Phaedrus* must sort out how the criticisms of *erōs* in Lysias' speech and Socrates' first speech relate to the palinode's praise of *erōs* as divine gift. Should we completely disregard the first two speeches' criticisms in light of Socrates' more accurate treatment of *erōs* in the palinode, or do these different accounts of erotic love relate to one another in a more nuanced way? While the criticisms of *erōs* in the first two speeches may appear to be mutually exclusive with the palinode's praise of it, I argue that the three speeches show us that *erōs* can be directed virtuously or viciously, just as rhetoric can be used to benefit others or to exploit them (260d). In section II.1, I argue that although Lysias' speech and Socrates' first speech claim to criticize all erotic love, they really only depict and criticize the ways in which those who lack virtue mishandle the *erōs* they experience, which becomes especially clear in light of the palinode speech. Plato's account of *erōs* as it is handled by those *without virtue* sets the stage for Socrates' account of how to handle *erōs with virtue* in the palinode, which I discuss in the next chapter. By exploring in the first two speeches how *erōs* can lead us to act viciously when we do not properly channel it, the ways in which it fosters virtue and wisdom (described in the palinode) become clearer thanks to the contrast. Through its three speeches and the ensuing dialogue, the *Phaedrus* illuminates the nature of *erōs* by reflecting on what it is, showing its virtuous and vicious manifestations, explaining what makes it beneficial or harmful, and discussing the goods (such as virtue) toward which it can lead. In this way, the *Phaedrus* provides a thorough examination of erotic love's role in human life.

Similarly, the first two speeches contrast the harmful madness of the lover with the supposedly calm, sensible "moderation" (*sōphrosunē*) of the nonlover, arguing that it is much better for one to give sexual favors to the nonlover. The palinode speech, however, criticizes this customary conception of *sōphrosunē* as mere "mortal moderation," a characteristic that simply enables an individual to scheme and calculate how to maximize his own pleasure by temporarily restraining himself. The *Phaedrus*' discussion of mortal moderation is one of the key instances (there are similar instances in the *Republic* and the *Phaedo*, cited above) where Plato summarizes his understanding of the popular, overly simplistic notion of self-restraint that the *Gorgias* and the *Phaedrus* refine and transfigure. Importantly, mortal moderation in the *Phaedrus* is not identical to Socrates' account of *sōphrosunē* in the *Gorgias*, even though both give emphasis to self-restraint. In the *Phaedrus*, just as the depictions of nonvirtuous *erōs* set the context for the palinode's praise of its potential benefits, so also do they provide a portrait of the conventional, imperfect notion of *sōphrosunē* so that the palinode can criticize the shortcomings of mortal moderation and lead us toward a deeper understanding of genuine *sōphrosunē*. Section II.2 analyzes the first two speeches' portrayal of mortal moderation, and it ends by discussing Socrates' critiques of this characteristic in the palinode. I conclude section II.2 by discussing the similarities and differences between mortal moderation and Socrates' account of *sōphrosunē* as self-restraint in the *Gorgias*.

II.1. *Erōs* Without Virtue

Lysias' speech and Socrates' first speech substantially contribute to the *Phaedrus*' ethical inquiries by illustrating nonvirtuous mishandling of *erōs*. Lysias makes dubious arguments that are primarily aimed at convincing Phaedrus to have sex with him, but Plato also includes important observations about nonvirtuous *erōs* in this speech. Lysias emphasizes that love often clouds our judgment, increases the intensity of our emotions, motivates us to act on these emotions in inappropriate ways, and makes us more likely to get upset over trivialities. It also describes how those in the grip of erotic love commonly behave in harmful or vicious ways by being possessive, jealous, and manipulative—for example, a lover might discourage his beloved from having friends due to his desire to have his beloved all to himself. While Lysias and Socrates' first speech both erroneously argue that *all* lovers behave in these ignoble ways, Socrates later points out that noble and "free" (*eleutheron*) lovers do not (*Phdr*. 243c–d). After he recalls this important point, Socrates illustrates in the palinode how we can direct the *erōs* we experience in a virtuous manner, which allows us to love others in a healthier way and avoid these misuses of love.

Lysias' speech does not define *erōs*, but instead lists many of the harmful behaviors exhibited by those in love in an effort to persuade its audience to give sexual favors only to nonlovers. Lysias observes that many lovers feel jealousy toward others who might attract the affection of their beloveds, and a nonvirtuous lover will likely act on this jealousy in harmful and manipulative ways. For instance, a nonvirtuous lover might harmfully manipulate his beloved by preventing him from forming valuable friendships: "For all kinds of things cause [lovers] to grieve, and they think that everything is designed to hurt them. Consequently, they try to prevent those they love from meeting other people, fearful lest a wealthy person will outspend them or an educated person outsmart them. They are forever on the lookout, guarding against the possible influence of anyone who might have some advantage or other. Persuading you to become loathsome to everyone else, they leave you without friends" (232c–d). With this example, Lysias' speech shows us how a lover can misuse, or respond poorly to, the *erōs* he experiences for his beloved. The jealous and possessive lover does everything in his power to prevent his beloved from entering a scenario where he could fall in love with somebody else; he is particularly on guard for those who have more attractive qualities than himself (such as more wealth or education). This nonvirtuous lover does not consider whether his actions are just or beneficial to the beloved—he seeks only to use whatever means possible to keep his beloved's loyalty or alleviate his fear of losing his beloved. Consequently, the beloved is "left without friends," an outcome that is detrimental for his well-being, since healthy friendships are a necessary component of a happy life.

Lysias' speech also stresses that *erōs* often prevents us from thinking soundly. A nonvirtuous lover's clouded thinking makes it likely that he will both assess his beloved's character poorly and adopt a distorted understanding of himself. Regarding the former mistake, the attraction the lover feels toward his beloved's good qualities can lead him to erroneously conclude that the beloved is excellent in every respect. In addition, he may constantly praise the beloved, even when the beloved does not deserve it, in an effort to make his beloved feel more affection for him: "Far beyond what is best, lovers will praise whatever you say or do, in part because they fear that you will come to loathe them, in part because passion clouds their judgment" (233a). The lover's excessive compliments for his beloved are fueled both by the infatuation that blurs his judgment and his fear of losing his beloved's affection. With respect to the nonvirtuous lover's self-understanding, he might acquire a falsely inflated opinion of his own level of excellence or worth when he wins over the person he loves. For instance, a nonvirtuous lover's overestimation of his own excellence is apparent when he brags to others about having sex with his beloved: "It is plausible that lovers (being inclined to think they are just as worthy of emulation by others as they are by themselves) will be excited to talk about their affairs and toot their own horn, revealing to one and all that they have not labored in vain" (231e–232a). Having attained the beloved's sexual favors that he desired so intensely, the nonvirtuous lover thinks of himself as "worthy of emulation," and he wants to be admired by others for having successfully fulfilled his desire. For these reasons, Lysias characterizes *erōs* as a sickness of the soul that causes ignorance and harm. Again, while Lysias argues that these observations are true of all people who experience *erōs*, Socrates will show that they are true only of those who do fail to channel *erōs* in a virtuous way.

Finally, Lysias' speech shows that when the intensity of erotic love fades, the nonvirtuous lover often behaves even more harmfully toward his beloved than before. Because they no longer experience the intense pleasures they felt when they were in love, nonvirtuous lovers will no longer flatter their beloveds, and they may even "seek a pretext for enmity when their desire has dried up" (234a). If he loses the desire to gain sexual or other erotic pleasures from his beloved, this sort of lover also loses the motivation to treat his beloved respectfully.[31] Worse still, if nonvirtuous lovers fall in love and begin a relationship with someone new, they "will treat their old loves badly if the new loves so desire" (231b). Such a drastic change in the way this kind of lover treats his ex-partner is evidence that he only ever saw his beloved as a means for fulfilling his own desire, and that he did not really care for his beloved's long-term well-being. Indeed, when the nonvirtuous lover ceases to experience *erōs* for his beloved, he regrets the time and resources he put into their relationship: "When lovers lose their passion, they come to regret whatever goods they may have conferred" (231a). Lysias uses these examples to support his thesis that all lovers are

31. Relatedly, Lysias adds that when the lover's initial attraction to his beloved's body fades, there may be nothing else that motivates him to remain in a relationship with the beloved: "Many lovers desire your body before they know your character or are familiar with your personal traits. So it isn't clear whether they will still wish to remain friends when they cease to desire you" (232e–233a).

inconstant and unworthy of trust, and that one should therefore have sex with a nonlover instead:

> And anyway, how is it plausible to hand over something so precious to someone with such an affliction that no experienced person would even try to cure it: for lovers certainly agree that they are sick rather than of sound mind [*sōphronein*] and they realize that although they are thinking poorly [*kakōs phronousin*] they are powerless to do anything about it. So how can these men, once they have regained their lost senses, possibly continue to hold those beliefs which they had when they were in the grip of love? (231c–d)

Lysias' speech characterizes all erotic love as a temporary "affliction" that causes the lover to behave in all kinds of ridiculous ways in order to gratify his own raging desire for the beloved. Lovers necessarily "think poorly" and lack "sound minds," unlike nonlovers, and love is therefore an overall harmful sickness of the soul that one should always avoid (I will return to Lysias' remarks about *sōphrosunē* in the next section, II.2).

Socrates' first speech criticizes the nonvirtuous uses and expressions of *erōs* along the same argumentative lines as Lysias' speech, and it has important pedagogical and philosophical functions in the dialogue. Socrates criticizes Lysias' speech for saying "the same thing two or three times over, as if he were not particularly adept at speaking in depth on the same theme" (235a), so Phaedrus challenges Socrates to "deliver a speech which is fuller and more appropriate" than Lysias' speech" (236b). On the surface, then, it appears that Socrates gives his first speech simply to take up Phaedrus' challenge. However, Socrates' first speech serves several important purposes in the broader context of the *Phaedrus*, even if he later claims to disown it, calling it "terribly clever" (*deinon*) and "irreverent" (*asebē*) to the god Eros (242d–e), which means that he "needs to be cleansed" (*kathērasthai anagkē*) by giving the palinode speech (243a). By giving a more thorough account of the ways people commonly misuse *erōs* than Lysias' speech did, Socrates' first speech further develops the *Phaedrus*' philosophical examination of the nature of *erōs* and its various manifestations—some beneficial, some harmful—in human life. Similarly, his first speech functions pedagogically by showing both Phaedrus and the reader a clearer account of the vicious abuses of *erōs,* which he will later contrast with his illustration of how to handle *erōs* virtuously in the palinode. Moreover, both of Socrates' speeches are magnificent displays of rhetorical skill and so support his claim that the philosopher knows how to use rhetoric better than anyone, which may help to attract Phaedrus (who already aspires to become an excellent rhetorician) toward the philosophical life.[32]

In keeping with Lysias' basic perspective, Socrates' first speech describes *erōs* as a "form of desire [*epithumia*]" (237d), an "illness" (238e), and a harmful type of madness. In the palinode, however, Socrates does not characterize *erōs* as merely one desire among others, as I will show in the next chapter. So, I suggest that Socrates' first speech describes *erōs* as an *epithumia* because it depicts only nonvirtuous *erōs*, which is primarily driven by the lover's desires (*epithumiai*) for sex, control of the beloved, the social recognition one gets from telling others about his relations with the beloved, and other associated desires. These desires and pleasures are Socrates' primary focuses when discussing love in the first speech, as I show in the next paragraph. Like Lysias' speech, Socrates' first speech assumes that madness is always bad and should therefore be avoided. According to this view, the moderation or sound-mindedness (*sōphrosunē*) of a nonlover is more beneficial than the mad behavior of a lover (I will return to the first two speeches' characterization of *sōphrosunē* in the next section, II.2). Again, though, this speech's conceptions of love, madness, and *sōphrosunē* are all incomplete and imperfect; as Socrates later makes clear in the palinode, love can also be directed virtuously, not all types of madness are harmful, and genuine *sōphrosunē* is not the calm, pleasure-maximizing calculation of the nonlover.

Importantly, Socrates' first speech emphasizes the *hubris* and selfishness of nonvirtuous love, painting the nonvirtuous lover as one who seeks only an excessive amount of pleasure for himself.[33] Early in the speech, Socrates defines *hubris*: "When desire [*epithumias*] irrationally drags us toward pleasures and rules over us, we call this excess [*hubris*]" (238a). He characterizes *hubris* as the state of being completely ruled by one's own desires and therefore striving for more pleasure than is appropriate, a concept that is similar to the *Gorgias*' notion of *pleonexia* discussed in the previous chapters. Socrates

32. Phaedrus states that he is impressed with Socrates' rhetorical ability at 258c.

33. In Scully's translation of the *Phaedrus* (2003), his glossary entry on *hubris* states: "*Hubris* ranges in meaning from 'wanton violence' including rape, arising from pride of might or passion, to 'lust,' to 'insolence' or 'arrogance.' It always violates a general Greek sense of moral or social order, and is officially punished therefore by the gods, if not by men" (127). Helen North (1966) notes that Attic tragedy often paints *hubris* as the opposite of *sōphrosunē* (150).

then claims that nonvirtuous love is based on the hubristic desire for erotic pleasures: "When passion without reason rules over straight minded opinion and is itself driven toward the pleasure of beauty [*hēdonēn kallous*], and, further, when the passion is violently moved by kindred desires [*genōn epithumiōn*] toward the beauty of the body and is victorious, it takes its name from that very force and is called love [*erōs*]" (238b–c). Socrates adds that a person in love is "ruled by desire and is a slave to pleasure," and therefore wants to "reap the greatest possible pleasure for himself from the beloved" (238e). Hence, nonvirtuous, hubristic love is wholly self-centered, since this sort of lover cares only about gaining a maximal amount of sexual pleasure or other similar benefits for himself, regardless of whatever harm he might cause to others in the process.[34]

Further, Socrates' first speech thoroughly displays how the hubristic, nonvirtuous lover harms the beloved's body, his goods, and his relationships with others, all for the sake of gratifying his own desires as much as possible. If a muscular and "vigorous" body is less sexually pleasing to the nonvirtuous lover than a "soft" one, he will discourage his beloved from exercising (239c–d). Similarly, a nonvirtuous lover hopes that his beloved will lose all possessions, friends, and relatives, because without such things, the beloved will be more dependent on the lover and thus more likely to give erotic pleasure (239d–240a); the hubristic lover "pray[s] for his boyfriend to remain wifeless, childless, and homeless for as long as possible, desiring to enjoy the fruits of the boy's sweetness for as long as possible" (240a).[35] Worse still, Socrates brings attention to the abuse that sometimes occurs

34. Socrates' first speech remarks that there are different kinds of *hubris* that have different names, but they all stem from the same fundamental disorder in the soul. That is, a soul is hubristic when it is "ruled" or "led" by its own immoderate desire for an excessive amount of some good. He claims that we give different kinds of *hubris* different names in accord with the primary kind of object toward which it is directed: "To be sure, excess [*hubris*] has many names—many limbs and many forms—and when one of these forms happens to be preeminent, a person takes its name, hardly a beautiful or praiseworthy name to have. When the passion for food, for example, rules over our best reasoning and our other desires, we call this gluttony and the person in the grips of this desire, gluttonous. Or take the tyrannizing passion for wine, which leads a drinker in that direction, it is clear what name to call him. And in regard to kindred cases of other desires, and the names of those kindred desires—when that desire is ruling for the time being—it is clear how each should be labeled" (238a–b).

35. Socrates adds that when the lover "has ceased loving he is untrustworthy from that moment forward" (240e), and he does not live up to the promises and oaths he made when he was in love (241a–b).

when *erōs* is not paired with virtue. The nonvirtuous lover might resort to verbal abuse when he is drunk: "Reproaches which are unbearable when the lover is sober become shameful as well when he is drunk and gives way to excessive and unchecked language" (240e). Unfortunately, the nonvirtuous lover might also "force himself on the beloved" to satiate his intense and frequent sexual desire (240c–d). In all of these examples, the common thread is the nonvirtuous lover's lack of care for the well-being of his beloved and his sole focus on using the beloved to gratify his own desires. Readers who have been in relationships with such lovers will unfortunately find Socrates' descriptions and examples all too familiar.

Perhaps most detrimental of all, though, is the harm a nonvirtuous lover can cause to the soul of his beloved by preventing him from pursuing education and self-cultivation. When summing up his argument about the abuses of the lover, Socrates emphasizes that the beloved's very own soul is the most valuable thing that a lover can damage, stating that the nonvirtuous lover is "especially harmful to the education of his soul, than which surely nothing is more esteemed, whether by humankind or the gods" (241c). In order to maintain his capacity to manipulate and control his beloved, the lover does everything in his power to prevent the beloved from becoming an independent, mature, and philosophically educated thinker:

> For a sick man, anything that offers little or no resistance is sweet, and anything that is equal or stronger is hateful. So a lover will not willingly put up with a boyfriend who is stronger or even on equal terms with himself, but he will make him weaker and more needy always. So, the ignorant are weaker than the wise, the cowardly are weaker than the manly, those incapable of speech-making are weaker than rhetoricians, and the slow are weaker than the quick-witted. Necessarily, then, either a lover is deprived of his immediate pleasures, or he enjoys and tries to instill evils such as these, whether they are cultivated or innate—and evils still worse than these—which harm the boy's mind. A lover can't restrain his jealousy or his impulse to prevent the boy from attending all sorts of occasions, especially the beneficial ones where he may best grow into a man. This is cause enough for harm, but the greatest harm occurs when the lover prevents the boy from attending an occasion where he might best refine his thinking. That is the divine love of wisdom [*theia philosophia*] and a lover must necessarily keep his boyfriend

> far from it, terrified to his marrow that the boy will grow to despise him. And so, a lover schemes to keep the boy totally ignorant and totally fixed on him, the boy being the sort who, in offering the greatest possible pleasure to the lover, would bring the greatest possible harm upon himself. (238e–239c)

The lover's jealousy leads him to watch the beloved "suspiciously at all times" (240e) and keep his beloved away from talented individuals who could provide valuable educational guidance. If the nonvirtuous lover can prevent his beloved from gaining the sort of education that would help him clearly see the extent to which the lover selfishly manipulates, oppresses, and damages his well-being, then the beloved will be less likely to reject and "despise" the lover's presence. Socrates' palinode speech later reveals that the mutual benefit each member of the virtuous, philosophic couple give one another is the polar opposite of the harm that the nonvirtuous lover causes his beloved by steering him away from self-cultivation and the "divine love of wisdom."

In sum, the first two speeches show that nonvirtuous *erōs* is devoid of genuine care for the well-being of another person. Instead, the person who lacks virtue hubristically aims to satisfy his own desires as much as possible, and he simply treats his erotic partner as a means to reaching this end. Socrates sums up this point succinctly with the following analogy: "A lover's friendship does not stem from kindness [*eunoias*] but from a kind of hunger and desire for satiety: as wolves adore lambs, so lovers are fond of a boy" (241c–d). While all (or at least most) people feel erotically attracted to a person who appears especially beautiful to them, some respond to their experience of *erōs* virtuously, as the palinode shows, but others respond to it in a predatory manner—like wolves—aiming to satisfy themselves any cost. Nonvirtuous *erōs* is ultimately self-directed, even if it appears that this kind of lover actually cares about the beloved's well-being. Aristotle draws a similar distinction between two kinds of "self-love"—one that is vicious, and another that is virtuous. Interestingly, in *Nicomachean Ethics* book 9, he associates the vicious kind of self-love with *pleonexia*:

> Now, then, those who bring self-love [*philautous*] into reproach call "self-lovers" those people who allot to themselves the greater share [*aponemontas to pleion*] of money, honors, and bodily pleasures, for the many long for these things and are serious about them on the grounds that they are what is best; hence too such

> things are fought over. Those who grasp for more [*pleonektai*] of these things gratify their desires and, in general, their passions and the nonrational part of their soul. Such is the character of the many. [. . .] Those who are self-lovers in this way, therefore, are justly reproached. (*EN* 1168b15–23)

The vicious kind of self-love aims solely to gratify the nonrational part of the soul as much as possible. This activity often leads to vicious action that harms others, since acquiring an excessive amount of goods so often involves unjustly taking them from others. The virtuous self-lover, though, takes care of his whole soul, especially the rational part, by living nobly, which necessarily involves benefiting others: "The good person ought to be a self-lover—he will both profit himself and benefit others by doing noble things—but the corrupt person ought not to be—he will harm both himself and his neighbors, since he follows his base passions" (1169a11–14). The nonvirtuous lover of Socrates' first speech closely resembles Aristotle's vicious self-lover in that both primarily aim to gratify their own desires at the expense of others.

Of course, Socrates' first speech generalizes its descriptions of *erōs* by saying that they are true of all "lovers." However, shortly after delivering his first speech, Socrates almost explicitly states that both Lysias' speech and his first speech are talking about erotic love *only as it is handled by people who are not virtuous*. Socrates tells Phaedrus that he has realized that his first speech is terribly flawed, and his description of the flaw is crucial for understanding the significance of his first speech:

> In fact, my good Phaedrus, you too recognize how shameless those speeches were, both the one from the book and the next one. If someone of noble and gentle character [*gennadas kai praos to ēthos*] happened to hear us saying that lovers get very irate over trivial matters and that they feel jealousy and ill-will toward their boyfriend, and if this someone was either in love with a character like himself or had once been loved, how could you think that he would not believe that he was listening to people who had been raised among sailors and had never seen a noble form of love among the free [*eleutheron erōta heōrakotōn*]? And he would be far from agreeing with our censure of Eros. (*Phdr*. 243c–d)

Socrates' statement implies that those who lack "noble and gentle characters" exhibit all of the behaviors that the first two speeches associate with erotic love. So, Socrates does not claim that his points about *erōs* in the first speech were wrong—instead, he claims that they apply only to the nonvirtuous kind of *erōs*. His first speech is wrong only insofar as it makes claims about all kinds of *erōs* instead of just the nonvirtuous, hubristic kind.[36] Later in the dialogue, Socrates confirms that the criticisms of nonvirtuous *erōs* in the first two speeches were warranted, since the kind of erotic love they focus on is different from the kind in the palinode (265e–266a).[37] *Erōs* is not bad in itself but becomes harmful when humans handle it hubristically and without virtue. In reality, *erōs* is "a god or at least as something divine" and, therefore, "he could not be bad in any way" (242e–243a). As Socrates will argue in the palinode, humans must use the guiding light of philosophy to discover the "divine" potential of *erōs*.

Finally, although the *Phaedrus* primarily focuses on ancient Athenian pederastic relationships,[38] many of its observations about the experience of erotic love may sound familiar to modern ears. For instance, many of the

36. Socrates also remarks that Lysias' speech does not "completely miss the mark" regarding its appraisal of *erōs*, and that "even the worst prose writer has some merit" (235e).

37. In this passage, Socrates states that the three speeches effectively identified two different kinds of *erōs*, rightly praising the one and criticizing the other: "To have the power, conversely, to cut up a composition, form by form according to its natural joints and not to try to hack through any part as a bad butcher might. Rather take the example of the two recent speeches which seized upon one common form to explain the loss of coherent thought; just as the body, which is one thing, is naturally divided into pairs of things with both parts having the same name (called, for example, left arm and right arm), so also the two speeches assumed that madness is by its nature one form in us, though capable of being divided into two parts. One of the speeches cut the part on the left and did not cease cutting until it found among these parts something called "left love" and then, with absolute justice, abused it; the other speech, however, led us to the madness on the right side and discovered there a love with the same name as the other but of some divine nature. Setting this before us, the speech praised it as the greatest cause of good for us" (265e–266a).

38. David Halperin's influential 1986 article "Plato and Erotic Reciprocity" makes an important point about recognizing the difference between traditional Athenian pederasty and Plato's own reflection on it. Plato's erotic dialogues offer critiques of the one-sided nature of the pederastic relationship, which was commonly seen as pleasurable only for the older lover. The *Phaedrus* provides an especially clear model of a better alternative to the traditional pederastic relationship through its description of the "philosophic couple," where both partners gain benefit from the joint pursuit of philosophy and virtue, as I discuss in chapter 4.

harmful behaviors discussed above are (unfortunately) prevalent in modern sexually intimate relationships between consenting adults. Almost everyone feels a strong erotic attraction toward another individual at some point in their lives, and some people act on their erotic feelings in healthy ways, while others act in the jealous, manipulative, and even abusive ways that are similar to those discussed in the first two speeches of the *Phaedrus*. Sadly, harmful behaviors in the context of erotic, intimate relationships are all too common, as many of us know from personal experience, public discourse about these issues, or depictions of such behavior in popular works of art. Then, as now, we can choose to handle the *erōs* we feel in either a virtuous or vicious way, and the *Phaedrus*' reflection on the difference between the two remains relevant to us. The first two speeches remind us that our desire to maintain a pleasant relationship with the person(s) we love can easily lead to common mistakes such as manipulation, verbal abuse, or other such harmful actions. As I discuss in the next chapter, the rest of the dialogue highlights ways we can support the well-being of those we love and avoid the mistake of using another person solely to gratify our own erotic desires.

II.2. Mortal Moderation

The first two speeches of the *Phaedrus* not only contribute to the dialogue's broader investigation of *erōs*; they also add to its account of *sōphrosunē* by painting an imperfect portrait of this virtue that represents conventional views about what it is. Socrates' palinode later criticizes this conception of *sōphrosunē* as mere "mortal moderation" and contrasts it with genuine or divine moderation. Through its three speeches and ensuing dialogue, the *Phaedrus* gives us a thorough reflection on *sōphrosunē,* since it scrutinizes common conceptions about it and provides substantial suggestions about its true nature. Lysias' speech depicts the nonlover as someone who has *sōphrosunē* due to his ability to restrain certain desires, his healthy and sane mind (i.e., he is not "mad"), and his cleverness. He claims that erotic love necessarily distorts or clouds our thinking, while *sōphrosunē,* by contrast, gives us the ability to work toward our own advantage clearly, calmly, and effectively:

> And anyway, how is it plausible to hand over something so precious to someone with such an affliction that no experienced person would even try to cure it: for lovers certainly agree that they are sick rather than of sound mind [*sōphronein*] and they realize that although they are thinking poorly they are powerless

> to do anything about it. So how can these men, once they have regained their lost senses, possibly continue to hold those beliefs which they had when they were in the grip of love? (*Phdr.* 231c–d)

In Lysias' view, souls in the "grip of love" are so infatuated with the beloved that their desire for erotic pleasure dethrones any previous priorities they may have possessed. He calls this state of mind an "affliction" that causes the lover to behave in all of the atypical and often harmful ways discussed in the previous section. Even if lovers have enough self-awareness to "realize" that they are "thinking poorly" and lack *sōphrosunē*, they nonetheless pursue the beauty and erotic pleasures that are so overwhelmingly attractive to them. For Lysias, *erōs* and *sōphrosunē* are mutually exclusive because the latter allows us to preserve our normal beliefs about how to behave in our own best interest, while the former causes us to abandon these beliefs.

In particular, *sōphrosunē* best enables the sort of thinking by which we can clearly calculate and maximize our own pleasure. Since the moderate nonlover is free from the bad influence of *erōs*, he can avoid the common mistakes of the lover and always determine the best way to please his sexual partner, which will in turn maximize his own pleasure: "But non-lovers don't blame love as an excuse for their neglect of family matters, nor do they keep a scorecard of labors endured, and they don't blame loved ones for problems with relatives. So actually when such ills are cleared out of the way, nothing is left but for non-lovers to do with zeal whatever they think would please their partners" (231b). Causing pleasure for the beloved will, of course, lead to more pleasure for the nonlover, since the beloved will want to give his sexual favors to the man who brings him the most pleasure in return. So, although the moderate person and the lover both pursue pleasure in Lysias' account, the moderate person can produce much more pleasure for himself and his beloved thanks to his clever planning, an activity that *erōs* prevents. As Socrates puts it, Lysias' speech at bottom praises the nonlover for being in his right mind (here Socrates uses the adjective *to phronimon*) and criticizes the lover for being "out of his mind" (*aphron*) (236a). The line of reasoning in Lysias speech assumes that the failure to effectively maximize pleasure is a sign that one lacks *sōphrosunē*.

A closely related way that Lysias describes the contrast between the moderate nonlover and the lover is that the former exhibits self-control or self "rule" (*kreitton*).[39] The main reason why Lysias praises self-control is

39. Like Callicles in the *Gorgias*, Lysias suggests that we not care too much about "public opinion" or human customs (*nomoi*) more generally if they interfere with our ability

that it allows the nonlover to act in a way that promotes both "immediate pleasure" and long-term "benefit": "If I have won you over, first of all I will keep your company, not [only] looking out for immediate pleasure but also for future benefits, because I am not weakened by love but am in full possession of myself [*emautou kratōn*]. Nor do I get irate over trivial matters, and only slowly build up anger from big problems, forgiving unintended mistakes and trying to forestall deliberate transgressions" (233b–c). The nonlover does not let himself get carried away by the present intense desire for erotic pleasure. Instead, he remains "in full possession" or control of his desires and emotions such that he can always carry out his plan to maximize pleasure for himself and the beloved over an extended period of time. According to Lysias, then, the moderate nonlover is the exemplar of the clever, calculating, and self-restrained individual who knows how to best satisfy his desires for the longest possible stretch of time.[40] In these respects, the conception of moderation in Lysias' speech is a representative example of a common way people conventionally conceive of moderation, both in antiquity and in the present day.

The conception of *sōphrosunē* that Socrates uses in his first speech is very similar to the one used by Lysias, but it adds a few important points. Like Lysias, Socrates paints the nonlover's soul as self-controlled and capable of clear thinking, and it describes the lover's soul as unsound, mad, and ill. However, Socrates introduces the idea that *sōphrosunē* is the opposite of *hubris*. Notably, moderation is also the opposite of *hubris* in the palinode, even though the palinode conceives of *sōphrosunē* in a very different way, which I discuss in the next chapter. *Erōs* is the cause of *hubris* according to Socrates' first speech, though the palinode will make the opposite case, saying that *erōs* as divine madness can lead to genuine *sōphrosunē* and the rest of the virtues.

Socrates' first speech uses a basic distinction between reason, which holds opinions about what is best, and our nonrational desires for pleasure to explain the difference between *sōphrosunē* and *hubris*.[41] He states:

to get what we want: "But non-lovers, possessing a measure of self-control [*kreittous hautōn ontas*], choose to do what is best rather than to follow in the foot-steps of public opinion" (232a).

40. Ryan Brown (2022) similarly observes that Lysias strongly associates *sōphrosunē* with self-restraint, which Socrates then criticizes and contrasts with his own account of this virtue (46).

41. Socrates' palinode speech offers a more sophisticated and detailed moral psychology that details the relationships between reason, *thumos*, and nonrational desires, as I will discuss in the next chapter.

> Further, one must realize that in each of us there are two forces which rule and guide us and that we follow both wherever they lead. One of them is our inborn desire for pleasure, the other an acquired opinion in pursuit of the best. Sometimes the two, lodged within us, agree; at other times, they quarrel. Then, sometimes one, sometimes the other gains the upper hand. When right opinion with reason rules and leads toward the best, we call this moderation [*sōphrosunē*]. But when desire irrationally drags us toward pleasures and rules over us, we call this excess [*hubris*]." (237d–238a)

The moderate person can restrain or "rule" his desires through "right opinion and reason" so that he acts in accord with what his reason identifies as "best." Since Socrates' first speech assumes the same perspective as Lysias' speech, what is "best" is simply the maximum amount of pleasure over a long period of time. The mad lover, on the other hand, hubristically seeks to satisfy his desires immediately, and these desires can overrule his reason's opinions about the best possible action. For example, the lover's overwhelming desire to make a sexual advance on the beloved would lead him to act on this impulse in an unattractive or even harmful way, while a moderate, self-controlled nonlover would be much more careful to act in ways that may not give him immediate pleasure but will ensure much more pleasure in the long run. When the lover ceases to experience *erōs* for his beloved, "he adopts a different principle for himself and a new champion, mind and moderation, replacing love and madness [*noun kai sōphrosunēn ant' erōtos kai manias*]" (241a), and he does not "honor the oaths and promises of his former mindless regime [*anoētou archēs*], now that he is a mindful and moderate person [*eschēkōs kai sesōphronēkōs*]" (241a–b). In sum, Socrates' first speech reaffirms and supplements Lysias' portrait of *sōphrosunē* as the characteristic that enables us to restrain desire for the sake of effectively achieving the greatest total amount of pleasure.[42]

42. At the beginning of the palinode speech, Socrates still uses the previous speeches' conception of *sōphrosunē* and madness to make his points about madness, but the speech will later criticize this conception. When stating one of the fundamental claims of the palinode, Socrates says that the first speech is not a "'genuine account' if it claims that one ought to grant favors to a non-lover rather than to a lover who is near at hand, just because one is of sound mind [*sōphronei*] and the other is mad [*mainetai*]" (244a). Then, he says: "First, the prophetess at Delphi and priestesses at Dodona do many good things for Greece, both in private and public matters, when they are mad, but when they are of sound mind and self-controlled [*sōphronousai*], they do next to nothing for our

In the palinode, Socrates' explicitly refers to the first two speeches' conception of *sōphrosunē* as "mortal moderation" and "slavish economizing." He criticizes the limitations mortal moderation places on one's soul, since those who possess it care only for "meager mortal benefits" such as acquiring pleasure or other conventional goods: "But a non-lover's intimacy is diluted by mortal moderation [*sōphrosunē thnētē*] and pays meager mortal benefits. It begets in his friend's soul a slavish economizing which most people praise as a virtue but will cause your soul to roam for 9000 years around the earth and beneath it, mindlessly [*anoun*]" (256e–257a). In the context of the palinode's reincarnation myth, Socrates claims that mortal moderation will cause the soul to "mindlessly" roam for nine thousand years, but this detail may symbolize the long-term harm to the soul that mortal moderation may cause in the span of a single life. Mortal moderation prevents an individual from harnessing the *erōs* he experiences in a way that will lead him toward wisdom, the rest of the virtues, and other benefits to the soul that Socrates discusses throughout the palinode:

> So, let's not fear madness itself, nor let us be confused by any argument which tries to frighten us into believing that a man of sound mind [*ton sōphrona*] should be chosen as friend over someone who has been stirred. Rather let that argument carry the day only after it has been shown that the gods do not send love [*eros*] to a lover and the beloved for their benefit. For our part we must show the opposite—namely that the gods grant such madness for our greatest good fortune. (245b–c)

Mortal moderation cannot provide the benefit to humans that the "divine madness" of *erōs* gives us when it leads to a "a regimented life and a love of wisdom," the actualization of virtue, the regrowing of the soul's wings, and reward in the afterlife (256a–b). As I show in the next chapter, the palinode suggests that *sōphrosunē* as it is characterized in the first two speeches

---

country" (244b). When describing madness, he states: "Madness itself, as the ancients testify, is more ennobling than moderation [*sōphrosunēs*], the one coming from a god, the other from man [*anthrōpōn*]" (244d). Similarly, when discussing the third type of madness, he claims: "The poetry of those who are mad will obliterate the poetry of a sound and self-controlled mind [*sōphronountos*]" (245a). All four statements closely associate *sōphrosunē* with self-restraint.

is not really *sōphrosunē* at all but merely a characteristic that appears to be *sōphrosunē* to those who do not understand the true nature of this virtue.[43]

As I mentioned in the introduction, there is some overlap in the accounts of mortal moderation in the *Phaedrus* and *sōphrosunē* in the *Gorgias,* but there are also key differences. In chapter 2 I argued that Socrates' characterization of *sōphrosunē* in the *Gorgias* focuses on self-restraint and placing limits on desires, because shedding light on the value of self-restraint has the most potential to pedagogically and morally benefit souls who have views and moral characters similar to those of Callicles. I argued that self-restraint in the *Gorgias* is a "civic virtue" (borrowing a term from the *Republic*), which is a necessary step toward genuine moderation and the rest of the virtues. The primary similarity between the conceptions of *sōphrosunē* in the *Gorgias* and mortal moderation is that both highlight the advantages of restraining nonrational desires and not acting in ways that are harmful (both to ourselves and others) in order to fulfill them. Both dialogues stress the practical, everyday benefits of being able to manage our desires in such a way that we do not live as slaves to them or allow them to consume our lives; the more our desires lead us to act in impulsive ways, the less satisfied we become over a long period of time. I have also noted that this is a primary feature of moderation according to the common conceptions of this virtue in both antiquity and the present day.

On the other hand, there are important differences between *sōphrosunē* in the *Gorgias* and mortal moderation in the *Phaedrus.* Mortal moderation is more closely aligned with the previously mentioned flawed, popular accounts of the moderation in the *Phaedo* and the *Republic* according to which moderation is the ability to restrain some desires for the sake of satisfying more highly prized desires in a kind of self-interested economic exchange. A central idea of Lysias' speech is that one can be a more effective hedonist by ruling over one's desires such that one can cleverly plan to satisfy them regularly over a long period of time. In the *Gorgias,* Socrates does not claim that self-restraint will maximize pleasure. It is true that Socrates, in a somewhat utilitarian manner, argues that *sōphrosunē* helps us avoid the harmful effects of *pleonexia.* But he also shows how giving limit to one's desires makes one's soul more excellent, which (according

43. In *Republic* VIII (553e–554e) and *Phaedo* (68c–69c), Socrates similarly criticizes the practice of restraining some desires for the sake of fulfilling others as a misguided and impoverished view of *sōphrosunē,* and he remarks that the majority of people hold this view.

to my interpretation) helps an individual transition toward genuine moderation.

In other words, self-restraint in the *Gorgias* is directed toward virtue and *eudaimonia* as its ultimate goals, whereas mortal moderation in the *Phaedrus* simply aims to maximize one's own pleasure in a strictly hedonistic sense. Indeed, I argue in chapter 4 that the *Phaedrus* itself distinguishes between the self-restraint that aims for virtue (described in Socrates' palinode) and the self-restraint involved in mortal moderation, which aims only to maximize one's own pleasure. When an individual cultivates harmony between the parts of the soul through habitual self-restraint and thus comes closer to a state of completeness and sufficiency, she prepares herself to achieve the self-knowledge, fulfillment, and illumination that accompany genuine *sōphrosunē*. In section II.1 of chapter 4, I argue that Socrates' palinode speech describes how habitual self-restraint can be a way to transition toward genuine *sōphrosunē*. Still, Socrates' critiques of mortal moderation's shortcomings in the *Phaedrus* also apply to self-restraint in the *Gorgias* insofar as the latter dialogue does not delve into the multifaceted nature of genuine *sōphrosunē*, nor does it explore the crucial benefits that moderation facilitates, such as self-knowledge, eudaimonic relationships, and insight into the sources of Being.

Conclusion

Through his artful depiction of Phaedrus, Plato shows us the type of person who can—and must—choose between the philosophical life and the life spent in pursuit of conventional goods. Phaedrus has the potential to pursue wisdom and virtue, as evidenced by his intellectual curiosity, his love for *logos*, and his propensity to experience wonder (among other traits), but he is also gripped by the seductive lure of wealth, pleasure, fame, and social power that accompany the conventional, sometimes abusive, use of rhetoric. In an attempt to guide Phaedrus toward the philosophical life, Socrates displays through his words and deeds how the philosopher can use rhetoric pedagogically. He composes speeches and leads a discussion that contains powerful images, arguments, and flirtation, tailoring his words to best fit the type of soul Phaedrus represents. If Socrates' rhetoric were to succeed, it would plant the seeds of insight about the value of wisdom and virtue in Phaedrus' soul, which Phaedrus can choose to nurture through his own efforts over the course of his life. The *Phaedrus*' main themes of *erōs* and *sōphrosunē* emerge in its first two speeches, which together show the harmful ways *erōs* manifests in the behavior of those who lack virtue. These two speeches present a conventional, flawed conception of "mortal" *sōphrosunē* through their portrayal of the selfish and calculating nonlover. As I will show in the next chapter, Socrates supplants this conception of moderation with his own superior, multifaceted account of *sōphrosunē* and its benefits.

Chapter 4

Genuine *Sōphrosunē* in *Phaedrus*

The first two speeches of the *Phaedrus* are crucial to Plato's project of thoroughly examining *erōs* insofar as they depict the ways people can misuse erotic love and harm their erotic partners if they lack virtue. Similarly, the first two speeches display the characteristic Socrates calls "mortal moderation," which consists in restraining some desires for the sake of fulfilling others and therefore maximizing pleasure for oneself. These speeches set the stage for Socrates' palinode speech, since it offers a contrasting account of how to handle *erōs* virtuously such that it leads us to become more virtuous, happier, and capable of having healthy intimate relationships.[1] His palinode likewise critiques mortal moderation and provides a substantial reflection on the true nature of *sōphrosunē* (which I have been calling "genuine *sōphrosunē*"), as I will argue in this chapter.

Yet, as we try to discover what genuine *sōphrosunē* is in the *Phaedrus*, several challenges confront us. As Socrates says at *Phaedrus* 263a, the most important terms, such as justice and goodness, are interpreted in a various number of ways by different people, and they are even interpreted differently by a single individual at different times. Socrates' own use of the term *sōphrosunē* admits of various possible interpretations. I point out the ambiguities contained in the palinode's comments about *sōphrosunē* to make clearer the difference between genuine *sōphrosunē* and mortal moderation.

1. Socrates calls his second speech a "palinode" because it aims to renounce and make up for the disrespect or blasphemy against Eros in his first speech (which was meant to be a better version of Lysias' speech). He claims that his second speech aims to show that Eros, the god personifying the erotic love experienced by humans, "could not be bad in any way" (242e).

One ambiguity is that some of the practices that Socrates associates with genuine *sōphrosunē* in the palinode appear similar to the practices he associates with mortal moderation. Specifically, Socrates discusses the importance of restraining desire at length in the passages about how the "black horse" of the soul, which symbolizes the soul's desires (*epithumiai*), must be habituated such that it will always obey the command of the charioteer (symbolizing reason) and not force the soul to have sex with a beloved boy. One could interpret these passages to mean that genuine moderation is simply following universal rules or commands, such as a rule to abstain from sex or other goods that we desire. In other words, it is possible to interpret genuine moderation in the palinode as restraining desire for the sake of following some universal rules given to us from an outside source, such as a wise person or a certain group of people. I argue that this is an incorrect way to interpret Socrates' reflection on the true nature of *sōphrosunē*. Genuine *sōphrosunē* is not reducible to certain behaviors or choices that are the means to the goal of obediently following the rules given to us from an authority. Instead, Socrates shows Phaedrus that *sōphrosunē* is the virtue through which we gain direct and pivotal insight about ourselves, the nature of the world, and the importance of the well-being of others.

Another ambiguity in the *Phaedrus*' account of *sōphrosunē* I address is Socrates' use of violent metaphors when describing the restraint and the training of the soul's desires (*epithumiai*). Using the chariot image of the soul, Socrates says in the palinode that the charioteer must "bloody" the black horse's "abusive tongue and jaws," and press "the legs and haunches of the horse hard upon the ground in pain" (*Phdr.* 254e). This passage might suggest that *sōphrosunē* is built on a kind of suppressive coercion of desire, or even a kind of self-violence. Such an interpretation would also entail that the moderate soul is always fighting against its own desires and never achieves a state of unity, agreement, or harmony. In my view, although Socrates' metaphorical discussion of habituating desire indeed uses violent imagery, this habituation does not describe the state of the soul for one who has fully achieved genuine *sōphrosunē*. Rather, I argue in section II.1 that these passages describe self-restraint, the same characteristic that Socrates equates with *sōphrosunē* in the *Gorgias* due to his pedagogical goals in that context. Self-restraint is a necessary transitional stage between the undisciplined soul and the genuinely moderate soul. While desires must be deliberately and forcibly restrained by the individual who aims to cultivate genuine *sōphrosunē*, the result of this process is a state of agreement between all three parts of the soul. When an individual becomes genuinely moderate, his whole soul, including his desires, becomes harmonious in a way that no longer requires forcible restraint (though inner harmony is only one facet of genuine *sōphrosunē* in the *Phaedrus*). Just as Socrates "divides" virtuous *erōs* from vicious, hubristic *erōs* in the *Phaedrus* (266a–b), so I will divide genuine moderation from self-restraint and mortal moderation through a careful interpretation of *Phaedrus*' reflection on *sōphrosunē*.

To aid my analysis of the *Phaedrus*' ethical reflections in this chapter, section I discusses the moral psychology that Socrates uses throughout the dialogue, paying special attention to his famous chariot image of the soul. According to the chariot image, the soul has three parts or aspects, namely the charioteer, symbolizing the soul's ability to reason, the white horse, symbolizing *thumos*, and the black horse, symbolizing the soul's desires (*epithumiai*). The other crucial element of Socrates' moral psychology is *erōs*, and Plato's conception of *erōs* in the *Phaedrus* is similar to the one at play in the *Gorgias* and *Symposium*, which I examined in chapter 1. *Erōs* is not a desire, feeling, or passion located in one part of the soul, but rather the attraction a whole soul experiences for that which appears best and most beautiful to her.[2] Using this tripartite conception of the soul, Socrates explains the nature of human vice. Much like the account of vice in the *Gorgias*, moral vice in the *Phaedrus* is rooted in ignorance of what is best and most beautiful, and this ignorance causes the soul to become disordered, disorganized, and unharmonized.

In section II, I examine the palinode's illustration of how one can respond virtuously to the *erōs* one experiences and, at the same time, cultivate genuine *sōphrosunē*. Although self-restraint is a necessary transitional step toward genuine *sōphrosunē* according to Socrates (as I argue in section II.1), it is different from genuine *sōphrosunē*, and so we must move past it to live a happier and more fully virtuous life. Far from the *mortal* moderation espoused by Lysias and criticized by Socrates, genuine *sōphrosunē* is bound up with the *divine*—in the context of an intimate relationship, *sōphrosunē* is expressed as the activity of treating the person one loves with "reverence" (*sebomai*) as an image of divine beauty. Another link between genuine *sōphrosunē* and divinity is that the person who possesses this virtue accurately sees himself as a limited, imperfect human being (thereby avoiding the *hubris* of those who live as if they are gods), but who also actively

2. Although the *Phaedrus* does not explicitly say so, Plato closely associates the good (*to agathon*) with the beautiful (*to kalon*). In the *Symposium*, Diotima implies that all good things are beautiful and vice versa (*Smp.* 204d–206a).

cultivates his own potential to become similar to the divine, a project that is best pursued in the context of a philosophical relationship and a philosophical life more broadly.

Finally, I shed further light on true *sōphrosunē* in section III by discussing three substantial benefits it brings oneself and others. In the context of an intimate relationship, treating the person one loves moderately involves helping him live a more virtuous, happy life in whatever way one can, a behavior that is the opposite of the harmful manipulation of the nonvirtuous lover depicted in the first two speeches. The "philosophic couple," as Socrates calls them, jointly engages in philosophical education and the cultivation of inner harmony, and their relationship is based on both erotic attraction and friendship (*philia*). Second, genuine *sōphrosunē* enhances self-knowledge; the person with this virtue accurately understands that his wisdom and virtue are imperfect and limited, and so he neither hubristically regards himself as greater than he is nor lives as if the fulfillment of his desires takes precedence above all else. Having an accurate view of his own limitations and imperfections, the person with true moderation instills the order and harmony of the divine in his own soul, and in this way becomes as much like the divine as is possible for humans. Third, *sōphrosunē* brings illuminating insight into divine Being, because the more similar to the divine we become through virtue, the more we share in the knowledge of the divine "in a way that is appropriate for us" (247d). I use the term "Being" to refer to the *Phaedrus*' discussion of the Forms in the palinode. Socrates refers to the Forms collectively as *ousia ontōs ousa* at 247c. Being is distinct from things that are in a state of "becoming" or constant flux. The Forms are the source of all determinate being and intelligibility that we find in the world (247c–e, 250b–c). In my view, Plato uses the term "Form" to refer to a wide range of related concepts throughout his corpus, but of particular importance for my purposes will be the discussion of the soul's relationship to Forms in the palinode. Socrates presents the soul's "vision" of the Forms as crucial for cultivating virtue and understanding reality so far as this is possible.

As I mentioned in the introduction and chapter 1, many point to the *Republic* or the *Philebus* as Plato's more mature, philosophically rigorous accounts of virtue or the good life. The *Republic,* for example, bases its account of virtue in an accompanying account of the soul, and it gives a thorough treatment of the relationship between each of the virtues. While the *Phaedrus* has much in common with the *Republic* regarding virtue and the soul, it explores these topics using a significantly different approach, especially in the heavily mythological, poetic, image-laden palinode speech. Scholars generally do not look to the *Phaedrus* as one of Plato's key reflections on virtue in general or on *sōphrosunē* in particular. It is widely acknowledged that the *Republic* contains a strong account of *sōphrosunē.* There Socrates uses the city-soul analogy and a tripartite conception of the soul to define it as "the friendship and accord" of the three parts of the soul, which comes about "when the ruling part and the two ruled parts [*thumos* and the desiring part] are of the single opinion that the calculating part ought to rule and don't raise faction against it" (442c–d). *Sōphrosunē* is the primary topic of the *Charmides*, a dialogue that spells out and offers a critical, nuanced reflection on six common ways that classical Greeks conceived of this virtue. The *Charmides* apparently ends in *aporia* and does not explicitly provide a final definition of the term, as Socrates refutes all six definitions offered by Charmides and Critias.[3] In my view, the *Phaedrus* also contains a substantial reflection on *sōphrosunē* and the virtuous life more broadly, offering a rich and relevant account of this virtue. In addition to being a strong account of *sōphrosunē* taken on its own, it is perfectly fitting for souls such as Phaedrus who are in a position to begin cultivating this virtue.

I. Moral Psychology, Ignorance, and Vice

As is the case with the *Gorgias*, the *Phaedrus*' insights about moral psychology are crucial for understanding its investigation of virtue. Socrates' famous chariot image is the primary means he uses for reflecting on three main parts of the soul, but he claims that this image describes only what the soul is "like," not what it truly is, since the latter would take a god and a long time to complete (246a). Section I.1 examines the important features of the charioteer, the white horse, and the black horse, which symbolize the soul's ability to reason, its *thumos*, and its nonrational desires (*epithumiai*), respectively. For Plato, these are the parts of the soul that are most relevant to moral life, since they all influence or at least factor into our decision-making, the formation of our values, and the habits we adopt. Our decisions, habits, and values in turn affect the moral structure of our soul insofar as these three parts can be in painful conflict with one another or in harmony.

3. Please see note 19 in the introduction for more on the *Charmides*.

Then, I examine the nature of *erōs* according to the *Phaedrus*. I argue that *erōs* is the attraction a whole soul experiences for that which appears best and most beautiful to it. Further, the *erōs* we experience can be handled well or poorly, and it can also be redirected toward different goods through guidance from others and education. In section I.2, I look closely at the *Phaedrus*' comments on the vicious and disordered soul. Without horses that are regimented and subordinated to the charioteer, the latter cannot perform its proper functions or accurately grasp what is, in reality, best and most beautiful. In a soul that lacks harmony, reason is confused and its "vision" obscured by the undisciplined desires, which leads to morally bad decisions and habits, and an even more disordered and unharmonized soul.

I.1. Moral Psychology

Since this chapter primarily focuses on Socrates' palinode speech, I will make some brief remarks about my approach to interpreting it. Importantly, my interpretive approach to the palinode is guided by important ideas from the second half of the *Phaedrus*. The palinode is not a story that is meant to justify certain rules of behavior, nor should we passively accept it as a literal revelation of truth. Otherwise, the palinode may act as a "cicadas' song" (259a) that could lull us into a dogmatic slumber. Philosophical inquiry is critical and dialectical in that it involves independently examining the speeches and arguments of others, as the discussion of dialectic (265d–266d) and the critique of writing (274c–278b) suggest to us (I will return to the critique of writing in section II.2), and we should adopt this philosophical attitude toward the palinode as well.[4] The images and the story that Socrates uses to make important points also have limitations, and we need to examine them through a critical lens. By doing so, we engage in the process of learning and seeing the truth for ourselves. I take it that the palinode's *muthos* about the gods, the soul as a winged chariot, the soul's activities before birth and after death, and other such aspects of Socrates' palinode should be understood as making natural (and not supernatural) points about the soul, virtue and vice, erotic relationships, self-knowledge, and the nature of reality. If we understand the palinode from this perspective, it can serve as a speech that "bears seeds," as Socrates says at the end of the dialogue, since it will live and develop in the souls of those who receive it critically.

4. Socrates claims to be a "lover" (*erastēs*) of dialectic at 266b, indicating that dialectical skill and training are essential for the philosopher.

By "cutting up" the palinode "form by form according to its natural joints" (265e), we uncover its most valuable insights about virtue.

The moral psychological framework that Socrates works with in his palinode is important for understanding the nature of self-restraint and why it is a step toward genuine *sōphrosunē.* Plato's famous image of the soul as a charioteer and a pair of horses allows for an illuminating exploration of the parts of the soul most relevant to moral life.[5] Importantly, though, Socrates is clear that the chariot image describes only what the soul is "like": "But we still need to discuss her [the soul's] form [*tēs ideas*]. It would take a god and a long time to examine in every detail what kind of thing the form is, but human beings in a shorter amount of time can describe what she is like. So, let's take this route. Let us liken [*eoiketō*] the soul to the innate power of a winged team of horses and a charioteer" (*Phdr.* 246a). It is extremely difficult for humans to have a complete, exhaustive understanding of the soul for several reasons. First, Socrates' contrast between the gods' abilities and our own highlights that our mental powers are limited, and our limitations become all the more apparent when we try to understand a subject as difficult as the soul. Second, the soul is unlike anything else in our experience insofar as we cannot perceive it through the senses, and it is a self-mover.[6] Because it is so dissimilar to anything else we experience, it is difficult to conceive of it without using images or metaphors. Third, knowledge of the soul's nature is a type of self-knowledge—since we *are* souls—which means that gaining this type of knowledge requires a difficult self-reflexive examination.

Socrates says in the passage above that he is discussing the soul's "form" (*tēs ideas*). In this context, he uses this term to mean the nature of the whole soul—that is, its qualities, what "kind of thing" it is, and so on. Later, though, at 253c–d he describes each of the three members of the chariot (the charioteer and each horse) using a similar term, *eidos*, which can be translated as "parts" or "forms" of the soul. Hence, the three important figures of the chariot symbolize three different parts of the soul

5. Interestingly, Socrates calls his whole description of erotic experience in the palinode an "image": "In some way, though I can't say exactly how, we offered an image of erotic experience and perhaps touched upon a truth in some instances and in others were wide of the mark, blending together a not totally unpersuasive account in a playful way—but also in a measured way and with due reverence—in a mythic hymn to your master and mine, Phaedrus, to Eros, the guardian of beautiful boys" (*Phdr.* 265b–c).

6. At the very beginning of the palinode, Socrates argues that the soul is an immortal self-mover (245c–246a).

(throughout my analysis, I use the terms "part" and "aspects" of the soul interchangeably). Socrates does not mean for the chariot image to fully represent every conceivable facet of the human soul. Rather, he focuses on the parts of it that are most relevant to his current discussion with Phaedrus, namely the parts of our mind that we must attend to and cultivate to become virtuous.[7] Because of the difficulties associated with understanding the soul, Socrates' palinode uses images from Greek religion and culture that Phaedrus is familiar with to create a "story" (*tou muthou*) (253c) about the soul that can have tremendous ethical and pedagogical value. Through this symbolic myth, he accessibly conveys insights about the structure of the human mind, especially regarding its aspects that are most important for understanding virtue, internal strife, and internal harmony.

I use the term "reason" for the part of the soul that the charioteer symbolizes, because Socrates associates the charioteer with the activity of "discursive thinking" (*dianoia*) at 247d and 249c–d and with "reasoning" (*logismō*) at 249c and 256a.[8] Socrates highlights two of the charioteer's primary abilities. First, it can apprehend the structure of reality, which Socrates symbolically dramatizes in his myth of the human soul's activity before becoming embodied. Human souls attempt to follow the gods on the journey to view Forms or "Being" (also called "the Plain of Truth," 248b): "But of the other souls, one follows a god very well and patterns herself after him, raising up the head of her charioteer to peer upon the place outside

7. In *Republic* IV, Plato suggests that the tripartite conception of the soul he uses in that context, which is very similar to the chariot image in the *Phaedrus*, may not cover every facet of the human soul. Socrates remarks that there might be "some other parts in between" the reasoning, thymotic, and desiring parts of the soul (443c–e). He also says that the tripartite conception of the soul does not give us a "precise grasp of it," and that there is "another longer and further road leading to it" (*R.* 435c–d), just as he says in the *Phaedrus* that it would "take a god and a long time to examine in every detail" (*R.* 246a) what the soul is. However, it is at least clear that the tripartite view of the soul helps us to gain working definitions of the virtues in *Republic* IV (Socrates says that he has "spied out" the virtues "at least sufficiently to form some opinion" [*R.* 432b]). Plato's tripartition highlights three core aspects of the human mind that are intimately connected to moral life.

8. Daniel Werner (2012) expresses the most common interpretation of what parts of the soul the charioteer and two horses symbolize: "The psychological image here generally corresponds to what we find in the *Republic*, namely, the tripartition of the human soul into rational, spirited, and appetitive parts" (59). While we should not import every detail of the *Republic*'s moral psychology into that of the *Phaedrus*, I agree that these are the three parts of the soul symbolized by the chariot image.

heaven, and she is carried around with the gods in the revolving motion, but even so, this soul gets confused by the horses and is scarcely able to gaze upon the things that are. Another soul, harassed by the horses, rises and falls, seeing some things and not seeing others" (248a). Some human souls can gain a fuller vision of the Forms than others (the cause of this is unclear), but all human souls "leave the sight of Being unfulfilled" (248b). The human charioteer is "weighed down" by the black horse (247b), which inhibits its ability to see the Forms and guide the chariot well.[9] The interrelations between the parts of the soul in this passage also applies to embodied human life; the horses' interference with the charioteer symbolizes how our understanding of reality can be obscured by vicious, misguided, inordinate desire, a topic I will return to in section III.3. The gods, on the other hand, view the Forms easily, since their chariots are "well-balanced and obedient to the rein," which means they make the "steep climb of heaven's vault" without any problems (247a–b). The human charioteer bears resemblance to the gods in that both drive teams of horses (though the gods can detach from their horses by putting them in a manger to feed, 247e) and both gaze upon real Being. It is difficult to tell if the charioteer *is* divine, since Socrates never says so explicitly, but it is *at least* the part of the human soul that most resembles the divine. Socrates claims that both the gods and human souls think discursively, and through this thinking the human soul can understand the divine and eternal Forms "in a way that is appropriate" for humans (247d), which may suggest that the charioteer is divine.[10]

---

9. Socrates' myth might suggest that *thumos* and *epithumia* are parts of the soul even without a body, since in the myth they are with the chariot even before the human soul becomes embodied, but it could also be the case that Socrates' purpose is not to give a serious account of the differences between embodied and disembodied souls. Indeed, I take it that Socrates' primary focus is the embodied soul, and he is not aiming to accurately describe a disembodied soul in the palinode. A major example of Socrates' concern for the embodied soul is his description of the very bodily experience of feeling sexual attraction toward another person and the various ways this experience can cause the parts of the soul to interact with each other (253e–255a).
In *Republic* X, Socrates compares the soul to the sea-god Glaucus, implying the possibility that *thumos* and the desiring part of the soul really belong to the body, not the soul (*R.* 611b–612a).

10. However, Socrates clearly draws a distinction between gods and human souls in the palinode: "On the nature of the soul, both in its human and divine forms, it is necessary first of all to consider the truth about what the soul experiences and what her activities are" (245c).

Second, the charioteer plays an important role in moral life. Reason can distinguish (or fail to distinguish) the difference between what is really good and what is only apparently good. The degree to which one's charioteer understands what is truly good and beautiful strongly influences her actions, decisions, and activities; the ends toward which she strives; and the way of life she chooses to pursue. Additionally, reason can relate to the other two parts of the soul in ways that either entail cooperative pursuit of a given end or inner conflict about what to do. Because of the unruly black horse, "chariot-driving must be difficult and irksome" (246a–b) for humans. Reason is most fit to rule the soul well, but it can be overpowered by the soul's desires. Only the white horse naturally cooperates with the charioteer, and these two can work together to control and train the black horse, a topic I explore in section II.1. For example, when the black horse urges the soul to make sexual advances on a beautiful person, the charioteer and the white horse can "resist" it "from a sense of shame and reason [*logou*]" (256a). Some souls' charioteers are better at fulfilling their knowing and leading functions than others, both before the soul is embodied and afterward—at 248a–b, for example, Socrates says that the charioteer's vice or badness (*kakia*) contributes to its inability to gain the same view of Being that the gods have. In any case, reason's capacity to understand what is truly good and beautiful, as well as its ability to control the other two parts of the soul, makes it the part that is most fit to lead the soul well, so long as it receives the proper education, guidance, and nourishment.

The white horse represents the soul's *thumos*, which the *Phaedrus* and the *Republic* (see especially *R.* 439e–440c) associate with anger, competitiveness, self-assertiveness, and the striving for honor or social recognition that comes from victory in the political realm, war, or contests.[11] As I mentioned in chapter 1, section I.1, the *Phaedrus*' moral psychology includes *thumos*, which makes its moral psychology significantly different from that of the *Gorgias*. In the *Phaedrus*, Socrates characterizes *thumos* as a natural ally of reason just as he does in the *Republic* (440a–b). Socrates highlights the benefits that *thumos* can bring to the soul:

> One of the horses, we said, was good, the other not, but we haven't discussed the excellence [*aretē*] of the good one or the vice

11. Jessica Moss (2005) defends the relevance of *thumos* in the *Gorgias* and the *Republic*, arguing that it is "central to Plato's ethical and psychological thought," since it is "indispensable to his conception of virtue" and his suggestions about the nature of shame (138).

> of the vicious one [*kakou kakia*]. We should do that now. Well, of the two, one stands in the position of greater beauty (i.e., on the right), in form erect and well-jointed, high-necked, hooked nose, white to behold, black-eyed, a lover of honor with a sense of moderation and shame [*timēs erastēs meta sōphrosunēs te kai aidous*] and a companion of true opinion, without need of the whip, ruled by command and word [*logō*] alone. (*Phdr.* 253d)

Along with the charioteer, the white horse makes the experience of shame possible, and it is crucial for helping the soul develop moderation through habitual self-restraint, as I will discuss in detail in section II. Socrates' remark that the white horse is "excellent" and the black horse is "vicious" should not be taken too literally—rather, as he explains later, *thumos* is especially helpful for cultivating virtue in the soul, while misguided *epithumia* (the black horse) is a major source of viciousness. The white horse is also a "companion of true opinion," which means that it aids the charioteer in carrying out an action it deems best when the black horse protests. Socrates mentions that the white horse is a "lover of honor," and at the end of the palinode he briefly discusses couples where both members lead "a more coarse way of life [than the philosophic life], one that loves honor and not wisdom" (256c). So, he acknowledges that it is possible to live in a way that allows *thumos* to have too much power in the soul, but he primarily focuses on the capacity of *thumos* to work alongside the charioteer for the betterment of the whole soul.

The black horse symbolizes the desiring part of the soul, or its many *epithumiai*. Presumably, this part of the soul includes all nonrational desires, such as those for wealth, property, food, and so on, but the desire for sexual pleasure is Socrates' primary focus in the palinode speech. In Socrates' myth, human souls in their pre-embodied lives struggle to follow the gods to the summit of heaven mainly because of the black horse: "The vicious horse [*ho tēs kakēs hippos*] is heavy and to the extent that it was not trained well it sinks earthward and weighs the charioteer down. At this point, the soul experiences extreme toil and struggle" (247b). The black horse is the part of the soul most associated with bodies or matter (it "sinks earthward"), probably because our desires are often for bodily objects and pleasures. This horse's lack of training inhibits the charioteer's ability to gain a fuller view of Being, and in this way it causes "extreme toil and struggle." Importantly, Socrates explicitly calls the black horse hubristic and emphasizes its natural disobedience: "But the other is crooked, bulky, poorly slung together, stiff-necked, thick-necked, snub-nosed, black-skinned, cloudy-eyed, hot-blooded, a companion of wantonness [*hubreōs*] and insolences, shaggy about the ears, obtuse, and scarcely obedient to whip or goad" (253e). The black horse can fuel an individual's hubristic behavior, since it is inclined to pursue excessive pleasure or pleasure that would be inappropriate in a given situation. Instead of being "obedient" to the charioteer's commands about what to do, the untrained black horse often fights against the charioteer.

Socrates gives more details about the black horse's qualities by giving a vivid example of what the soul experiences when it is sexually attracted to a beautiful person. When a lover's soul sees his beloved, his black horse "recalls the delight of sex." It then attempts to "force" the charioteer and white horse (and, in effect, the individual of which they are parts) to initiate sex:

> Therefore, whenever the charioteer beholds the eyes of his beloved—the sensation having thoroughly warmed the whole soul—and he begins to feel a tickling and a desire for the goad, the obedient horse, constrained as always by a sense of shame restrains itself [*aei te kai tote aidoi biazomenos eauton katechei*] from jumping upon the darling boy. But the other horse no longer minds the charioteer's goad or the whip as it bounds up and is carried along by force. It causes every kind of difficulty for its yoked partner and for the charioteer, forcing them to move toward the darling boy and to recall the delight of sex. (253e–254a)

The soul's *epithumia* for sexual pleasure becomes automatically inflamed at the sight of its beloved. The black horse is only slightly responsive to the restraint imposed by the charioteer and the white horse, and it persistently disagrees with them. Meanwhile, *thumos* becomes active and allies with reason in the attempt to restrain *epithumia,* giving rise to the experience of shame. Such inner conflict may cause an individual to feel anger toward his unruly desires. As Socrates puts it in *Republic* IV, "Anger sometimes makes war against the desires as one thing against something else" (*R.* 440a). If a given individual is in the habit of caving in to his *epithumia*, it is more likely that his *epithumia* will win the internal conflict. Later, Socrates provides details about how the charioteer and white horse can manage the black horse through habitual training, which I will discuss in section II.1.

Finally, *erōs* plays a key role in the moral psychology of the *Phaedrus*, just as it does in the *Gorgias*. Even though the theme of *erōs* is obviously a primary focus and ubiquitous theme of the *Phaedrus*, the conception of *erōs* presented over the course of the dialogue is very similar to that of the *Gorgias*. Throughout the *Phaedrus*, *erōs* is the attraction that the soul experiences for that which it regards as best and most beautiful. *Erōs* is a leader of the soul in that it compels us to pursue whatever appears to us as especially good and beautiful. We experience *erōs* toward those bodies we find particularly beautiful from a sexual perspective, but also toward nonhuman goods such as wealth, pleasure, fame, honor, or wisdom. The *Phaedrus* is not particularly clear about how many people or goods we can direct our *erōs* toward at one time, but it is probably a small number. As I discussed in chapters 1 and 2, Socrates says in the *Gorgias* that both he and Callicles love one person and one other type of good—Callicles loves a young man named Demos and the people of Athens, while Socrates loves Alcibiades and philosophy (481d). After Lysias' speech criticized all *erōs* as a harmful type of madness, Socrates' palinode responds that not all madness is bad, and that four types are actually gifts from the divine. When describing the second type of madness in the palinode, "mystical initiation ascribed to Dionysos" (265b), Socrates says that those who are "mad and possessed in the right way" bring great benefits to both themselves and others (244e–245a). This statement also applies to the fourth kind of madness, *erōs,* especially when we handle it in a virtuous manner. Depending on the degree to which we possess wisdom, we can experience *erōs* toward things that are truly good and beautiful, which will promote well-being for ourselves and others. Or, we can experience *erōs* toward people or things that are not as good as they appear, in which case *erōs* can often cause harm to ourselves and others, as I showed in chapter 3 (section II.1).

When handled well, *erōs* can lead us toward higher types of beauty and goodness. The initial attraction we feel toward physical beauty can act as a catalyst that begins a process of recognizing higher kinds of beauty and goodness. Socrates says that the source of all beauty is divine Beauty itself along with the other Forms, which are more lovable (or worthy of love) than anything else:

> And when we came here, we grasped [beauty] shining most clearly through the clearest of our senses, because sight is the sharpest of our physical senses. But thought [*hē phronēsis*] is not seen by it—oh, what awe-inspiring loves [*erōtas*] sight would provide if it could provide just as clear an image, as beauty does, of

> thought itself or of other lovely forms [*talla hosa erasta*]. But, as it is, beauty alone has this distinction to be naturally the most clearly visible and the most lovely [*erasmiōtaton*]. (*Phdr.* 250d–e)

Beginning with the beauty of the Forms' earthly images, some souls eventually begin to grasp and love the higher, divine, invisible beauty of the Forms themselves. Beauty is special among the Forms because its earthly images are so visible and striking. If images of beauty "remind" the soul (albeit vaguely) of divine beauty, it begins to experience *erōs* for divine beauty:

> Certainly, then, everything about our fourth madness is here: when someone looks upon earthly beauty and is reminded of the true [*alēthous*] beauty, he acquires wings; and when he tries those wings, eager but unable to take flight like a bird looking upward and he shows no concern for things below, there are reasons to think him touched with madness. Both for the person who has this madness and for the one who shares in it, this is the very best of all the divine possessions, and it comes from the best sources; and the lover hit with this madness is called a lover of beautiful people and beautiful things. (*Phdr.* 249d–e)

The more love we experience for the divine beauty and the other Forms, the less "concern" we have for lower, conventional goods "below." The philosophic soul described in this passage still loves "beautiful people and beautiful things"—that is, those that are most similar to divine beauty—but restlessly seeks to understand or somehow attain true beauty so far as is humanly possible.[12] Striving for divine beauty through the practice of philosophy can lead to the process of "regrowing" the soul's "wings," which symbolizes a radical change in one's way of life and moral character, as I explain below in sections II and III.

I.2. Ignorance and Vice

Socrates suggests that knowledge of the Forms is necessary to understand what is truly good, beautiful, just, and moderate, and this is precisely

12. Charles Griswold (1986) rightly argues that an important part of the lover's philosophical development and self-understanding is his realization that "what he really wants" is not the image of beauty in the beloved but beauty itself, and that this results from the recollection of divine beauty he experiences when seeing the beloved (119).

the knowledge that the vicious person lacks. So, an analysis of Socrates' discussion of the Forms in the *Phaedrus* will shed light on its account of vice. His discussion of the Forms is also relevant for many other ideas in the text that I will address below. The gods and the Forms are depicted as separate things in the context of Socrates' myth, but it is possible that the gods and the Forms are really one and the same, and Socrates' myth depicts them as distinct for other reasons.[13] Hence, I use the term "divinity" in my analysis as a synonym for Being or the Forms. "Being" is the primary term Socrates uses for the collection of all of the Forms (*Phdr.* 247b), and when speaking mythologically, he also refers to them as the "Plain of Truth" (248b). Being is "colorless, shapeless, and untouchable, visible to the mind [*nō*] alone" (247c) in contrast with the ever-changing, material world of "becoming" (247d–e). As I will discuss further below, the Forms give things in the world their determinate qualities or *way* of being, and so they are the source of the world's structure. Unlike sensible objects, they are not in a state of constant change, but instead they provide the stability in the world that allows for knowledge. As Socrates puts it, they are "the source of all true knowledge" (*tēs alēthous epistēmēs genos*) (247c), and "a human being must understand what is said in reference to Form" (249b). Socrates' remarks about the Forms entail that there is a true structure of the nature of things that is accessible to humans through knowledge, which means that the better we understand them, the better we understand the true nature of reality, including the true nature of goodness, beauty, justice, moderation, and so on.

The *Phaedrus* discussion of the Forms is not as rigorous or detailed as those contained in other dialogues such as the *Parmenides* or the *Sophist*, but it establishes several important points that support Socrates' purposes in this context. His palinode gives a relatively brief yet rich description of them:

> None of the poets here on earth have ever sung the praises of this place beyond heaven, nor will any ever sing of it adequately. But the hymn goes like this—for we must have the courage

13. As I will argue in section III below, one reason that Socrates might depict the gods as separate from the Forms is so that he can make the gods appear anthropomorphic and therefore easier to depict as models for humans to emulate. Additionally, in a puzzling remark, Socrates claims that "For thought is always according to her capability through memory, near to those things [the Forms] and by this nearness a god is divine" (249c). If nearness to the Forms makes the gods divine, then Socrates appears to strongly suggest that the Forms are divine in this context.

> to speak the truth, especially when the true nature of things is our subject. This is the place of Being, the Being that truly is—colorless, shapeless, and untouchable, visible to the mind [*nō*] alone, the soul's pilot, and the source of true knowledge [*tēs alēthous epistēmēs genos*]. Just as a god's discursive thinking is nourished by the mind and unmixed knowledge, so is the thought of every soul nourished by what is appropriate for her to receive. When much time has passed and she looks upon Being, she feels adoration [*agapa*] and when contemplating the truth, she is easily nourished and feels joyous, until the revolving motion carries her around in full circle to the originating point. In this circuit, the soul looks upon Justice itself [*autēn dikaiosunēn*], and she looks upon Moderation [*sōphrosunēn*] and she looks upon Knowledge [*epistēmēn*], but not the knowledge where Becoming [*hē genesis*] resides, nor the knowledge which changes from object to object regarding things which down here we call Being. Rather, it is the knowledge of the Being which really is. (*Phdr.* 247c–e)

Regardless of how one might interpret the true nature or qualities of the Forms, a crucial point about them is that they are the stable source and measure of all goodness and beauty in the world. The three Forms Socrates names are justice, moderation, and knowledge, all of which are good things that humans strive for, and he adds that "beauty shone brightly in the midst of those visions" (250d). The Forms serve as the unchanging standard against which we can measure what is truly good, beautiful, just, moderate, and so on. Hence, they give our lives meaning as the source of everything that is worth striving for, and we fail to experience fulfillment when we ignore them. Because the Forms are "simple and unchanging" (250b), they could be known in a way that the ever-changing material world of "Becoming" cannot, but they are difficult for the limited human mind to comprehend.[14]

---

14. Socrates later remarks that humans have to both reason and draw on their sense experience to gain some sense of the Forms: "Only a soul which has seen the truth can enter into our human form: for a human being must understand what is said in reference to form, that which, going from a plurality of perceptions is drawn together by reasoning into a single essence. This process occurs by recollecting those things which our soul once saw when traveling in the company of a god, looking with contempt at those things which we now say exist, and lifting up its head to see what really is" (*Phdr.* 249b–c).

We have to search them out and try to attain mental glimpses of them (they are "visible to the mind alone"), and such glimpses give us a better understanding of "the true nature of things." They are more fundamental than we are in the sense that justice, moderation, beauty, and goodness are not merely fabricated notions of the human imagination; they are real sources of meaning and value that we have to seek, find, and live in accordance with. We can either encounter the Forms and use them as a guide for living well, or we can live completely blinded to them.

The *Phaedrus* is largely consistent with the *Gorgias*' suggestions that moral vice is caused by ignorance about what is truly good, but the *Phaedrus*' reflection on this issue occurs in a much different context. Socrates mostly discusses the root of moral imperfection through his myth of souls as they were before becoming embodied. First, Socrates cites ignorance, "confusion," and weakness as the reason why disembodied human souls cannot live the life of the gods, who encounter no problems when it comes to beholding the Forms. While the gods' horses effortlessly bring them above the rim of heaven to gain a full view of the Forms (247a–e), the souls who later become embodied humans can gain only a partial glimpse:

> But of the other souls, one follows a god very well and patterns herself after him, raising up the head of her charioteer to peer upon the place outside heaven, and she is carried around with the gods in a revolving motion, but even so, this soul gets confused [*thoruboumenē*] by the horses and is scarcely able to gaze upon the things that are. Another soul, harassed by the horses, rises and falls, seeing some things and not seeing others. But all of the remaining souls seek the upward path and are eager to follow but they lack the means and are carried around below the surface, trampling each other and getting smashed about, each one trying to get in front of the other. Confusion [*thorubos*] and rivalry and great quantities of sweat are the result, some souls being maimed because of the charioteers' wrongdoing, while other souls have their wings shattered. In spite of this great effort, all souls, every one of them, leave the sight of Being unfulfilled, and, once departed, feed on the food of conjecture [*doxastē*]. (248a–b)

The human soul's horses, especially the black horse, prevent it from gaining the full vision of reality that the gods have. Human souls "lack the means" to live the life of the gods, try as they might, though some gain a fuller "vision" of Being than others. Nonetheless, all of them "leave the sight of Being unfulfilled," and therefore must "feed on the food of conjecture [*doxastē*]," meaning that they lack the knowledge about the nature of reality that the gods possess.

So, just as ignorance of what is truly good causes moral imperfection in Socrates' myth of the soul before it becomes embodied, so also is such ignorance the root of vice in its earthly life. The disembodied souls' lack of knowledge about the Forms, especially the three Socrates mentions explicitly—"Justice" (*dikaiosunēn*), "Moderation" (*sōphrosunēn*), and "Knowledge" (*epistēmēn*) (247d)—causes their moral imperfection (i.e., their lack of justice and moderation) and lack of wisdom. They are then born into a human body in a similar state of ignorance and moral imperfection: "But whenever a soul cannot see the truth and is thus unable to follow the path, and by some misfortune gets weighed down and burdened by forgetfulness and wrongdoing [*lēthēs te kai kakias*], in her heaviness sheds her feathers and falls to earth" (248c). Given these details, Socrates' myth of the soul's pre-embodied life represents the view that human souls are born in a state of ignorance about the true nature of reality, especially with regard to what is truly good, just, beautiful, moderate, and so on, and therefore these truths must be learned or "recollected" through philosophical education. If a soul remains in ignorance about what is truly good, it will pursue what falsely appears to it as best (such as pleasure, wealth, and so on) and therefore inevitably develop the vicious characteristics that result from a life spent solely in pursuit of such goods.

Further, Socrates' palinode cites the body as a major source of the limitations that our souls have to overcome if we want to lead a better and happier life on earth. The body inhibits the soul's capacity to understand important matters such as goodness, beauty, and moderation, but some are able to eventually conquer these obstacles. Although Socrates does not explicitly say what it is about the body that adds to the soul's struggle to understand reality, we might reasonably assume that he is referring to the constant care and maintenance that a body requires, the disturbances from pain, illness, or fatigue to which it is prone, or the ways it prevents us from thinking for a long period of time (Socrates makes this point in the *Phaedo* at 65c). In any case, the body makes the "vision" of Being difficult to regain:

> Formerly, however, it was possible to look upon beauty [*kallos*] in its radiance when in a blessed chorus-dance we in Zeus'

> entourage, and others in the company of other gods, witnessed a blest [*eudaimoni*] sight and spectacle and we were initiated into what it is lawful to call the most blest of the mysteries. Celebrating these inspired rites, we were whole and untouched by those evils [*kakōn*] which lay in wait for us later. Being fully initiated and looking upon whole, simple, unchanging, and blessed visions in pure light, we were ourselves pure [*katharoi ontes*] and unmarked by what we now carry around and call a body, a thing which imprisons us like an oyster shell. (*Phdr.* 250b–c)

Socrates uses the metaphor of "purity" to describe the difference between souls who are ignorant of what is truly good or beautiful and those who have wisdom and the rest of the virtues. Embodied humans can "purify" their souls of their ignorance and moral imperfections through the cultivation of virtue and the practice of philosophy, since these activities allow us to gain as much insight as possible into the Forms, or sources of Being, as I will discuss further below. With a better understanding of what is truly good and beautiful, souls recognize that the lower, conventional goods are not as valuable as they once appeared, and they now care about them to the appropriate degree. In so doing, they avoid the overvaluing of conventional goods such as pleasure, wealth, and honor that leads to vicious strife with others who also wrongly think that these are the highest goods in life.

Although all humans are born in a state of ignorance, Socrates is clear that it is easier for some people to purify themselves by learning about and cultivating internal beauty through the virtues. Souls who "witnessed Being the most in heaven" before their embodiment (members of "Zeus' entourage," 252e)—who are later "planted into the seed of someone who will become a lover of wisdom, or a lover of beauty, or of something musical and erotic" (248d)—are more easily "reminded" of the Forms than those who did not and those who were born into bad circumstances on earth. He states: "But it is not easy for every soul from her earthly perspective to recall those distant things, especially for those souls which saw them briefly or had bad luck when falling here, so that when they were turned toward injustice [*to adikon trapomenai*] by some company or other here they naturally forgot the sacred things they had seen there. To be sure, few souls are left for whom that memory is sufficient" (250a). Injustice and the rest of vice cloud or inhibit the soul's ability to have the pivotal experience of mentally glimpsing divine beauty at the sight of its earthly image, an experience that can lead us toward genuine virtue, as I discuss in section II. Owing either to their inborn inclinations, the bad influence of their environments, or a combination of the two, many souls will never be inspired by earthly beauty to pursue a better understanding of Beauty itself or to cultivate it in their own souls by living philosophically.

The palinode also returns to the first two speeches' theme of *hubris*, arguing that this quality results from a lack of understanding about the true nature of goodness, beauty, and how we should live in order to cultivate inner goodness and beauty. Socrates' concept of *hubris* is consistent in his first and second speeches, even if his conception of its opposite, *sōphrosunē*, is very different in each speech. When someone regards sexual pleasure as the best thing he can achieve and acts accordingly, Socrates calls this attitude hubristic:

> Thus, the person who has been corrupted or who is not a recent initiate is not conveyed quickly to beauty itself, that is, he is not carried from here to there quickly. When looking at beauty's namesake here, such a person fails to experience true reverence [*sebetai*] as he gazes but yields to pleasure and tries to mount and to spawn children according to the law of a four-footed animal. In company with wantonness [*hubrei*], he shows no fear or shame [*ou dedoiken oud' aischunetai*] as he pursues unnatural pleasure. (250e–251a)

The hubristic soul is not led toward true beauty and goodness due to its ignorance and imperfection, it and feels no "fear or shame" in the presence of the beloved, a reaction that would prevent the soul from being dominated by its desires and seeking to satisfy them no matter what. Socrates calls the black horse hubristic at 254e, and so the soul who is dominated by its black horse is likewise hubristic. Socrates later contrasts the hubristic lover with the philosophic soul's reaction to physical beauty. The experience of "reverence" at the sight of beauty is the key difference between the two types of soul, a topic that I return to in section II.

In my view, the *Phaedrus*' moral psychology and its account of vice can aid our personal efforts to understand (and perhaps alter) our own motivations and the aspects of our minds that influence our decision-making, form our habits, and shape our moral character. Socrates' schema for the morally relevant aspects of the soul can make sense of the painful inner strife or conflict we might experience in our daily lives. If we tend to unreflectively follow our impulses or emotions, the sort of self-cultivation through rehabituation that

Socrates talks about could lead to a deeper sense of inner harmony and a happier life. In addition, Socrates' view of vice as rooted in ignorance could significantly improve interpersonal life, especially when it comes to dealing with those who cause harm to us or to anyone we care about. Even if one is not convinced that Socrates' understanding correctly explains the root of *all* vicious actions (such as radical acts of evil), experience shows us that, at the very least, it applies to a large number of more commonplace acts of injustice. If we adopt the view that humans cannot help but pursue what we *think* is best, yet we so often fail to understand what is *actually* best for ourselves and others, then we are more likely to forgive and empathize with one another. From this perspective, those who commit vicious deeds need punishment that is helpful and educational more than anything else. As I discussed in chapter 1, that is why Socrates argues that punishments given by a justice system should aim for rehabilitation rather than revenge. In a similar way, interpreting vicious action as a misguided pursuit of the good could contribute to healing the many harmful social divisions we create between ourselves and perceived enemies.

II. Genuine *Sōphrosunē*

In section II.1, I argue that habitual self-restraint, dramatized by Socrates in his palinode by way of his chariot image for the soul, is a practice that is distinct from genuine *sōphrosunē* but that nonetheless helps one transition toward it. The philosophically inclined soul temporarily feels "reverence" (*sebomai*) at the sight of his beloved, who is an image of divine beauty. This initial experience of reverence inspires him to give order and harmony to his soul by rehabituating the black horse. Habitual self-restraint firmly establishes the charioteer as the leader of the soul, helps one to avoid the *hubris* that arises from living with a soul led by its black horse, and prepares the way for internal harmony. In section II.2, I argue that, in contrast to the mortal moderation depicted in the first two speeches, Socrates depicts genuine *sōphrosunē* as a characteristic that is closely tied to the divine. In the ideal intimate relationship, *sōphrosunē* is expressed by consistently treating the person one loves with reverence—the moderate, harmonized soul always supports the beloved's efforts to become a wiser, more virtuous, and happier person. Moreover, the genuinely moderate person clearly sees how he stands in relation to divine perfection. That is, he accurately regards himself as an imperfect, limited human, unlike the hubristic and vicious person who thinks he knows more than he does and lives as if the fulfillment of his own desires is the only thing that matters. At the same time, the person with genuine *sōphrosunē* sees himself as something capable of becoming more like the divine through virtuous and philosophical activity, and therefore earnestly devotes himself to this project over the course of an entire life.

II.1. Self-Restraint as a Transition to Genuine *Sōphrosunē*

Although every soul is at least susceptible to experiencing *erōs*, Socrates is clear that only the philosopher (or the potential philosopher) is "reminded" of divine beauty when he perceives the beauty of another person. This recollection occurs because the beauty of the person for whom the philosophic soul experiences *erōs* is an "image" of divine beauty:

> Whenever [a few souls] behold an image [*homoiōma*] of the things there, they are thoroughly startled and they are no longer themselves and they do not recognize the sensation that they are having because they cannot perceive it sufficiently [*mē hikanōs diaisthanesthai*]. There is no shine in the images here on earth of justice [*dikaiosunēs*] and moderation [*sōphrosunēs*] and the other things honorable for souls, but through the dim organs of the senses a few people, and they with difficulty, approach these images [*eikonas*] and behold the original of the thing imaged. (*Phdr.* 250a–b)

Alongside the erotic love they feel for their beloveds, philosophic souls are suddenly "startled" by the presence of something unusually beautiful that a beloved calls to their minds, an experience that takes them out of their normal perspective (they are "no longer themselves").

Earthly "images" of beauty stand out among earthly images of other Forms, because the perception of physical beauty through the senses strikes the soul more powerfully than other images. In other words, through a physical perception of beauty, invisible divine beauty becomes temporarily present (though in a way that is difficult to comprehend) to the minds of souls who are most fit for the philosophical life.

The philosophic lover's vague sense of something divine, which it struggles to understand, fills it with "fear" and "reverence." Importantly, this experience helps the philosophic lover see the beloved's beauty as connected with divine beauty in some way: "But the recent initiate, someone who has amply observed things from the past realm, at first shudders and feels something of those old terrors come over him [*hupēlthen auton deimatōn*] when he sees a god-like [*theoeides*] face or any part of the body which is a good imitation of beauty. Later, looking more, he feels reverence [*sebetai*] as if he were before a god" (251a). The more the lover looks at the beloved, the more he understands that the beloved's beauty stems from the source of all beauty, namely the divine Form of Beauty. He "feels reverence" for divine beauty, and he is prompted to treat his "godlike" beloved as a god deserves to be treated. By contrast, "the person who has been corrupted or who is not a recent initiate is not conveyed quickly to beauty itself, that is, he is not carried from here to there quickly" (250e), and therefore sees the beloved's beauty only as a means for his own erotic satisfaction. The corrupted person does anything he can to have sex with a person for whom he feels erotic love, failing to "experience true reverence as he gazes," and instead he "yields to pleasure" (250e). In sum, the philosophic soul has a special potentiality in relation to physical beauty, since he or she has the capacity to recognize and feel reverence for divine beauty in addition to erotic attraction.[15]

If the philosophic lover decides to treat his beloved in a reverential way thanks to the "reminder" of divine beauty, then he will begin the process of habitually restraining and ruling over his sexual desire so as to prevent it from dictating how he treats his beloved. When the philosophical soul experiences reverence for divine beauty at the sight of the beloved's beauty, in addition to the initial flash of reverence and fear or awe, he also experiences "shame" (*aischos*), a term that is used in the *Phaedrus* in a way that is similar to the way it is used in the *Gorgias*. The experience of shame aids the project of reining in our nonrational desires, as I discussed in chapter 2. Before the philosophic soul has begun the process of self-restraint as a transition to *sōphrosunē,* the sight of the beloved causes a mixture of inner experiences, including sexual desire (symbolized by the black horse's excitement), fear, astonishment, reverence, and shame. He must then decide how to handle this confusing and distressing combination of experiences:

15. John Ferrari (1987), in his classic book on the *Phaedrus*, aptly describes the philosophic soul's special reaction to the sight of physical beauty: "A person's beauty naturally prompts you to care, not just about their beauty, but about them-as-beautiful. [. . .] The philosophic character, prompted by the boy's beauty to think of him as lovable, cannot (we shall see) justify loving him on the grounds of his physical beauty alone, nor on any grounds short of the possibility of jointly pursuing with him the worthiest kind of human life" (147).

> At the beginning, the [charioteer and white horse] resist feeling forced to engage in terrible and unlawful acts, but finally when they find no end to this vice they follow along passively, both of them yielding and agreeing to do whatever is commanded. They approach the boy and see the darling's face, flashing like a lightning bolt. With this sight the charioteer's memory is carried toward the essence of the beautiful [*tēn tou kallous phusin*], and once again he sees beauty itself standing alongside moderation [*sōphrosunēs*] on a holy pedestal. Overcome with fear and reverence [*edeise te kai sephtheisa*] by the sight, the charioteer's memory recoils on its back and is compelled simultaneously to pull back on the reins with such violence that both horses naturally sit on their haunches, one willingly because it does not resist, but the wanton one [*hubristēn*] is extremely unwilling. When both withdraw some distance from the boy, one from a sense of shame and astonishment [*aischunēs te kai thambous*] bathes the entire soul with sweat; the other, having scarcely regained its breath and no longer feeling pain from the bit and the fall, starts in a fury to abuse and to curse the charioteer and its yoke-mate excessively for cowardice and lack of manliness. (254b–d)

Along with "fear and reverence," the sense of "shame and astonishment" felt by the charioteer and the white horse (reason and *thumos*) rein in the black horse, because they team up together to "pull back on the reins" and prevent the lover's soul from acting on its sexual desire, even as the black horse hubristically "curses" the other two. This symbolic dramatization of the soul's inner conflict illustrates that the philosophically inclined lover can either decide to let the black horse win, so to speak, by pursuing sex with the beloved at any cost, or he can decide to habitually restrain his sexual desire until he firmly rules over it and no longer feels compelled by it to have sex with the beloved at inappropriate times.

Through habitual self-restraint, the philosophic lover can eventually develop genuine *sōphrosunē*, a characteristic I explore more fully in the next section (II.2). For now, I focus on Socrates' vivid description of how habitual self-restraint leads to agreement between all three aspects of the soul such that one no longer needs to restrain oneself. At 253c–255a, Socrates uses the chariot image to illustrate how we can properly habituate the soul's sexual desire so that it never become the ruler of the soul. To avoid the hubristic mistakes of the nonvirtuous lover, Socrates claims that the charioteer, with the aid of the white horse, must habitually discipline and train the black horse to obey the charioteer's commands, which will eventually cause the black horse to "cease its wanton excess [*tēs hubreōs*]" (254e). Excessive desires "enable viciousness to enter the soul," and therefore they must be "enslaved" (256b) by reason over and over again until all parts of the soul harmonize:

> Forcing them against their will to advance again, the black horse steps back, but barely, as they plead to put off the advance for a time. But when that agreed-upon time is up and the other two pretend to have forgotten, it reminds them both: forcing, snarling, dragging, it makes them approach the darling again to deliver the same words, and when they are near, it pulls forward, head down, tail straight back, biting on the bit, shameless [*anaideias*]. Even more resentful than before, the charioteer falls back as if recoiling from a starting gate, still more violently yanking back on the bit in the wanton horse's [*tou hubristou hippou*] mouth. Bloodying its abusive tongue and jaws, he presses the legs and haunches of the horse hard upon the ground in pain. Only when it has suffered this same treatment repeatedly does the despicable creature cease its wanton excess [*tēs hubreōs*]. Humbled, in the end it follows the charioteer's plan [*tē tou hēniochou pronoia*], and when it sees the beautiful boy it is devastated by fear [*phobōi diollutai*]. Then at last it actually happens that the lover's soul follows the darling with awe and a sense of shame [*aidoumenēn te kai dediuian*]. (254d–255a)

The philosophic lover rules his desire so that it never leads him to have sex with his beloved in a way that could be harmful or exploitative (254e–255c).[16]

---

16. See footnote 85 of Scully's (2003) translation of *Phaedrus* at 255b, where he explains why the term *homilia* here can be translated as either "social intercourse" or sexual intercourse. I agree with Scully's suggestion that Plato deliberately leaves the meaning of the term ambiguous. At 255e–256a, Socrates describes what the souls of each person in the philosophic couple experience (especially what their horses do) when they lie down beside each other. Each person has a "desire to see" the other, and he says that they touch and kiss one another. On the other hand, he says that the philosophic couple "resist" the impulse of their black horses in this situation (256a). He also claims that lovers of honor have sex with one another "perhaps when drunk or in some other careless hour," and they therefore fall short of the moral perfection of the philosophic couple (256c–d). In any case, I think it is ultimately unclear whether the homosexual

After forcefully restraining sexual desire often enough, his sexual desire begins to decrease in intensity and does not overstep reason's "plan" (*pronoia*, 254e) about when it is best to have sex, who it is best to have sex with, how often, and so on. Habitual self-restraint thus causes his desires to always remain subordinate to his reason's decisions regarding what is best. In this way, habitual self-restraint is a "prerequisite" for genuine *sōphrosunē*, just as learning rhetorical techniques is a prerequisite for learning the true art of rhetoric (268a–269c). Unlike mortal moderation, the habitual self-restraint described in this passage is not the practice of restraining some desires in the present so others can be satisfied in the future—instead, self-restraint aims to bring the soul to a state in which all of its parts agree about the best course of action in a given situation. Socrates' example focuses on the decision of when or whether to have sex, but a fully harmonious soul would not, presumably, experience inner conflict about moral decisions. When the philosophically inclined lover achieves genuine moderation, he always feels reverence and awe for the image of divine beauty in the beloved and treats him as one should treat something divine, an idea that I discuss further in sections II.2 and III.1.

II.2. Genuine *Sōphrosunē* as Reverence and Becoming Like the Divine

In addition to criticizing mortal moderation and the nonvirtuous handling of *erōs*, Socrates' palinode shows that *erōs* can lead us to transcend conventional notions of moral excellence to discover its true nature. Socrates' argument may at first appear paradoxical—*erōs*, which he calls a type of divine "madness" (*mania*), can lead us to develop one of madness' opposites, namely *sōphrosunē*, the most literal meaning of which is "sound-mindedness."[17] An intense erotic attraction toward someone or something that strikes as unusually beautiful can be a profound experience that leads us to see the world and our previ-

---

philosophic couple ever have sex with each other according to Socrates. Articles that give insightful analyses of this topic include Halperin (1986), Tafolla (2018), and Brown's "The Lovers' Formation in Plato's *Phaedrus*" (2022).

17. Dominic Scott (2011) summarizes scholarly discussions about the sense in which the philosophic lover is "mad" according to Socrates in the palinode. He helpfully suggests that Socrates' use of the term *mania* here is a "playfully misleading" (181) use of rhetoric that uses the first two speeches' assumptions about love to convincingly support an opposite conclusion, that is, that love is beneficial instead of harmful.

ous opinions from a new perspective. Socrates states explicitly that such an experience can shed light on the flaws in socially established beliefs: "There [are] two forms of madness, one caused by human illness, the other by a divine upheaval of customary beliefs [*theias exallagēs tōn eiōthotōn nomimōn*]" (*Phdr.* 265a). As I discussed in the previous chapter, customary beliefs both in ancient Athens and in contemporary society associate moderation with choosing not to indulge our desires as much as we might want in order to get something else we desire—the conventionally moderate person avoids overeating for the sake of appearing fit, chooses not to drink too much alcohol to avoid a hangover, does not spend too much money today so he can save for a larger purchase tomorrow, and so on. One of Socrates' primary aims in the *Phaedrus* is to illustrate how *erōs*, when handled well, helps us see the self-restraint advocated in the first two speeches as "slavish economizing" that severely hampers the soul's potential for growth. At the same time, he shows that the genuine *sōphrosunē* that the virtuous and philosophic handling of *erōs* can lead us toward it is substantially different from and much more valuable than the conventional misconceptions about this important moral characteristic.

As I discussed in the previous section, handling *ēros* virtuously is intimately bound up with the experience of "feeling reverence" (*sebomai*) at the sight of beauty due to its intimate relation to divine beauty.[18] The term *sebomai* is closely tied to "piety" (*eusebia*), and the theme of reverence and piety appears frequently throughout the *Phaedrus*.[19] Socrates calls his first speech "terribly clever" (*deinon*) and "irreverent" (*asebē*)" to the god Eros (242d–e), and says that he "needs to be cleansed" (*kathērasthai anagkē*)" by giving the palinode speech (243a). After delivering the palinode, Socrates confirms that he atoned for his impiety, since it expressed "due reverence": "In some way, though I can't say exactly how, we offered an image of erotic experience and perhaps touched upon a truth in some instances and in others were wide of the mark, blending together a not totally unpersuasive account in a playful

18. Paul Woodruff and Betty S. Flowers (2001) have a helpful text on the value of reverence in the ancient world and its connections to modern life. They rightly point out that the Greeks, including Plato, often regard reverence as the opposite of *hubris* (1–2). This point fits well with the *Phaedrus*' contrast between hubristic *erōs* and moderate *erōs* that is based on reverence for the beloved.

19. "Piety" (*eusebia*) is the same term that is the primary focus of Plato's *Euthyphro*. For more information on piety in Plato and ancient Greece more broadly, see Emlyn-Jones (1990) and Sedley (1999).

way—but also in a measured way and with due reverence [*metriōs te kai euphēmōs*]—in a mythic hymn to your master and mine, Phaedrus, to Eros, the guardian of beautiful boys" (265b–c). Socrates also offers prayers at key points in the conversation, including one to Eros at the end of the palinode (257a–b) and one to Pan at the very end of the dialogue (279b–c). Much like the palinode's many images, symbols, and metaphors, Socrates' prayers and reverence to the gods may be a symbolic representation of the piety that is bound up with moderation. Genuine moderation requires piety, but not in the sense associated with traditional Greek religious practices—rather, one is pious and reverent when she appropriately appreciates the image of divinity that is present in both others and herself.

Genuinely moderate *erōs*, therefore, consists in persistent reverence for the image of divine beauty in the beloved. The moderate lover reverently treats his beloved as someone with divine dignity, "waiting on him" in "every possible way as if he were a god" (255a). The initial brief experience of reverence at the sight of divine beauty can be turned into a more stable state of mind, which leads to virtuous living and a thriving erotic partnership. As I indicated above, the soul with uncultivated philosophical potential "at first shudders and feels something of those old terrors come over him when he sees a god-like face or any part of the body which is a good imitation of beauty," but the more he looks and reflects on the image of divine beauty in the beloved, "he feels reverence [*sebetai*] as if he were before a god" (251a). If this lover can continue to see his beloved as someone so valuable, he will treat his beloved without *hubris*, but instead with a fostering respect. Instead of using the beloved as a means to his own satisfaction, he displays virtue by treating his beloved with kindness, adoration, and friendliness (I expand on these points in section III.1). The person possessing genuine *sōphrosunē* accurately sees that there is something more fundamental or important than his own desires, and in this way *sōphrosunē* is the opposite of *hubris*.

Through *sōphrosunē* we accurately see ourselves as imperfect yet valuable—just like the beloved, we are an image of divine beauty who possesses the ability to become more similar to the divine. By seeing that we pale in comparison to divine perfection, we can recognize the ways in which we need to cultivate wisdom and the rest of the virtues. Inspired by his beloved, the moderate lover tries to "pick up" the "habits and practices" of the gods (i.e., virtuous ones) and help his beloved to do the same:

> And in this way when they make contact with a god through memory, they are possessed by him and pick up his habits and

> practices [*ta ethē kai ta epitēdeumata*] to the extent that humans can share in the divine. As they attribute the cause of these feelings to the beloved, they adore [*agapōsi*] him even more dearly; and, if they draw their inspiration from Zeus, then like inspired Bacchants following Dionysos they pump this inspiration into the beloved's soul and make him as similar as possible to their god. (253a–b)

The genuinely moderate person does not hubristically behave as if he were a god by treating others however his desires dictate. The philosophic couple instead take up the practice of philosophy together and provide mutual benefit as they seek resemblance with the divine by way of virtue, ideas that I will discuss in further detail in section III.

Genuine *sōphrosunē* thus helps us thrive in many spheres of our lives in addition to our intimate relationships. When discussing the virtuous use of rhetoric later in the dialogue, Socrates says that we can express moderation and piety through our words and deeds in political life:

> A moderate man [*ton sōphrona*] does not put himself through this labor in order to speak and to act [*legein kai prattein*] in the company of human beings, but to put himself in a position to say what is gratifying to the gods and at all times to act in a gratifying manner to the best of his ability [*alla tou theois kecharismena men legein dunasthai, kecharismenōs de prattein to pan eis dunamin*]. For certainly, Tisias, men wiser than we say that a man of intelligence [*ton noun*] must not concern himself with gratifying fellow slaves, except in a secondary way, but rather with gratifying masters who are good and from good stock. (273e–274a)

Unlike conventional rhetoricians who strive solely to persuade as many people as possible and gain popular acceptance, the moderate person "gratifies the gods"—a metaphor for behaving virtuously—with his *logoi* and his actions that affect other members of society. He does not have inordinate desires for conventional goods such as political power, popularity, and wealth, goods that the person with mortal moderation prioritizes above all else. Even though managing sexual desire is a main focus of the *Phaedrus*, Socrates also indicates in his prayer to Pan that moderation gives measure to our desires for money and the goods that wealth can buy: "Dear Pan and ye other gods who dwell here, grant that I become beautiful within and that my worldly belongings be in accord with my inner self. May I consider the wise man [*ton sophon*] rich and have only as much gold as a moderate man [*ho sōphrōn*] can carry and use" (279b–c). Through the inner harmony of the soul that moderation and the rest of the virtues provide, one becomes "beautiful within," and such a soul is most able to make the best use of external goods. The moderate person has no desire to pursue an excessive amount of money, and she uses what she has in a way that is most beneficial for herself and her community.

The genuinely moderate person, like the person who possesses the art of rhetoric (and not just its prerequisites), effectively assesses each unique situation she faces and responds in an excellent way. She does not refer to an external authority, a universal moral formula, or a generalized set of rules that determine how to act for her, such as the universal rule to never give sexual favors to a nonlover that Lysias proposes. Instead, she independently finds the action or decision that each situation calls for, since no supposedly universal set of rules can be applied to every single unique situation.[20] Since she does not rely on an external authority to decide what to do, the virtuous person develops herself through habitual practice to become the sort of person who is best at discerning and executing whatever the virtuous action might be in her real-life context. Though Socrates does not explicitly discuss this situational element of moral virtue in the *Phaedrus*, he makes analogous points about *technē* that can illuminate the nature of moral virtue. As I discussed in chapter 3, the person who possesses an art such as medicine, music, or tragedy writing pays close attention to "the proper arrangement of parts," fitting each of them "appropriately in relation to the other and the whole" (268d). For some arts, such as rhetoric, one must also know when to apply one's art, how it must be applied, the appropriate length of time required to apply it, the best ends toward which to persuade someone, and the sort of person(s) who will be most receptive to a certain sort of speech. She must also have practical experience in applying

20. Aristotle likewise makes this point in *Nicomachean Ethics* II, arguing that we cannot be as precise in our theoretical inquiries about ethics as we can in other disciplines such as mathematics: "But let it be agreed to in advance that every argument concerned with what ought to be done is bound to be stated in outline only and not precisely. [. . .] Matters of action and those pertaining to what is advantageous have nothing stationary about them [. . .]. Instead, those who act ought themselves always to examine what pertains to the opportune moment [when it presents itself]" (1104a1–9).

this knowledge (271d–272b).[21] Even though moral virtue is not a *technē*, Socrates' description of what distinguishes someone as possessing a *technē* also applies to *sōphrosunē*—whether it comes to assessing one's own level of wisdom and virtue, how to behave in an intimate relationship, how to handle external goods, how to use one's words and rhetoric, how to best act in the *polis*, or how to best manage one's desires, the moderate person gives the best response to whatever an issue calls for.

Relatedly, Socrates' reflection on writing at the end of the dialogue can enhance our understanding of the difference between genuine *sōphrosunē* and mortal moderation. Applying some of Socrates' remarks about writing to the *Phaedrus*' passages about genuine *sōphrosunē* and mortal moderation sheds light on why genuine *sōphrosunē* is not achieved or enacted by following universal rules or the teachings of others. Socrates points to the rigidity and inflexibility of the written word as one of its major limitations: "You might suspect that [written words] would speak as if they understand something, but if you ask them about anything in the text in hopes of learning something, the words signify only one thing, and always the same thing" (275d–e). In my view, we can extend this point to rules of conduct or universal formulas that aim to give a definite, correct choice in every situation. No matter how well intentioned and well thought out rules of conduct happen to be, they invariably fail to account for the unique particularities of every single situation. Moreover, if the person who aims to follow them does not understand why they should be followed or why a certain action is actually best, he is prone to misapplying the rule and, as a result, ignorantly committing a morally bad action (or, at least, failing to make the best decision).

For these reasons, composing and following rules of conduct is not the focus or goal of the person who cultivates genuine *sōphrosunē* in the context of the philosophical life. One does not become moderate by simply

21. Aristotle also acknowledges that virtuous action must take into account many different variables in a given situation: "[Moral virtue] is concerned with passions and actions, and it is in these that excess, deficiency, and the middle term reside. For example, it is possible to be afraid, to be confident, to desire, to be angry, to feel pity, and, in general, to feel pleasure and pain to a greater or lesser degree than one ought, and in both cases this is not good. But to feel them when one ought and at the things one ought, in relation to those people whom one ought, for the sake of what and as one ought—all these constitute the middle as well as what is best, which is in fact what belongs to virtue. Similarly, in the case of actions too, there is an excess, a deficiency, and the middle term" (1106b17–25).

following the teachings of the dead, written word in a thoughtless way. Instead, she cares for her own soul and the souls of others through living, critical dialogue and dialectical inquiry, which leads to real "knowledge [*epistēmas*] of what is just, beautiful, and good" (276c). The person with genuine virtue artfully considers all of the relevant facets of the unique situation she faces, and she acts based on her understanding of both *what* is best and *why* it is best. Rather than referring to the written words of others, the genuinely moderate person possesses the sort of *logos* that is "written with knowledge in the soul of one who understands; this is able to defend itself and it knows when and to whom it should speak, and when and to whom it shouldn't" (276a). Virtue is not the ability to follow dogmas but a matter of direct insight through which we understand ourselves, care for our souls in the best possible way, and promote the well-being of others.

In addition to closely associating *sōphrosunē* with reverence for divine beauty, the *Phaedrus* makes further connections between *sōphrosunē* and divinity insofar as cultivating it (along with the rest of the virtues) is how we make ourselves more similar to the divine.[22] The moderate person tries to make his soul like the divine beauty he strives for as much as possible, and he helps his beloved pursue this end in any way he can. The metaphor of "regrowing" the soul's "wings" is the main symbol Socrates uses for becoming similar to the divine through the virtuous handling of one's erotic attraction to beauty:[23]

> And let us consider why the feathers fall off a soul and drop away. The explanation is something like this. By its nature the wing's natural capacity is to convey what is weighty upward and to roam among the stars where the race of the gods dwell, and, most of all bodily parts, it has a share in the divine—the

22. Socrates' "digression" in the *Theaetetus* similarly associates piety with becoming like the divine: "That is why a man should make all haste to escape from earth to heaven; and escape means becoming as like God as possible [*phugē de homoiōsis theōi kata to dunaton*]; and a man becomes like God when he becomes just and pure, with understanding [*homoiōsis de dikaion kai hosion meta phronēseōs genesthai*]" (*Tht.* 176c). Sedley (1999) helpfully investigates the concept of becoming like God in Plato.

23. Socrates claims that losing its wings is the reason a given soul becomes embodied in the first place. Prior to that, it lived a life similar to the gods, helping them "govern the cosmos": "When she is perfect and winged, a soul roams among the stars and governs the cosmos at large. But when she has lost her feathers, a soul is carried along until she lays hold of something solid where she settles in and acquires an earthly body" (246c).

> divine which is beautiful, wise, good, and everything of this sort [*to de theion kalon, sophon, agathon, kai pan hoti toiouton*]. The soul's feathers are especially nourished and increased by these, but diminished and utterly destroyed by shame, vice and such opposites. (246d–e)

If the soul's wings have "a share of the divine," and the divine is beautiful, wise, and good, then regrowing the soul's wings symbolizes making one's soul as good, wise, and beautiful as possible through the development of virtuous characteristics.[24] Fully actualizing our capacity for "thought" through philosophy helps us become "nearer" to Forms and the divine:[25]

> As is just, only the discursive thinking of a philosopher [*hē tou philosophou dianoia*], the one who is in love with wisdom, grows wings. For thought is always according to her capability through memory, near to those things [the Forms] and by this nearness a god is divine. And only a man who correctly handles such reminders and is perpetually initiated into these perfect mysteries is truly perfect [*teleous aei teletas teloumenos, teleos ontōs monos gignetai*]. But standing apart from zealous human pursuits and being near to the divine, he is admonished by the many for being deranged, because they fail to see that he is divinely possessed, having the god within [*enthousiazōn*]. (249c–d)

The true philosopher "correctly handles" the erotic attraction he feels toward physical images of divine beauty, and they bring his *dianoia* closer to understanding the divine. The more he is "initiated" into the "perfect mysteries" of Being, the more perfect he becomes (he would have to do this "perpetually" to become "truly perfect"); gaining as much understanding of the divine as he can, his soul's "wings" are "nourished," and he becomes moderate and beautiful within. In other words, he has "the god within"

24. Other passages in the palinode about the soul "patterning herself" after a god's nature (248a, 252d–253b) are instances where Socrates characterizes the cultivation of virtue as becoming like the divine. I discuss these passages in section III.3 below.

25. As I noted in section I.2 above, it is possible to construct an interpretation of Socrates' myth according to which the Forms and the gods are not really separate things but instead two symbols that represent two different aspects of the same divine reality. This question is not central for my aim, which is to show that virtue makes us more similar to the divine, whatever the nature of divinity might be.

him. This process is cyclical—the more similar to the divine he becomes, the better he understands it, and the better he understands it, the more divine he becomes.

Making the same point about becoming like the divine in a different way, Socrates claims that the pre-embodied soul's limited vision of the Forms "nourishes" its wings. He states: "The reason for this great haste to see the Plain of Truth and find its whereabouts is that the pasturelands there happen to be just right for the best part of the soul, and that the wing which makes it possible for the soul to become airborne is nourished thereby" (248b–c). If gaining a better understanding of the Forms also "nourishes" the soul in one's embodied life, then a properly nourished soul symbolizes a moderate soul. In *Republic* VI, Socrates claims that when one's desires increase for one kind of good, they necessarily decrease for other kinds. When one becomes a lover of wisdom and learning, one also becomes more moderate:

> But, further, we surely know that when someone's desires incline strongly to some one thing, they are therefore weaker with respect to the rest, like a stream that has been channeled off in that other direction. [. . .] So, when in someone they have flowed toward learning and all that's like it, I suppose they would be concerned with the pleasure of the soul itself with respect to itself and would forsake those pleasures that come through the body—if he isn't a counterfeit but a true philosopher. [. . .] Such a man is, further, moderate [*sōphrōn*] and in no way a lover of money. (*R.* 485d–e)

This point is analogous to the one Socrates makes in the palinode. The more we love learning about or "gaining nourishment" from the Forms or the divine, the less we care about accumulating the lower goods of the body and the more moderate we become.

While becoming similar to divinity may sound like an unrealistic goal for an imperfect, limited human being, it can benefit us as an ideal to strive for, even if it is not something that we can fully attain. The way of life through which humans can become as virtuous as possible according to the *Phaedrus* is the philosophical life (see 249c–d and 256a–b above), especially when one partakes in a philosophic relationship (249a), but the *Phaedrus* gives several indications that it is not a project that we can complete. Socrates is clear that we can make progress toward this ideal, and the closer we get to the ideal, the better our lives become. However, he does not claim that humans can ever fully reach this end in one lifetime. In his palinode's myth concerning reincarnation, he says that most souls take ten thousand years to "return to the same spot whence she started," unless one "loves wisdom without deceit, or loves a boy at the same time as he loves wisdom": "If in the third 1,000 year circuit these souls choose the same life three times in succession, they sprout wings in the 3,000th year and depart" (248e–249a). Socrates' claim that completely regrowing the soul's wings takes more than one lifetime suggests that a human will never attain the complete wisdom of a god in the span of one lifetime. For this reason, Socrates describes the person who uses rhetoric philosophically in the following way: "To call him a *wise* person [*sophon*], Phaedrus, is too much, and only befitting a god, it seems to me. But a lover of wisdom [*philosophon*] or a name of this sort would be more appropriate and harmonious with his nature" (278d). The philosopher is in between ignorance and wisdom—he is wise enough to know that he lacks the wisdom of a "god," and so he loves what he lacks. He can make progress toward achieving godlikeness by becoming virtuous and practicing philosophy, but so long as he remains human, he will never possess wisdom in the complete way that a god would and will therefore remain a lover of wisdom (an argument Diotima makes in the *Symposium*, 203c–204b).

The *Phaedrus*' reflection on why *sōphrosunē* is crucial for inner harmony and *eudaimonia* has much in common with that of the *Gorgias*, but it gives a fuller illustration of the ideally virtuous and philosophic life. Socrates explains why, in his view, the philosophic couple leads the best possible life a human can have:

> So if the better parts of discursive thinking [*tēs dianoias*] prevail, as they lead toward a regimented life and a love of wisdom [*tetagmenēn te diaitan kai philosophian*], then all involved enjoy a blessed and harmonious [*makarion men kai homonoētikon*] life here on earth. Self-composed and master of themselves [*egkrateis autōn kai kosmioi ontes*] they have enslaved what enables viciousness [*hō kakia*] to enter the soul and they have liberated what allows excellence [*hō aretē*] access. [. . .] There is no greater good than this that either mortal moderation [*sōphrosunē anthrōpinē*] or divine madness can provide a human being. (256a–b)

The philosopher's life is "regimented" in that it is organized around the pursuit of wisdom and virtue as its top priority. His soul is led by his "thinking" rather than his desires, so he pursues the goods (such as virtue, philosophical education, and healthy relationships) that are, in reality, most beneficial for himself and others. As Socrates argues in the *Gorgias*, virtue protects us from the self-destructive misery of living as a slave to our own desires, whether this results from leading the pleonexic way of life represented by Callicles or the life of mortal moderation represented by Lysias. Instead, moderation and the rest of the virtues make us "self-composed" and "masters" of ourselves, such that all aspects of our souls are "harmonious" with one another. This way of being helps us reach the state of completeness and sufficiency gestured toward in the *Gorgias,* both of which give rise to *eudaimonia*, a long-term, stable sense of fulfillment accompanied by flourishment in all of the important private and interpersonal spheres of our lives. Socrates suggests in both dialogues that virtue provides inner harmony, but in the *Phaedrus* this harmony is more fully described as the truly moderate, divine activity of "thinking," living, and loving others in an excellent way over the course of one's life.

In addition to Socrates' insights about *sōphrosunē* expressed in the *words* he speaks to Phaedrus, Plato depicts Socrates as an exemplar of moderation in his *deeds* throughout the dialogue. Socrates' behavior adds to the *Phaedrus*' account of *sōphrosunē* by giving us a concrete example of an individual expressing this virtue through his actions.[26] He is highly aware of his own mortal limitations, and cares more about attaining deeper self-knowledge than debunking every myth with a materialistic explanation as the "clever" (*deinos*) sophists do (229c–e). If Socrates' flirting is an indication that he feels erotic attraction for Phaedrus, he does not make the mistake of the hubristic, nonvirtuous lover by immediately attempting to sexually seduce him. Instead, he tries to benefit Phaedrus' soul by using philosophical rhetoric to turn him toward the path to virtue and philosophy, as I discussed in chapter 3. He treats Phaedrus reverently and stresses the importance of piety through his palinode and his symbolic prayers to Eros and Pan. Like the moderate, philosophic lover in his palinode, he tries to help a younger, less mature philosophic soul reach his full potential and become more similar

26. Helen North (1979) insightfully surveys what she calls *sōphrōn* heroes and heroines in Greek literature, and she includes Socrates as one of the main ones (33–54). In a recent article on the *Phaedo,* David Ebrey (2023) argues that Plato presents Socrates as a "philosophical hero, a replacement for traditional heroes such as Theseus and Heracles" (153).

to the divine. Though Socrates is aware that he lacks the wisdom that a god would have, he has made progress toward his goal of becoming wise. Without such progress, he would not be able to compose the speeches or lead the philosophical dialogue in the highly insightful way that he does. He actualizes his capacity to be an individual who thinks and lives with a well-organized, harmonious soul, pursuing wisdom instead of the much more common goal of conventional goods.

Moderation's connection to piety, wisdom, and the just treatment of others raises the often-discussed issue of the unity of the virtues. That is, many wonder whether having one of the virtues requires that we have all of the others according to Plato.[27] In my view, the *Phaedrus* does not provide a clear answer to this question. However, it is at least clear that the virtues besides *sōphrosunē* that Plato talks about most frequently—wisdom, courage, justice, and piety—are all connected to *sōphrosunē* in some way, and my analysis of *this virtue* has shed light on the relationship it has with each of the others. When we look at the difference between the self-restrained person and the genuinely moderate person in the *Phaedrus,* the latter is clearly wiser than the former, since he has self-knowledge and a better understanding of reality. The moderate person is pious because of the reverence he shows for the image of divine beauty in the beloved. While courage is not a focus of the *Phaedrus*, one can see how the moderate, philosophic lover is more courageous than the hubristic lover of the first two speeches. The hubristic lover harmfully manipulates his beloved due (at least in part) to his fear of rejection. Motivated by this cowardice and his desire to gain as much pleasure as possible from his beloved, the nonvirtuous lover does whatever he can to maintain control over his beloved, while a moderate lover respects his beloved's autonomy and helps him become more independent. The moderate lover therefore courageously makes himself vulnerable to the pain of rejection. Finally, justice is mentioned almost as often as *sōphrosunē* in the *Phaedrus* (for example, see 247d, 250a, and 250b). The moderate person behaves justly toward others, especially the person he loves in the context of the *Phaedrus*, by working for their benefit rather than their harm for the

27. Aristotle argues in *Ethics* book VI that possessing practical wisdom necessarily entails possessing all of the virtues: "For all of the virtues will be present when the one virtue, prudence, is present" (*EN* 1145a1–2). Modern scholars also take interest in this question as it arises in Plato. For example, Thomas C. Brickhouse and Nicholas D. Smith (1997) examine passages from *Protagoras*, *Laches*, and *Euthyphro* where this issue comes up.

reasons discussed above. These just actions stem from a harmonious soul in which each part plays the role for which it is best suited.[28]

As I indicated in the introduction of this chapter, the *Phaedrus* significantly adds to our contemporary reflections on the value of moderation and virtue ethics more broadly, and there are several core ways that we can apply its insights to our own lives. Rather than being the whole of moderation, self-restraint is only the beginning of living moderately—regularly restraining our desires in a way that requires inner struggle is a habit that should lead toward a happier and more peaceful psyche. Moderation makes one's inner life more harmonized by minimizing internal strife. Apart from inner harmony, the connections Plato makes between moderation and other spheres of life shows how this virtue improves relationships and self-knowledge. Moderation shapes how we relate and connect to one another and is therefore vital for healthy relationships and community. In our intimate relationships or in interpersonal life more generally, the habit of revering the value and dignity of others leads to healthy and stable relationships, as such an approach prevents many common mistakes that stem from using others as a means for fulfilling our own desires. As I discussed in the previous chapter, the abuses that can result from erotic love outlined in the *Phaedrus* sound all too familiar to our modern ears, and moderation can be an antidote to these abuses now as much as it was in ancient Greece. With regard to the *Phaedrus*' conception of moderation as recognizing oneself as a limited being, realizing that we will never have an omniscient, godlike understanding of the world is an important part of living philosophically. Because of our human limitations, we will never have an all-encompassing understanding of the world that an omniscient deity would. However, we can make progress toward this ideal through the cultivation of virtue, gaining a better sense of the path as we move farther along and discern more about the sources of structure and meaning in the world that Plato calls the Forms. Regardless of one's views about the nature of divinity (or whether there is such a thing), "becoming like God" can at least be understood as living seriously through moral self-cultivation, caring for the benefit of others, and philosophical seeking.

28. According to Socrates in *Republic* IV, an individual is just when "each of the parts in him minds its own business" (443b). The person with a just soul behaves justly toward others because his reason correctly identifies what action is best in each situation, and the other parts of his soul assist reason in carrying out this action, or they at least do not interfere. In the *Phaedrus,* Socrates also remarks in the palinode that each of the gods attend to their own business (247a).

III. The Benefits of Genuine *Sōphrosunē*

The *Phaedrus* illustrates how *sōphrosunē* helps us thrive in several important spheres of private and interpersonal life. Each of the following sections is devoted to one of the primary benefits that the dialogue touches on. In section III.1, I explain why, according to the palinode, moderation helps one participate in a healthy intimate relationship wherein each partner is committed to the benefit of the other's soul. Socrates elaborates some essential features of a virtuous, eudaimonic relationship through his description of the "philosophic couple." This sort of relationship provides mutual benefit through its balance of erotic attraction and friendship (*philia*), with each person fostering the other's pursuit of happiness (*eudaimonia*), wisdom, and the rest of the virtues. Relatedly, genuine moderation is crucial for self-knowledge, which I discuss in section III.2. The *Phaedrus* shows why the moderate relationship involves self-examination from both practical and metaphysical points of view. The more self-knowledge we gain, the better we are able to understand our own limits and to avoid the detrimental mistakes of *hubris*. Moderation helps us discern what we know and what we do not know, which allows us to pursue knowledge of the most fundamental and pressing issues, especially deeper knowledge of ourselves, before delving into more secondary concerns. Although we need others to help guide us toward the virtues, they are not reducible to propositional knowledge that we can simply receive from another person. In section III.3, I argue that transforming the soul through cultivating virtue enhances the soul's capacity to apprehend reality, which can help us gain insight into the sources of Being, or the Forms. Attaining virtue transforms one's character and mind such that it is not clouded by its own desires or disharmony. Purified and godlike, the virtuous soul gains a clearer view of reality, albeit one that remains human and therefore limited.

III.1. Eudaimonic Relationships

As I showed above, Socrates' palinode illustrates how genuine *sōphrosunē* can help us avoid the misuses of *erōs* highlighted by the first two speeches. One of the major differences between the nonvirtuous, hubristic lover and the genuinely moderate, philosophic lover is that the latter treats his beloved with "awe and a sense of shame" (*aidoumenēn te kai dediuian*) (*Phdr.* 254e), as well as reverence. The reverence, awe, and sense of shame one experiences in the presence of the beloved motivates him to prioritize the beloved's well-being over the satisfaction of his own erotic desires. The philosophic soul initially experiences reverence when another person's beauty briefly makes divine beauty present to his mind, and if he lives in such a way that persistently shows reverence toward that person, then he expresses *sōphrosunē* in the context of an intimate relationship. Unlike the nonvirtuous, hubristic lover, he does not let his desire for erotic pleasure lead him to act in ways that are detrimental to the beloved's well-being. In this way, reverence is the antidote to *hubris*—the experience of reverence and a sense of shame help us tame our *epithumiai* (the black horse). The moderate lover's reverence indicates that he fully understands the value of his beloved's soul and seeks to promote his well-being as far as possible.

In the philosophic relationship, the *erōs* that each member experiences for the other is accompanied by friendship (*philia*) and kindness (*eunoia*). In contrast to the harmful manipulation of the nonvirtuous lover, the moderate lover offers genuine, caring "friendship" (*philia*) and all of the "great and divine blessings" it brings (256e). Describing the beginning of the philosophic couple's relationship, Socrates states:

> Because the boy is now waited on in every possible way as if he were a god, and the lover is no longer pretending but truly feels his servitude, the boy is naturally friendly [*philos*] to the one who offers him such attention, even if earlier he thrust away from the lover, when he had been misled by his schoolmates and others who said that it was shameful to be near him. But with the passage of time, his age and necessity compel the boy to admit the lover into his company, as it has never been ordained by fate that vice be dear to vice [*kakon kakō philon*] or that good should not be dear to good [*agathon mē philon agathō*]. When the boy admits him, accepting his conversation and company (or intercourse) [*logon kai homilian*], the lover's kindness [*eunoia*] being near now astonishes the boy as he perceives how all his other friends and relatives [*alloi philoi te kai oikeioi*] put together do not offer a fraction of the friendship [*philias*] of his godly-inspired friend [*entheon philon*]. (255a–b)

The moderate lover is a friend in that he sincerely desires happiness for his beloved's own sake, regardless of what sacrifices he might have to make for the beloved or how it might affect their relationship.[29] This lover's "kindness" is sincere and "astonishing" because of how much time, attention, and energy he is willing to invest. Instead of trying to control and satisfy his own desires immediately in ways that can be harmful, the moderate lover bravely prioritizes the well-being of his beloved. He treats his beloved "as if he were a god," another indication that reverence toward the person one loves is what distinguishes moderate erotic love from the nonvirtuous, hubristic sort.

In the early stages of the philosophic couple's relationship, the kindness and friendship of the person who falls in love first can lead the beloved to gradually develop erotic feelings and his friendship in return. Socrates continues:

> When the lover continues over time to be kind and to remain by his side, even to the point of touching in the gymnasium and other places of companionship [*homiliais*], a spring from that flow which Zeus in love with Ganymede called Desire [*himeros*] gushes over the lover, part of its waters entering into him and part of it overflowing when he has become full [. . .] the stream waters the pathways of the feathers, urges them to sprout, and fills the beloved's soul in turn with love [*erōtos*]. The boy is then in love, but he is at a loss to say with what. He doesn't know what he has experienced, nor is he able to explain it, but just as a person who has contracted an eye-disease from someone is unable to name the alleged cause, so he does not realize that in his lover he is seeing himself as though in a mirror. When that man is near, his pain ceases, as it does for the man. But when the man is absent, the boy yearns and is yearned for, again in

29. Aristotle argues that wishing for a friend's well-being for the friend's own sake is characteristic of complete, virtue-based friendships: "But complete friendship is the friendship of those who are good and alike in point of virtue. For such people wish in similar fashion for the good things for each other insofar as they are good, and they are good in themselves. But those who wish for the good things for their friends, for their friends' sake, are friends most of all, since they are disposed in this way in themselves and not incidentally. Their friendship continues, then, while they are good, and virtue is a stable thing. Each person involved is good simply and for the friend, since good people are good simply and beneficial to one another. So too are they pleasant, for the good are both pleasant simply and pleasant to one another" (*EN* 1156b7–15).

> the same ways, as he experiences a "return-love," an image or copy of love. He calls and considers this to be friendship, not love [*ouk erōta alla philian*]. Like the man, only less intensely, he desires to see, to touch, to kiss, to lie down beside. And then, as is likely, soon afterwards he does these very things. (255b–e)

The moderate lover's kind and friendly treatment of the beloved healthily cultivates the relationship with his beloved from the beginning, never pressuring the beloved to return his affection or have sex with him. Socrates explains the reason why the beloved returns this love and affection in a puzzling way—the beloved sees his own beauty reflecting off the lover's face "as though in a mirror" and experiences an "image" of his lover's erotic attraction. In any case, the exact reason why the one returns the other's love is not crucial for my purposes. The important point is that the moderate lover patiently and bravely waits for the beloved to freely experience *erōs* and offer friendship in return, which may or may not happen. If the beloved begins to grow seriously interested in his lover, it is because he recognizes the value of his lover's friendship and guidance, and not because the beloved is persuaded or manipulated into having sex. The moderate lover's virtue eventually becomes apparent to his beloved, and if the beloved is also good (not vicious), they naturally form a happy and healthy intimate relationship. The beloved's "wings to sprout" as he experiences a disorienting mixture of friendly and erotic feelings, and he too may decide to adopt the philosophical way of life in pursuit of virtue and godlikeness with his partner.

III.2. Self-Knowledge

Since genuine *sōphrosunē* involves accurately seeing oneself as an imperfect being who has the potential for godlikeness, the more we develop this virtue, the more self-knowledge we attain.[30] Plato introduces the theme of self-knowledge in the opening discussion of the *Phaedrus* by having Socrates make the following remark: "Phaedrus, I know you as well as I know myself; and if I don't know Phaedrus, I've forgotten myself also" (*Phdr.* 228a).

30. Helen North's (1979) study of *sōphrosunē* in Greek literature distinguishes between moral *sōphrosunē* (similar to self-restraint) and intellectual *sōphrosunē*, the latter of which is closely connected with self-knowledge and the ability to avoid the mistake of *hubris* (38–39). The conception of *sōphrosunē* in the *Phaedrus* covers both senses of the term.

Socrates demonstrates that he knows Phaedrus well by correctly predicting what Phaedrus had been doing all morning and the reason why he was taking a walk in the country (228a–c). He knows Phaedrus' interests, character, habits, and values, so at the very least he knows similar things about himself. Having a good sense of our own moral character, habits, values, skills, talents, inclinations, flaws, and so on is valuable for the sake of our well-being. Without this kind of self-knowledge, we are unaware of what we know and what we do not know, an all-too-common and costly mistake that Plato so often reminds us of, especially in the *Apology*, where Socrates' description of his encounters with the politicians, poets, and craftsman (21a–23a) makes this point most explicitly.[31] Further, we need it to clarify our own moral strengths and weaknesses, and in general what goods (both those of the soul and those of the body) we must acquire to live better lives. The person with *sōphrosunē* neither overestimates nor underestimates herself in these respects, but instead has a clear, accurate understanding of her own soul.

Knowing one's own individual moral character, habits, values, talents, inclinations, flaws, and so on is one important part of self-knowledge in the *Phaedrus*, but it further suggests that we can gain knowledge of ourselves from a metaphysical standpoint as well. In other words, understanding of the nature of the human soul is another sense in which we can gain self-knowledge. Early in the dialogue, Socrates claims that one of his top priorities is inquiring about his own nature:

> All those nonbelievers employing some boorish sophistication will make everything conform to probability and they also will need a great deal of free time. But for me there's no such leisure. And, my dear friend, the reason is this: I am still not able to "know myself," as the Delphic inscription enjoins, and it seems laughable for me to think about other things when I am still ignorant about myself. So leaving those matters aside, I believe whatever people say these days about those creatures, and don't

31. Similarly, at the end of the *Theaetetus*, Socrates explicitly connects *sōphrosunē* with the ability to correctly determine what one knows and what one does not know. He tells Theaetetus that although he has failed to discover an adequate definition of knowledge, his conversation with Socrates has made him more "modest" (*sophrōn*) insofar as he will be less inclined to think he knows what he does not know (*Tht.* 210c).

> inquire about them but about myself. For me, the question is whether I happen to be some sort of beast even more complex in form and more tumultuous than the hundred-headed Typhon, or whether I am something simpler and gentler having a share by nature of the divine and the un-Typhonic. (229e–230a)

Socrates' contrast between the "complex," "tumultuous" Typhon and the "divine," which is "gentler" and "simpler," is difficult to interpret in light of his claims about the soul later in the dialogue. His palinode speech argues that human souls have a share of the divine (or at least they do when they have "wings") and that human bodies are images of divine beauty. However, he also likens the soul to a charioteer and two horses, which is something "complex in form" insofar as it is composed of three parts. Further, in his discussion of rhetoric, he says that the soul possesses multiple "forms" (*eidē*), and that its "number of forms" and their "quality" explain why "some people are of this sort and others of that sort" (271d, see also 270c–d). Socrates claims in the passage above that he is "still ignorant" about himself and therefore still inquiring about his own soul. Yet, his palinode shows that he indeed does have knowledge of the soul to some degree, or at least enough knowledge to give a sophisticated, imagistic account of the soul. Perhaps his knowledge of the soul and his claim of ignorance about it suggest that self-knowledge is similar to the ideal of godlikeness—it is not easy to gain it fully, but we can make progress by gaining some limited understanding of it, and we must continually work toward it over the course of an entire life.

The *Phaedrus* shows that the self-knowledge we gain from *sōphrosunē* helps us to know what type of soul we are.[32] Socrates' reincarnation myth in the palinode suggests that some types of human souls are born with certain potentialities and or proclivities that others lack. So, the type of soul one is born with determines what potentialities he can actualize:

> In the first generation of a soul's fall to earth, she can never be planted into a brute animal, but the soul which has witnessed Being the most in heaven shall be planted into the seed of

32. Ferrari (1987) insightfully points out that an individual's initial reaction to physical beauty can help him to gain self-knowledge: "You can learn who you are by considering your unconsidered reaction to an encounter with someone beautiful, and thus gain the opportunity to foster and justify the life appropriate to the kind of character you take yourself to be" (147).

> someone who will become a lover of wisdom, or a lover of beauty, or of something musical and erotic. The second best soul shall be planted into the seed of a future law-abiding king or a military man, or a ruler; the third best, into the seed of a political man, or an estate manager, or a money-maker; the fourth best, into the seed of one who loves toil, or a gymnast, or a doctor; the fifth best, into the seed of a prophet or seer or priest of mystic rites. In the sixth best soul a poet resides, or someone concerned with imitation; in the seventh, a craftsman or farmer; in the eighth, a sophist or demagogue; in the ninth, a tyrant. In all these men, the one who lives justly has a better portion; the one who lives unjustly, a worse portion. (248d–e)

Socrates uses the reincarnation myth to make the point that different types of people are born with different inclinations toward various goods, different types of work for which they are suited, and so on. Just as virtue allows us to actualize our uniquely human potentialities (as opposed to those of other species) according to Aristotle (*Ethics* I, 1097b22–1098a13), so also does it perfect the individual's unique characteristics in the *Phaedrus*. Socrates does not suggest that each soul is unique in the sense that it is completely different from every other individual, but instead that different types of people have different sets of propensities. He claims that it is possible to live "justly" in any type of life, or as justly as possible given the way of life it leads (which is difficult to imagine in the case of sophists, demagogues, and tyrants), but the philosophic soul clearly has the most opportunity to live the best possible human life for the reasons discussed in section II.

The self-knowledge possessed by the person with *sōphrosunē* makes it easier for her to actualize her unique potentialities. We can gain self-knowledge in the context of an intimate relationship in which both partners cultivate moderation. Socrates expresses this point in the context of his myth about souls following different Olympian gods before becoming embodied. He claims that we must learn which god we followed and seek someone who was also a follower of that god, a statement that mythologically expresses the view that we can have a fruitful relationship with someone whose soul has qualities and propensities similar to our own. Once two similar souls find each other, they "do everything they can" to help each other become "as similar as possible to their god":

> Each walks in the footsteps of the god he chooses joining in that choral dance, living out his life in honor of that god, and

> imitating him to the best of his abilities for as long as he remains uncorrupted and is in his first incarnation here on earth. He behaves this way to all: both to those he loves and to everyone else. Each person, then, chooses his Love from among the beautiful after his own tastes, and sculpts and fits that person out like a statue as if he were a god for him to honor and to worship with secret rites. The followers of Zeus search for a beloved who is noble and Zeus-like in his soul, and they ask whether the beloved is by nature a lover of wisdom and a ruler. Whenever they find him, they fall in love and do everything they can to help him become such a person. But if lovers have not practiced this kind of service before, they now try their hand at it and learn from any source, finding their way on their own. As they follow the scent and search within themselves to discover the nature of their god, they have an easy time of it because they are fiercely driven to gaze upon the god. And in this way when they make contact with a god through memory, they are possessed by him and pick up his habits and practices to the extent that humans can share in the divine. As they attribute the cause of these feelings to the beloved, they adore him even more dearly; and, if they draw their inspiration from Zeus, then like inspired Bacchants following Dionysos they pump this inspiration into the beloved's soul and make him as similar as possible to their god. (252d–253b)

Different types of people will cultivate different characteristics that correspond to (using the terms of the myth) the god they followed before they were born, adopting that god's "habits and practices." Those who followed Zeus are best suited to be philosophers and rulers, those who followed Hera "seek a beloved who is regal in nature," and the followers of each of the other Olympian gods "proceed in the manner of their god," but Socrates does not name each of their special qualities (253b). Couples help each other "search within themselves to discover the nature of their god," and once they find it, they help one another in the project of "sculpting" their own souls to become more like their common deity. The moderate lover behaves virtuously toward all people, "both to those he loves and to everyone else." Those who successfully develop their innate capacity for virtue in turn perfect their other unique personal characteristics, such as their talents, personality traits, and other such aspects of one's identity. So, rather than erasing one's individuality, virtue enhances one's incipient personal qualities.

III.3. Insight into Being

In addition to eudaimonic relationships and self-knowledge, *sōphrosunē* and the rest of the virtues also put us in a position to gain illuminating insight into Being, or the Forms. The Forms that Socrates mentions by name are Beauty, Justice, Moderation, and Knowledge, which implies that gaining a better understanding of Being is also bound up with knowledge about how to live justly and moderately as well as knowledge of the goods that are truly best and most beautiful. The vicious person who is ignorant about what is truly good is missing something important about the true nature of reality. According to Socrates' myth, the soul's internal order and virtue affect its ability to see the Forms before becoming embodied: "But of the other souls, one follows a god very well and patterns herself after him, raising up the head of her charioteer to peer upon the place outside heaven, and she is carried around with the gods in the revolving motion, but even so, this soul gets confused by the horses and is scarcely able to gaze upon the things that are. Another soul, harassed by the horses, rises and falls, seeing some things and not seeing others" (248a). In my view, the interrelations between the parts of the soul in this passage can be used to describe how different types of embodied humans gain more or less insight about the Forms depending on their virtue or lack thereof. Those who have the internal order of *sōphrosunē* (symbolized by horses who are obedient to the charioteer) are able to gain a clearer view of reality. The disorder of the vicious soul, on the other hand, obscures and skews his view of reality, symbolized by his unruly horses dragging his charioteer downward and away from its view of Being. The moral purity of the soul affects its ability to see the "pure" Forms according to Socrates, saying that the "evils" (*kakōn*) that necessarily accompany embodiment prevent us from "looking upon whole, simple, unchanging, and blessed visions in pure light" (250b–c). To understand the true nature of goodness, beauty, moderation, and so on, one must make his soul better, more beautiful, and moderate by giving harmony to his own soul.

As I argued in section II.2, even though an embodied human cannot have the complete understanding of the divine Forms that the gods have, the purer a human soul becomes through virtue, the more it is able to understand about the nature of reality. Socrates depicts the gods' way of life as a model for humans to emulate in this regard.[33] The gods exemplify the internal harmony of *sōphrosunē*, which allows them to steadily "gaze" on the Forms:

> But when the gods go to the feast and banquet, they make the steep climb to the arch of heaven's vault, a journey which the gods' chariots make with ease as they are well-balanced and obedient to the rein. But other chariots can barely follow. [. . .] But when those souls which we call immortal reach the summit of heaven, they go to the edge and stand on the rim; there the revolving motion carries them around as they stand and gaze on things outside the heavens. (247a–c)

The gods are models of a harmonious, virtuous, and happy life—they each "attend to their own business," presumably by "taking care" of everything in the heavens (246e–247a), and they contemplate Being without any struggle or interference from their horses. The gods' horses are "well-balanced and obedient to the rein," and after the gods finish gazing on Being, they "return home" and take the horses to the "manger" to feed (247e). Just as the gods' "discursive thinking" (*theou dianoia*) is "nourished by the mind [*nō*] and unmixed knowledge [*epistēmēn akēratō*], so also is "the thought of every soul nourished by what is appropriate for her to receive" (247d). By practicing philosophy, humans can gain a limited share of divine knowledge—a degree of knowledge that is "appropriate" for us—especially in privileged moments of insight wherein we temporarily gain some illumination about the nature of reality. In a cyclical manner, such experiences contribute to the process of becoming more like the divine (regrowing the soul's wings), and the more like the divine we become, the better we understand Being. Socrates expresses this point mythologically by saying that the "pasturelands" of the Plain of Truth "nourish" the soul's wings (248b–c). In the context of the *Phaedrus*, then, the ideal philosophical life emulates Socrates' depiction of the gods by performing the cyclical activities of living virtuously and contemplating Being.

Moderation as a way of gaining insight into Being may sound counterintuitive, or at least strange, to many modern readers of Plato. Although Socrates discusses this idea by way of his myths about the soul's life before

33. I thank Ronald Polansky for sharing his unpublished notes on the *Phaedrus*, as they were very helpful for thinking through these important threads in the palinode.

it was born and its fate after death, I have explained how his primary focus is really our current lives. In my view, the stability that virtue brings to our minds can give us a clearer view of reality—one that is less clouded by our erroneous assumptions, intense emotions, or all-consuming desires. Since we are finite humans who live temporally, we must constantly renew our sense of purpose or meaning. By seeking wisdom, we become more attentive to the reasons why we pursue certain ends, and gaining insight about what is *really* worth pursuing renews and reanimates us. Even if we sometimes go through long periods in which our lives or the world seem devoid of meaning or sense, brief periods of illumination, clarity, or insight into Being might come to those who seek them out by pursuing moderation and wisdom.

Conclusion

Using the tripartite conception of the soul and his accompanying analysis of its structure when it lacks knowledge, harmony, and virtue, Socrates builds a rich account of *sōphrosunē* that we can still draw from today. Human souls experience the compulsion of *erōs* toward the goods and the individuals that appear most valuable to us, but philosophical reflection and self-cultivation can redirect our *erōs* and change how we respond to it in our decisions and actions. Socrates uses philosophical rhetoric to explain these ideas while he simultaneously attempts to guide Phaedrus' soul toward a deeper love for wisdom and the rest of the virtues. Socrates' palinode primarily focuses on how *sōphrosunē* is expressed in the context of an intimate relationship in order to illustrate the important features of this virtue's true nature. To cultivate genuine *sōphrosunē,* one who is in love must habitually restrain his desires so that he does not make the same mistakes as the nonvirtuous lover, who manipulates and harms the beloved for the sake of his own gratification. The experience of reverence for the beloved, as an image of divine beauty, initially motivates this process of self-restraint. But self-restraint eventually transforms the lover into someone who constantly reveres and works alongside his beloved in a lifelong pursuit of the godlikeness that comes from *sōphrosunē* and the philosophical life more broadly. The multifaceted Platonic virtue of *sōphrosunē* not only fosters happy and healthy intimate relationships but also increases one's own self-knowledge, since it requires us to know our own limitations even as we seek to overcome them so far as possible. Through this transformative improvement of the soul, we grow more similar to the divine and therefore gain deeper insight into Being.

it was born and its fate after death, I have explained how his primary focus is really our current lives. In my view, the stability that virtue brings to our minds can give us a clearer view of reality—one that is less clouded by our erroneous assumptions, intense emotions, or all-consuming desires. Since we are finite humans who live temporally, we must constantly renew our sense of purpose or meaning. By seeking wisdom, we become more attentive to the reasons why we pursue certain ends, and gaining insight about what is really worth pursuing renews and reanimates us. Even if we sometimes go through long periods in which our lives or the world seem devoid of meaning or sense, brief periods of illumination, clarity, or insight into Being might come to those who seek them out by pursuing moderation and wisdom.

Conclusion

Using the tripartite conception of the soul and his accompanying analysis of its structure when it lacks knowledge, harmony, and virtue, Socrates builds a rich account of *sophrosune* that we can still draw from today. Human souls experience the compulsion of *eros* toward the goods and the individuals that appear most valuable to us, but philosophical reflection and self-cultivation can redirect our *eros* and change how we respond to it in our decisions and actions. Socrates uses philosophical rhetoric to explain these ideas while he simultaneously attempts to guide Phaedrus' soul toward a deeper love for wisdom and the rest of the virtues. Socrates' palinode primarily focuses on how *sophrosune* is expressed in the context of an intimate relationship in order to illustrate the important features of this virtue's true nature. To cultivate genuine *sophrosune*, one who is in love must habitually restrain his desires so that he does not make the same mistakes as the nonrational lover, who manipulates and harms the beloved for the sake of his own gratification. The experience of reverence for the beloved, as an image of divine beauty, initially motivates this process of self-restraint. But self-restraint eventually transforms the lover into someone who constantly reveres and works alongside his beloved in a lifelong pursuit of the goodness that comes from *sophrosune* and the philosophical life more broadly. The multifaceted Platonic virtue of *sophrosune* not only fosters happy and healthy intimate relationships but also increases one's own self-knowledge, since it requires us to know our own limitations even as we seek to overcome them so far as possible. Through this transformative improvement of the soul, we grow more similar to the divine and therefore gain deeper insight into Being.

Conclusion

This book began with a close examination of the significance of Callicles, a character who feels familiar to the modern reader in several important ways. Callicles praises and attempts to justify limitless consumption, domination, and satisfaction as the key to a good life. Analyzing his moral character shed light on the *Gorgias*' depiction of reason and desire, its examination of the nature and cause of moral vice, and its insights about how the relationship between reason and desire in one's soul can affect the type of moral character he develops. I argued that Callicles is an example of the tyrannical soul that Plato outlines in the *Republic*, and that the root of his problem is his lack of knowledge about what is truly best for his soul, which leads him to erroneously regard *pleonexia* and unlimited satisfaction as the highest good. His ignorance and habitual vicious choices cause his desires to become inordinate and directed solely toward (what I called) the "lower" goods, primarily pleasure, wealth, political power, and popularity. He aims to persuade the masses to support him for the sake of his own gratification. His desires for victory and domination become amalgamated with these desires, with the result that he wants to accumulate the lower goods by dominating and taking from those he perceives as weaker. The disorder of Callicles' soul is such that his reason acts only as a slave to his desires, as it is reduced to finding the means to satisfy the ends set by his desires. Worse still, these ends are always out of reach, since his desires have no limit. He also formulates clever arguments in an attempt to justify his commitments, as he demonstrates in his conversation with Socrates. He appeals to the supposed natural order of things by asserting that it is just for the strong to dominate the weak, but his view implies that there is no real, universal measure for virtue or source of value that we should seek out. Instead, the satisfaction of the individual's own desires is the sole and ultimate goal of life.

Studying Callicles is worth our time, since he is not a straw man that Plato sets up for Socrates to destroy. Rather, Callicles gives a seductive presentation of some ideas that many people suspect are true. For this reason, I discussed in chapter 1 how modern versions of Callicles' views and moral persona can be detected in many individuals today. Callicles represents those who hold that pleasure is synonymous with happiness and commit themselves to (more or less) unfettered hedonism. Such individuals often seek as much wealth and political power as possible, since they are the best means for gratifying one's desires for wealth, physical pleasure, fame, domination, security, and so on. To use Callicles' words, such people let their desires grow as large as possible and seek the power to constantly fulfill them. This Calliclean outlook shapes some of our collective cultural attitudes about what it means to succeed. For example, many contemporary societies claim to value liberalism, saying that all citizens should be free to pursue whatever we think is best so long as we do not unjustly harm one another. However, our culture idolizes "outlaws," or strong individuals who take what they desire and disregard any laws or individuals who stand in the way. As I mentioned in chapter 1, many individuals may never take major, serious steps toward living the way of life Callicles praises, but many might at least suspect that, if they could get away with it, an unjust life that guarantees extreme wealth, power, and excesses would be the best possible life. The *Gorgias* still offers compelling reasons for why an unjust life would be intrinsically miserable and self-destructive.

Chapter 2 examined Socrates' critique of Callicles views, the alternative views he defends, and how these views are especially well suited to souls like Callicles. Defending a position that is the polar opposite of Callicles' in many respects, Socrates argues that the life characterized by *pleonexia* inevitably leads to pointless misery, and that there are a set of goods that are most essential for human happiness regardless of one's identity, namely the virtues, philosophical education, friendship, and inner harmony. Socrates' core views have substantial implications for social justice issues such as gender equality, criminal justice, and the true nature of power, because it follows from these views that both men and women are equally capable of becoming virtuous and happy, that criminal justice should aim for educative rehabilitation rather than revenge, and that true power comes from the ability to achieve happiness through virtue, not the ascent to a higher social class or political office. Socrates' deeds throughout the entire dialogue instantiate his views about just punishment. Since punishment's primary goal should be to benefit the persons punished through education, Socrates himself attempts to discipline Callicles in this way over the course of their conversation. Socrates' philosophical rhetoric in the *Gorgias* combines arguments with rhetorical tactics that aim to influence Callicles' reason and his nonrational desires. One of its primary goals is to help Callicles cultivate his sense of shame about his own moral vice, which may in turn motivate him to care for virtue. I argued that my interpretation of Socrates' philosophical rhetoric in the *Gorgias* is equivalent to the "true art of rhetoric" (*Grg.* 517a) and the "work of a good citizen" (*Grg.* 517b–c) that he mentions late in the dialogue. When discussing the nature of *sōphrosunē* with Callicles, Socrates emphasizes the importance of limiting and restraining desire as an antidote to the unfulfilling misery of a life dedicated to *pleonexia.* As I argued in chapters 3 and 4, self-restraint is analogous to a "civic virtue," a concept used in the *Republic* (429d–430e, 619c–d), and it is distinct from the genuine *sōphrosunē* of the *Phaedrus.* However, it is a necessary step toward attaining the robust Platonic conceptions of true virtue and happiness (*eudaimonia*), and it is the characteristic that souls like Callicles need most given their current state.

Plato has Socrates give effective critiques of the Calliclean worldview and a compelling alternative to it. Socrates' words are not just attempts to correct a particular person at a particular time. Rather, no matter when or where we live, unlimited desires bring us deep dissatisfaction and inevitably lead us to harm those who stand in the way of what we want. Giving limit to one's desires through self-restraint makes it possible to experience a sense of completeness, sufficiency, and inner harmony. Further, when we do not spend all of our time pursuing the objects of our unlimited desires, we open the possibility of caring for others, building our friendships, and furthering our education. For those who do not care if their vice harms others, Socrates' arguments show why committing injustice causes serious damage to *oneself*, as is most vividly apparent in the case of the tyrannical soul. Socrates also seriously challenges the view that there is no real, universal measure for goodness with his remarks about the beautiful order of the natural world. This aspect of Plato's thought prompts us to recognize that there is value apart from (or, that is not born from) our own desires, but is instead external to us and shared with others. The implications of Socrates' views in the realm of social justice are obviously important to us today as we continue to struggle with issues surrounding gender equality and criminal justice reform. Finally, by paying close attention to the pedagogical dimension of Socrates' words and his use of philosophical rhetoric, we are reminded that philosophical exchanges never happen in a vacuum, but instead between concrete individuals who are always in the process of learning. To benefit students, the educator must take into account the specificities or unique characteristics of those whom she aims to impact.

In chapter 3, my focus turned to the *Phaedrus* for the sake of illuminating how that dialogue's differing contexts shaped Socrates' philosophical rhetoric, his account of virtue, especially with regard to *sōphrosunē*. Phaedrus represents a significantly different type of soul than Callicles. On the one hand, he is tempted to pursue a way of life that is similar to the one Callicles endorses insofar as he is enamored with the way Lysias uses rhetoric and the lavish lifestyle of the conventional rhetorician. On the other hand, Phaedrus shows signs that he is a philosophical soul, or that he at least has the potential to become one. These signs include his love of spoken and written *logos*, his eagerness to participate in conversation, his experience of wonder at various points in the conversation, and his interest in the same topics that philosophers care about. Next, I explored the similarities and differences between philosophical rhetoric in the *Gorgias* and the *Phaedrus*. Socrates sums up his philosophical rhetoric in the *Phaedrus* with his concept of soul-guiding, an important component of which is the ability to classify the various types of speeches and souls. The knowledge of speeches and souls allows the rhetorician to match the speech to the soul that will find it most persuasive, and his persuasion aims toward ends that promote justice or the general benefit of those he persuades. Socrates performs philosophical rhetoric over the course of the entire dialogue with Phaedrus by using fitting types of *logoi* that have the most potential to guide Phaedrus' soul toward a better understanding of and a deeper care for virtue and philosophy.

Chapter 3 also showed how Lysias' speech and Socrates' first speech play a crucial role in the dialogue's investigation of the nature of *erōs* and *sōphrosunē*. While these speeches claim to describe the behavior of all lovers, Socrates later states that they really only described those who handle the *erōs* they experience in a vicious, hubristic, and self-serving way, and not the "noble form of love among the free" (*Phdr.* 243c). The speeches thus contribute to the dialogue's investigation of *erōs* by showing how it is often poorly handled, and the palinode later shows how to harness or direct the *erōs* one experiences virtuously. Similarly, Lysias' speech provides an example of mortal moderation, which is a common way to conceive of *sōphrosunē*. Mortal moderation amounts to the ability to restrain some desires for the sake of fulfilling others and the ability to calculate how doing so will result in the greatest overall amount of pleasure for oneself. Crucially, the description of mortal moderation sets up Socrates' critique of this characteristic and his contrasting notion of genuine moderation in the palinode.

Many modern individuals suffer from the misuses of erotic love that stem from characteristics that are very similar to what the *Phaedrus* calls mortal moderation, vice, or *hubris*. Indeed, these behaviors have been and continue to be so common that they are seen by many as acceptable or at least unavoidable. Those who experience serious problems in intimate relationships are often harmed by a partner's manipulation or control tactics, unreasonable jealousy, or discouragement from spending time with family and friends, to name just a few examples. Often, lovers behave in these ways out of fear that their partners will leave them, or they want to maximize the erotic pleasures they get from their partners (or both). Such behavior is rooted in the erroneous view that satisfying one's own desires is more important than any other end. Lovers may harm the well-being of their partners if it allows them to maintain control and experience steady satisfaction. Socrates' vision of the ideal relationship as rooted in *sōphrosunē* in the palinode might allow us to think through healthier approaches to fostering our intimate relationships.

Finally, chapter 4 began by examining the moral psychology of Socrates' palinode and noting its key difference with that of the *Gorgias*, namely the incorporation of *thumos* into its analysis of the most morally relevant aspects of the soul. I showed that the *Phaedrus*' account of moral vice is consistent with the *Gorgias*, especially with regard to ignorance of the good as the root of vice, despite the different contexts of the *Phaedrus*. When discussing Socrates' famous image of the soul as a charioteer with two horses, I paid special attention to the passages describing the restraint of the black horse (which symbolizes the soul's *epithumiai*). The black horse must be restrained habitually in order to transition toward the eventual harmony of the soul that one attains when she has cultivated genuine *sōphrosunē*. I showed that genuine *sōphrosunē* is related to multiple different spheres of life, all of which are unified by the notion of divinity. In the context of an erotic, intimate relationship, the moderate lover treats his beloved, who is an image of divine beauty, with the reverence that would be due to a god by always working for the sake of the beloved's benefit. For Socrates, this genuinely moderate way of handling one's *erōs* is essential for a happy and healthy relationship. The moderate person also avoids *hubris*—he does not mistake himself as a god among men by thinking he knows more than he does or that the satisfaction of his own desires should take precedence over the well-being of others. Moderation therefore helps us gain self-knowledge and awareness of our mortal limitations. Third, cultivating moderation along with the rest of the virtues is the activity through which the soul becomes as similar to the divine as possible in two important senses. Through moderation we attain the internal harmony of the divine, which in turn allows us to understand the sources of Being, or the Forms (as the gods do in Socrates' myth) in a way that is appropriate for us.

The *Phaedrus* gives us important insights that are missing from contemporary conversations about moderation. Some may conceive of the virtue of moderation in a way that approximates the *Phaedrus*' notion of mortal moderation. We often think of moderation as limiting the amount of food we eat, the alcohol we drink, or the products we buy for the sake of bodily health, appearing more fit, saving money, taking less from others, or avoiding further damage to the environment. Socrates shows why such activities are, at bottom, a way of calculating how to maximize pleasure, as we trade smaller pleasures for larger ones. The self-restraint involved in these cases is certainly valuable for the reasons mentioned above, but we can gain a more sophisticated and meaningful notion of moderation by looking to the *Phaedrus*. In my view, regardless of one's views about the nature or existence of the divine, Plato can guide our thinking about the characteristic we need to see ourselves as we are. Platonic moderation allows the individual to see himself clearly as one human being among many, not as a god among mortals. The genuinely moderate person is keenly aware that he is far from omniscient, and he is less likely to see others as objects for his use or satisfaction. In relation to erotic love, cultivating moderation is not the practice of suppressing our desires but a way of caring for ourselves along with those we love. The inner harmony one can achieve through moderation prevents hubristic desire or the false conceit of knowledge from skewing our view of the world so that we can see it with clarity and openness.

Bibliography

Arendt, Hannah. "Thinking and Moral Considerations: A Lecture." *Social Research* 38, no. 3 (1971): 417–446.

Aristotle. *Metaphysics.* Translated by Richard McKeon. New York: Random House, 2001.

———. *Nicomachean Ethics.* Translated by Robert C. Bartlett and Susan D. Collins. Chicago: The University of Chicago Press, 2011.

Barney, Rachel. "The Sophistic Movement." In *A Companion to Ancient Philosophy,* ed. Mary Louise Gill and Pierre Pellegrin, 77–97. Oxford: Blackwell, 2006.

———. "Thrasymachus and Callicles." In *The Stanford Encyclopedia of Philosophy,* ed. Edward N. Zalta. Fall 2017 edition. https://plato.stanford.edu/archives/fall2017/entries/callicles-thrasymachus/.

Benardete, Seth. *The Rhetoric of Morality and Philosophy: Plato's* Gorgias *and* Phaedrus. Chicago: University of Chicago Press, 1991.

Billings, Joshua, and Christopher Moore. Introduction to *The Cambridge Companion to the Sophists,* edited by Joshua Billings and Christopher Moore, 1–29. New York: Cambridge University Press, 2023.

Blondell, Ruby. *The Play of Character in Plato's Dialogues.* New York: Cambridge University Press, 2002.

Brandwood, Leonard. *The Chronology of Plato's Dialogues.* New York: Cambridge University Press, 1990.

Brickhouse, Thomas C., and Nicholas D. Smith. "Socrates and the Unity of the Virtues." *The Journal of Ethics* 1 (1997): 311–324.

Brouwer, Mark, and Ronald Polansky. "The Logic of Socratic Inquiry: Illustrated by Plato's *Charmides.*" *Socrates* 2400 (2004): 233–245.

Brown, Ryan M. "The Liberation of Virtue in Plato's *Phaedrus.*" In *Arete in Plato and Aristotle: Selected Essays from the 6th Interdisciplinary Symposium on the Hellenic Heritage of Sicily and Southern Italy,* ed. Ryan M. Brown and Jay R. Elliott, 45–74. Siracusa, Italy: Parnassos Press, 2022.

———. "The Lovers' Formation in Plato's *Phaedrus.*" *Epoché* 27 (2022): 19–50.

Bryan, Jenny. "The Role of Lysias' Speech in Plato's *Phaedrus*." *The Cambridge Classical Journal* 67 (2021): 1–24.

Burnyeat, Myles F. "First Words." *Proceedings of the Cambridge Philological Society* 43 (1997): 1–20.

Cicero, Marcus Tullius. *De Finibus Bonorum et Malorum*. Translated by H. Rackham. Cambridge: Harvard University Press, 1967.

Cotton, A. K. *Platonic Dialogue and the Education of the Reader*. New York: Oxford University Press, 2014.

De Romilly, Jacqueline. *The Great Sophists in Periclean Athens*. Oxford: Clarendon Press, 1998.

Derrida, Jacques. "Plato's Pharmacy." In *Dissemination*. Translated by Barbara Johnson. Chicago: University of Chicago Press, 1981.

Dodds, E. R. Gorgias*: A Revised Text with Introduction and Commentary*. Oxford: Oxford University Press, 1959.

Ebrey, David. "The *Phaedo* as an Alternative to Tragedy." *Classical Philology* 118 (2023): 153–171.

Emlyn-Jones, C. "Socrates, Plato, and Piety." *Mediterranean Studies* 2 (1990): 21–28.

Ferrari, G. R. F. *Listening to the Cicadas: A Study of Plato's* Phaedrus. Cambridge: Cambridge University Press, 1987.

Foucault, Michel, Alessandro Fontana, and François Ewald. *The Hermeneutics of the Subject: Lectures at the College de France, 1981–1982*. London: Palgrave Macmillan US, 2001.

Friedlander, Paul. *Plato: An Introduction*. Translated by Hans Meyerhoff. New York: Pantheon Books, 1958.

Fritz, John. *Plato and the Elements of Dialogue*. Lanham: Lexington Books, 2016.

Gill, Mary Louise. "Plato's *Phaedrus* and the Method of Hippocrates." *Modern Schoolman* 80 (2003): 295–314.

Gordon, Jill. *Turning Toward Philosophy: Literary Device and Dramatic Structure in Plato's Dialogues*. State College: Pennsylvania State University Press, 1999.

Griswold, Charles L. *Self-Knowledge in Plato's* Phaedrus. New Haven: Yale University Press, 1986.

Hadot, Pierre. *What Is Ancient Philosophy?* Translated by Michael Chase. Cambridge: Harvard University Press, 2002.

Halperin, David. "Plato and Erotic Reciprocity." *Classical Antiquity* 5 (1986): 60–80.

Howland, Jacob. *Glaucon's Fate: History, Myth, and Character in Plato's* Republic. Philadelphia: Paul Dry Books, 2018.

Irani, Tushar. *Plato on the Value of Philosophy: The Art of Argument in the* Gorgias *and* Phaedrus. Cambridge: Cambridge University Press, 2017.

Irwin, Terence. *Plato's Ethics*. New York: Oxford University Press, 1995.

Jenks, Rod. "The Power of Shame Considerations in Plato's *Gorgias*." *History of Philosophy Quarterly* 29, no. 4 (2012): 373–390.

Kahn, Charles H. *Plato and the Socratic Dialogue*. Cambridge: Cambridge University Press, 1996.

———. "Plato's Theory of Desire." *Review of Metaphysics* 41, no. 1 (1987): 77–103.

Kamtekar, Rachana. *Plato's Moral Psychology: Intellectualism, the Divided Soul, and the Desire for the Good.* Oxford: Oxford University Press, 2017.

Kant, Immanuel. *Groundwork for the Metaphysics of Morals.* Translated by Allen W. Wood. New Haven: Yale University Press, 2002.

Kerferd, G. B. *The Sophistic Movement.* Cambridge: Cambridge University Press, 1981.

Mackenzie, Mary Margaret. *Plato on Punishment.* Los Angeles: University of California Press, 1981.

McCoy, Marina. "Love and Rhetoric as Types of *Psychagōgia.*" In *Platonic Love from Antiquity to the Renaissance,* ed. Carl Séan O'Brien and John Dillon, 49–63. New York: Cambridge University Press, 2022.

———. *Plato on the Rhetoric of Philosophers and Sophists.* New York: Cambridge University Press, 2008.

McPherran, Mark L. "Justice and Piety in the Digression of the *Theaetetus.*" Ancient Philosophy 30, no. 1 (2010): 73–94.

McTighe, Kevin. "Socrates on Desire for the Good and the Involuntariness of Wrongdoing: *Gorgias* 466a–468e." *Phronesis* 29, no. 3 (1984): 193–236.

Metcalf, Robert. *Philosophy as Agôn: A Study of Plato's* Gorgias *and Related Texts.* Chicago: Northwestern University Press, 2018.

Miller, Mitchell. *The Philosopher in Plato's* Statesman. Las Vegas: Parmenides, 1980.

———. *Plato's* Parmenides: *The Conversion of the Soul.* Princeton: Princeton University Press, 1986.

Moore, Christopher. *Socrates and Self-Knowledge.* Cambridge: Cambridge University Press, 2015.

———. *The Virtue of Agency:* Sōphrosunē *and Self-Constitution in Classical Greece.* New York: Oxford University Press, 2023.

Moss, Jessica. "Shame, Pleasure and the Divided Soul." *Oxford Studies in Ancient Philosophy* 29 (2005): 137–170.

———. "Soul-Leading: The Unity of the *Phaedrus,* Again." *Oxford Studies in Ancient Philosophy* 43 (2012): 1–23.

Munn, Mark. *The School of History: Athens in the Age of Socrates.* Los Angeles: University of California Press, 2000.

Nails, Debra. *Agora, Academy, and the Conduct of Philosophy.* Boston: Kluwer Academic, 1995.

———. *The People of Plato: A Prosography.* Indianapolis: Hackett, 2002.

Nietzsche, Friedrich. *The Will to Power.* Translated by Walter Kaufmann. New York: Random House, 1967.

Nightingale, Andrea Wilson. "Divine Epiphany and Pious Discourse in Plato's *Phaedrus.*" *Arion: A Journal of Humanities and the Classics* 26, no. 1 (2018): 61–94.

———. "Plato's *Gorgias* and Euripides' *Antiope*: A Study in Generic Transformation." *Classical Antiquity* 11, no. 1 (1992): 121–141.

North, Helen. *From Myth to Icon: Reflections of Greek Ethical Doctrine in Literature and Art.* Ithaca: Cornell University Press, 1979.

———. *Sōphrosunē: Self-Knowledge and Self-Restraint in Greek Literature.* Ithaca: Cornell University Press, 1966.

Nussbaum, Martha. *The Fragility of Goodness: Luck and Ethics in Greek Tragedy and Philosophy.* Cambridge University Press: New York, 1986.

Plato. *Apology.* Translated by G. M. A. Grube. Rev. by John M. Cooper in *Complete Works.* Edited by John M. Cooper. Indianapolis: Hackett, 1997.

———. *Charmides.* Translated by Christopher Moore and Christopher C. Raymond. Indianapolis: Hackett, 2019.

———. *Euthyphro.* In *Complete Works.* Translated by G. M. A. Grube. Edited by John M. Cooper. Indianapolis: Hackett, 1997.

———. *Gorgias.* Translated by James H. Nichols Jr. Ithaca: Cornell University Press, 1998.

———. *Phaedo.* Translated by Eva Brann, Peter Kalkavage, and Eric Salem. Indianapolis: Focus, 1998.

———. *Phaedrus.* Translated by Stephen Scully. Indianapolis: Focus, 2003.

———. *Philebus.* Translated by Dorothea Frede. Indianapolis: Hackett, 1993.

———. *Republic.* Translated by Allan Bloom. 3rd ed. New York: Basic Books, 2016.

———. *Statesman.* In *Complete Works.* Translated by C. J. Rowe Edited by John M. Cooper. Indianapolis: Hackett, 1997.

———. *Symposium.* Translated by Alexander Nehemas and Paul Woodruff. Indianapolis: Hackett, 1989.

———. *Theaetetus.* Translated by M. J. Levett. Rev. by Myles Burnyeat in *Complete Works.* Edited by John M. Cooper. Indianapolis: Hackett, 1997.

———. *Timaeus.* Translated by Donald J. Zeyl. Indianapolis: Hackett, 2000.

Rademaker, Adriaan. Sophrosyne *and the Rhetoric of Self-Restraint: Polsemy and Persuasive Use of an Ancient Greek Value Term.* Boston: Brill, 2005.

Rowe, Christopher. "The Argument and Structure of Plato's *Phaedrus.*" *The Cambridge Classical Journal* 32 (1986): 106–125.

———. *Plato and the Art of Philosophical Writing.* Cambridge: Cambridge University Press, 2007.

Ryan, Paul. *Plato's* Phaedrus: *A Commentary for Greek Readers.* Norman: University of Oklahoma Press, 2012.

Sallis, John. *Being and Logos: The Way of Platonic Dialogue.* Pittsburgh: Duquesne University Press, 1975.

Sanday, Eric. "Challenging the Established Order: Socrates' Perversion of Callicles' Position in Plato's *Gorgias.*" *Epoché* 14, no. 2 (2012): 197–216.

Scott, Dominic. "Philosophy as Madness in the *Phaedrus.*" *Oxford Studies in Ancient Philosophy* 41 (2011): 169–200.

Scott, Gary Alan. *Plato's Socrates as Educator.* Albany: State University of New York Press, 2000.

Sedley, David. “The Ideal of Godlikeness.” In *Plato 2: Ethics, Politics, Religion, and the Soul,* ed. Gail Fine, 309–328. Oxford: Oxford University Press, 1999.

Serafim, Andreas. “Revisiting Sexual Invective: Demosthenes as *Kinaidos* in Aeschines’ Speeches.” *Classics Ireland* 23–24 (2016): 1–30.

Shaw, J. Clerk. “Punishment and Psychology in Plato’s *Gorgias.*” *Polis: The Journal for Ancient Greek and Roman Political Thought* 32, no. 1 (2015): 75–95.

Sheeley, Kristian. “Philosophical Rhetoric as Paideia in Plato’s *Phaedrus.*” In *Paideia and Performance,* edited by Heather Reid, Henry Curcio, and Mark Ralkowski, 145–162. Siracusa, Italy: Parnassos Press, 2023.

Tafolla, Vince. “Philosophical Eroticism, or How Socrates Made Me a Man.” *Ancient Philosophy* 38 (2018): 289–304.

Tarnopolsky, Christina H. *Prudes, Perverts, and Tyrants: Plato’s* Gorgias *and the Politics of Shame.* Princeton: Princeton University Press, 2010.

Trivigno, Franco. “Putting Unity in Its Place: Organic Unity in the *Phaedrus.*” *Literature and Aesthetics* 19, no. 1 (2009): 153–182.

Tsouna, Voula. *Plato’s* Charmides: *An Interpretative Commentary.* New York: Cambridge University Press, 2022.

Werner, Daniel S. *Myth and Philosophy in Plato’s* Phaedrus. New York: Cambridge University Press, 2012.

———. “Plato’s *Phaedrus* and the Problem of Unity,” *Oxford Studies in Ancient Philosophy* 32 (2007): 91–137.

Williams, Bernard. *Shame and Necessity.* Oakland: University of California Press, 1993.

Woodruff, Paul, and Betty S. Flowers. *Reverence: Renewing a Forgotten Virtue.* Oxford: Oxford University Press, 2001.

Woolf, Raphael. “Callicles and Socrates: Psychic (Dis)harmony in the *Gorgias.*” *Oxford Studies in Ancient Philosophy* 18 (2000): 1–40.

———. *Plato’s* Charmides. New York: Cambridge University Press, 2023.

Yunis, Harvey. *Plato*: Phaedrus. New York: Cambridge University Press, 2011.

———. *Taming Democracy: Models of Political Rhetoric in Classical Athens.* Ithaca: Cornell University Press, 1996.

Index

aischos, 16, 30, 68, 87, 95
akolasia, 17, 31, 37, 48, 98, 101, 103–104
Alcibiades, 7n10, 32n22, 33, 36, 93, 96–97, 116, 134, 167
Apology, 50, 97n34, 197
Aristotle, 2, 15, 22n2, 28n14, 31, 31n20, 45n41, 45n43, 60n52, 71n3, 76n11, 78, 80, 82–83, 95–96, 102n, 103n40, 118–119, 132, 143–144, 184n, 185n, 191n, 195n, 199

Barney, Rachel, 10n13, 10n15, 23, 60n52, 61n55, 65, 74, 120n14
black horse, 156, 157, 159, 163–171, 174–179, 194, 209

chariot image, 156–162, 175
charioteer, 156–175, 178–179, 198, 201, 209
cicadas, 117, 123, 160
civic virtue, 16, 68n, 87, 101, 109, 151, 207
cosmos, 28–29, 49, 63n59, 71n4, 74–75, 106–107, 186n23
craft, 26, 28, 32, 60n53, 72, 79, 88–89, 106; craftsman, 26n13, 50, 71n4, 72, 106, 197, 199. See also *empeiria* and *technē*
critique of writing, 160, 185

demos, 33, 36, 38n33, 61, 92
Derrida, Jacques, 111
dialectic, 55–56, 126, 133, 160; dialectical, 8, 131–134, 160, 186
Diotima, 33–34, 43, 72n, 76n11, 117n, 157n, 189
discipline, 14, 17, 31–34, 70, 75, 76, 99–100, 156, 160, 179, 184n, 207. *See also* punishment

empeiria, 26–27, 32, 44n40, 88
epithumia, 24–29, 32–40, 44–46, 52, 54, 58, 67, 90, 93, 140, 156–159, 163n9, 165–166, 194, 209
eudaimonia, 12, 21, 27, 34, 46, 50, 54, 68, 70, 71n3, 77–80, 103, 152, 189–193, 207
eudaimonic relationships, 20, 110, 152, 193, 201

Forms, 13, 24n9, 50, 70, 72, 112n5, 158, 162–163, 167–176, 187–188, 192, 198, 201–202, 210
Foucault, Michel, 107n42

Gorgias (character), 10, 25–27, 38–39, 41, 60, 84, 88, 90

Hadot, Pierre, 76n10, 107n, 117n, 128n26
hubris, 16–18, 20, 106, 140, 141n34, 148–149, 157, 147, 175, 181n18, 182, 193–194, 196n, 209

immoderation, 8, 16–19, 22, 31, 37, 52, 68, 84, 98n35, 101, 103–104
inner harmony, 1, 4, 16–19, 46, 49, 51, 68, 80–81, 85, 103, 106, 157–158, 175, 184, 189–190, 192, 206–207, 210

Kant, Immanuel, 109n

limit, 3, 22, 30, 47–48, 59, 63, 68, 70, 101, 104–107, 109, 113, 151, 205–207. *See also* unlimited
logos, 23, 25–32, 55, 57, 59, 67, 89, 92–93, 94, 99, 114, 117, 125, 129–130, 152, 186, 208
Lysias, 4, 10–11, 20, 109–153, 157, 167, 184, 190, 208
Lysis, 81

Metaphysics (Aristotle), 118–119
moral psychology, 23–27, 67, 148n41, 159–166, 174, 209

Nicomachean Ethics (Aristotle), 2, 22n2, 28n14, 31n20, 78, 96–97, 143, 184n
Nietzsche, Friedrich, 65
nomos, 10–11, 19, 59– 63, 73–74, 77, 101

Phaedo, 12, 14–15, 55–57, 102, 112, 136, 151, 172, 190
Philebus, 2, 14, 23n6, 35n28, 47, 49, 111n3, 117, 158
philosophic couple, 45n42, 143, 145n38, 158, 179n, 180n16, 183, 189, 193–195
physis, 10–11, 19, 59, 61–63
pleonexia, 16–17, 19, 37, 40, 47, 57, 59, 60–68 *passim,* 75–76, 99–106, 113, 140, 143, 151, 205–207
Polansky, Ronald, 6n7, 6n8, 13n, 39n35, 87n20, 95n31, 202n33
Polus, 24n8, 25–28, 38–39, 41–42, 46–47, 51, 77, 79, 84–86, 90, 97, 99–100
Protagoras, 10, 60, 61n55, 96n33
psychagōgia, 33n23, 124n18
punishment, 31–32, 40, 43, 54–55, 68, 71, 73–74, 77, 84, 86, 92, 99–100, 175, 206. *See also* discipline

rhetoric: philosophical, 23, 67, 69, 87–95 *passim,* 112–115, 125–135, 190, 203, 207–208; art of, 67, 89–91, 125, 128–134, 180, 184, 207

sex, 110, 121, 136, 138–140, 156, 166, 177, 178, 179, 179n, 180, 196
self-knowledge, 12, 13n18, 80, 98, 110, 158, 161, 190–193, 196–201, 210
social justice, 71, 83, 206–207
Sophist, 31n19, 95
sophists, 10–12, 19, 36, 57, 59, 60–65, 76, 88, 89n23, 119–120, 190, 199
Statesman, 5n3, 29n, 63
Symposium, 33, 43, 72n, 76n10, 76n11, 91, 96, 115, 117n, 124n17, 134, 157, 189

technē, 26–27, 29, 32–33, 44, 63, 71, 79, 88, 127–130, 184–185
Theaetetus, 10–11, 61n54, 63, 72–73, 77, 118, 186n22, 197n
Thrasymachus, 26n13, 42, 120
Timaeus, 71n4, 74n8, 84, 128

thumos, 18, 24, 34–35, 39, 148n41, 157, 159, 163n9, 164–166, 178, 209
tyrannical soul, 8, 17, 19, 25, 40, 41–46, 57–59, 62n57, 72
tyrant, 35, 40–42, 44, 51, 58, 85, 199
unlimited, 17, 19, 23–24, 29–30, 32, 37, 38, 45n40, 54, 58, 60, 62, 70, 81, 83, 106. *See also* limit

white horse, 157, 164–166, 178–179. See also *thumos*